HOW TO TUNE & MODIFY YOUR
FORD
5.0-LITER MUSTANG
1979-1995

D1597145

Steve Turner

MOTORBOOKS
INTERNATIONAL

DECATUR PUBLIC LIBRARY

JUL 0 1 2005

DECATUR, ILLINOIS

This edition first published in 1999 by Motorbooks International, an imprint of MBI Publishing Company, Galtier Plaza, Suite 200, 380 Jackson Street, St. Paul, MN 55101-3885 USA

© Steve Turner, 1999

All rights reserved. With the exception of quoting brief passages for the purposes of review, no part of this publication may be reproduced without prior written permission from the Publisher.

The information in this book is true and complete to the best of our knowledge. All recommendations are made without any guarantee on the part of the author or Publisher, who also disclaim any liability incurred in connection with the use of this data or specific details.

We recognize that some words, model names and designations, for example, mentioned herein are the property of the trademark holder. We use them for identification purposes only. This is not an official publication.

Motorbooks International titles are also available at discounts in bulk quantity for industrial or sales-promotional use. For details write to Special Sales Manager at Motorbooks International Wholesalers & Distributors, Galtier Plaza, Suite 200, 380 Jackson Street, St. Paul, MN 55101-3885 USA.

Library of Congress Cataloging-in-Publication Data

Turner, Steve.
    How to tune & modify your Ford 5.0-liter Mustang/Steve Turner.
        p. cm.—(MBI Publishing Company PowerPro series)
    Includes index.
    ISBN 0-7603-0568-4 (pbk.: alk. paper)
    1. Mustang automobile—Motors—Modification. I. Title. II. Series.
TL215.M8T87   1999
629.28'722—DC21   99-14538

On the front cover: Though running with stock heads and cam, Brian Vander Haagen's 1995 Mustang Cobra boasts a dyno-proven 400 rear-wheel horsepower! Topping the list of mods to this Cobra is a Vortech supercharger. *Dale Amy*

On the back cover: "The Boss is Back!" Ford proudly boasted with its first 5.0-badged mustang in 1982. The two-barrel-carbed, 157-horsepower 5.0 was no Boss 302, but it heralded Ford's returned commitment to marketing the Mustang as a *performance* car. *Ford Motor Company*

Designed by Bruce Leckie

Printed in the United States of America

Contents

Acknowledgments

It is accepted practice to say that a book was written by one person. In fact this book simply has my name on its cover. Truth be told, there were many individuals who contributed to the completion of this work. Some donated time, some shared photos, others let me work while other things fell by the wayside, but without all of them, this book wouldn't have made it into your hands. If I miss anybody, please forgive me.

Combined with the never-ending job of working on a magazine, this project commanded what little free time I had left. Of the thanks to be given, Jeanine Sams, the love of my life, deserves the majority. In addition to standing by me through thick and thin, she allowed me the freedom to spend large chunks of time working on this project when I should have been spending time with her.

Of course, I never would have even had the opportunity to write this book without the support of three at Super Ford—Tom Wilson, editor, Steve Statham, former managing editor, and Donald Farr, group editor. These three let me have a shot at a summer internship at Super Ford magazine. It eventually blossomed into the job I have today, which put me in a position to learn more than I could have imagined about 5.0-liter Mustangs and Fords of all kinds.

Even though he's already mentioned as one of the three, special thanks go to friend and editor Tom Wilson for providing me the freedom and guidance to grow as a writer and editor. I know that simply putting up with my wisecracks was a test. Tom ultimately nominated me to write this book, and without his chassis and suspension knowledge and photographic assistance, the chore would have been far more difficult.

Others providing invaluable photographic aid were my friends Chuck James, staff photographer at EMAP-Petersen Publishing, Mark Houlahan, technical editor at Mustang Monthly, and Donald Farr. The 5.0-liter Mustang marketplace is so vast and diverse, committing it all to film is a task beyond one man. A thousand thanks for pitching in, guys!

So many companies provided product photography and information that there is not enough room to mention them in this space. To all those who did so, especially without me having to pester you, thank you so much. I didn't use nearly the number of pictures I received, borrowed, and took, but each was instrumental in boiling down 5.0 modifications into the backbone of this book.

If any one person went out of her way for photography, it was Pamela Przywara, at the Ford Motor Company Archives. Pamela took extra time and didn't forget about me over her vacation to dig up the crucial photos for Chapter 1. Today 5.0-liter Mustangs are either modified to the nines or run-down to the exclusion of photo-worthiness. Since hunting down the pristine stock 5.0s would have further delayed the production of this book, I most appreciate Pamela's extra efforts.

Speaking of delays, I would be remiss not to thank editors Zack Miller and John Adams-Graf of MBI Publishing. Zack took on a first-time author on one recommendation and gave him a fair shake. When Zack's plate overflowed, John inherited the hair-pulling task of shepherding the book through production.

Also, I would be remiss not to thank the countless shop owners, technical experts, tuners, engine builders, and the like for sharing their knowledge over the years. Those who spent interminable hours pouring their knowledge into my tape recorder, you know who you are. Thanks for letting me behind the scenes.

Lastly, to my parents: I hope this makes a bit of that college tuition worthwhile! Thanks.

Introduction

Others might argue the point, but to me the 5.0-liter Mustang embodies the American spirit more than any other vehicle. In stock form, this iteration of the Mustang lineage offered good looks, affordable performance, and, more importantly, gobs of potential.

It was the good looks of the 1982 Mustang GT that caught my adolescent eye. Ford's advertising screamed, "The Boss Is Back." Though the 1982 GT might seem like a mild car these days, it signaled the end of a dark, dark era in the history of Mustang. The evil spawn of OPEC's 1970s gas crunch, the 1974–78 Mustang II was the ugly pony cursed with questionable styling and lackluster performance. The 1982's bold front fascia, faux ram-air scoop, and marine-based 302 captured my imagination and Mustang loyalty.

At the time, I just thought the Mustang was a cool car. Little did I know the 1982 was three years into the seminal performance rush that made Fords a force in the aftermarket. It seemed Ford was bent on repairing the damage of the Mustang II era. The company continued to improve the car throughout its lifespan, and even sweetened the pot with aftermarket leadership via the Motorsport SVO division.

All of that only made the cars more appealing. By the time I was actually able to buy a 1982 Mustang GT, in 1988, the car was well worn, but it felt good to realize a dream. By then that dream had been jaded by the even better, fuel-injected 1987 and newer Mustangs. I so longed for the increased power and the high tech allure of EFI that when a friend totaled his 1987 Mustang GT, I took out a loan and bought his drivetrain and had it swapped into the 1982. Though the car was showing its age on the outside, the modern engine and five-speed transmission made it the best of both worlds for a college student with a part-time job.

Sadly, a hailstorm eventually totaled the 1982, so I finally got a real EFI Mustang—a 1989 LX coupe. I loved the looks of the new aero nose and I really loved the myriad of parts available to modify the car. Naturally I started right away, adding a pair of Flowmaster mufflers and, eventually, a K&N air filter and aftermarket wheels and tires. It was all my credit card would bear, but I did read and reread every Mustang magazine I could get my hands on, dreaming of future modifications.

After college, I was fortunate enough to get a job at Super Ford magazine. I never would have imagined in 1982 that I would someday make my livelihood by writing about performance Fords, particularly 5.0 Mustangs. The car/engine combo's popularity as a factory-built starting point for modification grew to support five magazines and countless small businesses, mail-order outlets, and speed shops.

In those magazines and from those businesses, a wave of aftermarket parts swelled to service the burgeoning legions of 5.0 fans like me. The 5.0 did what no other Ford engine had—it challenged the small-block Chevy for parts availability and performance.

All of that inertia gives the 5.0 Mustang the true American personality. You can take the powerful but flawed platform of the 1979–95 cars and build whatever you want: a show car, a drag car, a road race car, a top speed car, or the most popular choice, a hot street car.

This book will attempt to paint the 5.0 aftermarket with a broad brush. It would be impossible to show you how to install or modify every part produced for the 5.0 Mustang. That could fill a whole series of books. Instead, I will attempt to show you what's available for 5.0 Mustangs and how to choose the best pieces for your combination. More specifically, the book will zero in on bolt-on performance and appearance parts for street and dual-purpose street/performance 5.0s, particularly the overtly popular 1987–93 EFI 5.0s. For more information on racier engine combinations and modifications, you should check out Tom Wilson's book, *How to Build and Modify Ford Fuel-Injected 5.0 V-8 Engines*. Of course, you should purchase a Ford shop manual for your Mustang before embarking on any modifications.

With any luck, you'll enjoy this book as much as I enjoy writing about and tinkering with 5.0 Mustangs. So, grab your shop manual, get your tools, and go to work.

History

This book will serve you best once you have formed a rudimentary knowledge of 5.0 Mustangs. Before you plan to modify a 5.0 Mustang, it's good to have a basic idea of what you're starting with, and if you want to buy a 5.0 Mustang to modify, it's good to know what to seek out

The 1979–95 Mustangs are all built on some version of Ford's Fox platform. This chassis was the result of Ford's initiative to build a one-size-fits-all car to serve as a two-door sports car and a four-door family car; the first examples were the 1978 Ford Fairmont and Mercury Zephyr.

A shared platform means that many of the incremental improvements over the years offer a great deal of backward compatibility. Thus, you can easily modify an earlier 5.0 Mustang to match or surpass a later model. This is especially true of the 1979–93 cars; the 1994–95s have a number of specialized components.

1979

Concerned with improving its Corporate Average Fuel Economy numbers, Ford introduced the first Fox-bodied 5.0 Mustangs in 1979. The sharp-edged styling was a definite improvement over the

rounded Mustang II design, and the wind-tunnel-tested aerodynamics aided the CAFE cause. The design change was obviously a well-received move, as the Mustang was chosen as the pace car for the Indianapolis 500. In celebration, Ford produced 11,000 Indy Pace Car replicas. These came standard with several appearance parts, including a front air dam, hood scoop, Recaro front seats, a rear spoiler, a pop-up sunroof, and a unique paint scheme. It was available with a turbocharged four-cylinder, but the 302 was a no-charge option.

Under the hood, they weren't

Marking the first year of the 5.0 Mustang's 16-year run, the 1979 Mustang's edgy aerodynamics separated it from the round jellybeans of the woeful Mustang II era. The first Fox Mustang was chosen for the 1979 Indy 500 Pace car. Replicas, like this one, were available with 5.0 V-8s or turbo four-cylinders. *Ford Motor Company*

The darkest era of the Fox-bodied Mustang was the two-year period when the 5.0 vanished. Anticipating another oil shortage, Ford replaced the 5.0 with a 4.2-liter, 255-cubic inch engine packing only 140 horsepower. *Ford Motor Company*

really 5.0 Mustangs as we know them today. The 302-cubic-inch V-8 was a carryover from the Mustang II. Though the two-barrel carburetor was from the previous year, the 302 did gain a serpentine accessory belt and an improved exhaust system with revised cast-iron manifolds and a single 2 1/2-inch tailpipe. With the improvements, the 8.4:1 302 produced 140 horsepower at 3,600 rpm and 250 lb-ft of torque at 1,800 rpm.

Backing up the 302 option were three transmission possibilities: a three-speed manual, an optional four-speed manual, or a Cruise-O-Matic three-speed automatic. Similarly, there were three suspension choices: standard, han-

dling, and special. The suspensions were designed to complement the tires on the car—bias-ply, radial, and Michelin TRX respectively. Special handling and 302 cars all received rear sway bars affixed to the lower control arms.

All V-8 1979s were equipped with 3.45:1-geared 7.5-inch rear ends, while all 1979s had 10.06-inch front disc brakes and 9-inch rear drums.

1980–1981
Oddly, Ford took two steps back in 1980 and 1981. Anticipating another oil crunch, Ford replaced the 302 with a 255-cubic-inch, 4.2-liter V-8. The reduction in bore size resulted in a 23 horsepower drop,

to 117 from the 1980–81 V-8s. Since there was no 5.0 for this period, there isn't much to say other than Ford souped up the Mustang with stickers, paint, and body panels. In fact, some of the Indy Pace Car equipment, including the Recaro seats, became optional in 1980.

1982
Ford was certainly onto something with the Fox Mustang styling, but it didn't really put all the pieces together until 1982. It fused the 1979 Indy Pace Car air dam and spoiler with the 1980–81 Cobra hood scoop, added a new grille, and, most importantly, stuck a 5.0 badge on the side of the 1982 Mustang GT.

A 5.0 badge first graced a Mustang fender in 1982, when Ford's ad campaign proclaimed "The Boss is Back." The two-barrel-carbed, 157-horsepower 5.0 was no Boss 302, but it marked Ford's return to marketing the Mustang as a performance car. *Ford Motor Company*

Ford's advertising proclaimed "The Boss Is Back," and even though it wasn't quite up to the previous Boss Mustangs, the 1982 GT made overtures to that performance heritage, thanks to the incorporation of the first 5.0-liter High Output V-8. The 5.0 adopted the 351 Windsor firing order, gained a camshaft from Ford's marine engine program, and added a dual-snorkel air cleaner. The engine also changed balance in 1982, going to a 34-ounce-inch damper and 50-ounce-inch flywheel.

Though its compression ratio dipped a bit to 8.3:1, the 5.0 HO still gained 17 horsepower over the 1979 302. Its 157 horsepower and 240 lb-ft of torque were certainly enough to get enthusiasts excited, though some were disappointed by the two-barrel carburetor, as pre-production rumors slated a four-barrel for the HO.

The 5.0 HO was also available as an option in non-GT cars, but it was always accompanied by a single-rail-overdrive four-speed manual transmission. A 3.08:1 geared Traction-Lok 7.5-inch rear end was also standard on 5.0 Mustangs. Power steering, power brakes, and traction bars were also part of the 5.0 package. The handling suspension was standard, while the TRX suspension was optional.

1983

Enthusiasts finally got what they wanted in 1983—a Holley four-barrel carburetor. The 600-cfm carb coupled with the requisite matching intake, a larger twin-snorkel air cleaner, and enlarged exhaust ports brought the 1983 5.0 up to 175 horsepower. Besides horsepower, the engine received a one-piece rear main seal, replacing the leak-prone two-piece arrangement. Behind the rear main seal, the Mustang finally added another much-needed option. This model

Ford enacted a drastic, rounded makeover on the 1983 Mustang. While the rounded nose and reversed hood scoop set it apart from previous 5.0 Mustangs, the four-barrel carburetor and 175-horsepower rating were a sigh of relief to performance fans. Convertibles were also reborn in '83.

A more streamlined grille opening and GT insignias in the side moldings set the 1985 apart from the previous models. Topping out at 210 horsepower thanks to a new roller camshaft, the 1985 Mustang GT closed out the carbureted 5.0 era as the best yet. *Ford Motor Company*

year marked the first year of the T-5 five-speed transmission, although the SROD four-speed was still available.

Externally, Ford designers treated the 1983 Mustang to a smoother, more rounded front end than the 1982. Part of the smoothing included a new hood scoop with its opening facing the windshield, rather than the forward-opening, ram-air-style hood on the 1982 GT. Out back, designers treated the 1983 to longer, smooth-faced taillights. Convertibles rejoined the Mustang line-up in 1983 as well.

1984

It was the 20th anniversary of the Mustang, and Ford celebrated it with stickers. They sold a limited production run of GT-350 Mustangs, available with a 5.0 or turbocharged 2.3. These cars sported Shelby White paint with maroon stripes and GT-350 stickers. The previous GT's hood scoop was a casualty of change, but other than the anniversary cars and a new, rounded rear spoiler, 1984s Mustangs marked the start of Ford occasionally skipping a model year before invoking any substantive upgrades.

Though the cars didn't change much, a few important additions joined the Mustang line-up. It was the first year of the Mustang LX model, and the first year of a fuel-injected V-8 Mustang. Central fuel injection was standard on automatic-equipped 5.0s. CFI cars had 10 fewer horsepower than their carburetted brethren. They also gave up any hope of modification, as the CFI cannot compensate for increased airflow. In short, if you are looking to tune or modify a 5.0, stay away from those equipped with CFI.

1985

Ford further rounded the edges on 1985 Mustangs. The cars received a new front fascia with a simpler grille treatment and integral driving lights. New moldings were also part of the update, and GTs featured "GT" etched into the molding just aft of the doors.

While the exterior was certainly an improvement, the good news was under the hood. The 5.0 V-8s received roller camshafts and matching roller lifters. These changes plus stainless-steel, short-tube headers; redesigned accessory pulleys; and a Y-piped, dual-muffler exhaust spiked horsepower up to 210 at 4,400 rpm from 1984's 175. Torque also swelled from 245 to 270 lb-ft of torque at 3,200.

Though both automatic- and manual-transmission 5.0 Mustangs came withroller cams and forged aluminum pistons, the CFI-equipped automatic 5.0s still had a

Despite the naysayers criticizing the move to fuel injection in 1986, the 1987 5.0 Mustang was the vehicle that began the 5.0 craze. Mustangs were available in light, trimmed-down LX and heavy, ground-effects-laden GT packages. Both versions were available with the 225-horsepower 5.0-liter engine. *Ford Motor Company*

distinct performance disadvantage, sporting only 165 horsepower and 245 lb-ft of torque. A running production change, including improved induction and exhaust, bumped the CFI ratings up to 180 horsepower and 260 lb-ft.

To handle the increased power, the suspension was upgraded with larger sway bars and a new quadra-shock rear suspension, featuring two horizontal dampers designed to dampen wheel hop. GTs also came standard with new 15-inch "10-hole" wheels wearing Goodyear Gatorback radials.

Inside, 1985 interiors were upgraded with new sports seats and a steering wheel similar to those in the turbocharged, four-cylinder Mustang SVO produced from 1984 to 1986.

1986
Externally, the 1986 Mustang appeared to be another one of those carryover model years, for aside from the third brake light mounted on their rear decks, 1986s looked just like 1985s. This time, however, the upgrades were more than subtle.

Most drastic of the changes was Ford's adoption of sequential electronic fuel injection. Replacing the carburetor, or throttle body in the case of CFI, and short-runner manifold was a long-runner intake with individual fuel injectors for each intake runner/cylinder. Air enters the long-runner intake through a 58-millimeter throttle body and is greeted with fuel from 19-pound/hour fuel injectors controlled by Ford's speed-density EEC-IV processor, which infers airflow by looking at rpm, manifold pressure, air/fuel ratio, and other readings; it can accept some minor performance modifications before drivability suffers.

Under the new induction sat new cylinder heads built with high-swirl combustion chambers designed to improve emissions. The heads held back performance,

even with the addition of a dual exhaust—replete with 2 1/4-inch tailpipes—and a jump in compression ratio to 9.2:1, thanks to flat-top pistons with no valve reliefs. Horsepower dropped to 200, but torque, thanks to the long-runner intake, rose to 285 lb-ft. In response to the extra grunt, Ford enlarged the clutch diameter from 10 to 10 1/2 inches and added the durable 8.8-inch rear end, replacing the long-standing 7.5-inch rear.

1987
After nearly being put out to pasture in favor of a car built by Mazda and Ford (known cynically at the time as a Mazstang, it eventually became the now-defunct Probe), the Mustang came back better than ever in 1987. Most obvious of the changes was a new aero front end designed to bring the Mustang into the modern era and improve its coefficient of drag. GTs received a new closed grille, front air dam with integral driving lights, side

Following the 1989 California 5.0s, all 1989 5.0 Mustangs were equipped with mass airflow sensors connected to the EEC-IV processor. This sensor measures incoming air and allows the processor to compensate for improved airflow—and letting the performance genie out of the bottle. *Ford Motor Company*

skirts, rear bumper cover, and wing and larger rear side windows. New turbine wheels and "cheese grater" taillights were also part of the GT revamp.

Mustang LXs equipped with 5.0s came standard with the 10-hole wheels from the 1986 GT and new jeweled taillights. In all, the 5.0 LX was a smoother, cleaner-looking package. This model upgrade wasn't restricted to new urethane body parts, though. The 5.0 V-8 received some much-needed performance upgrades including a larger 60-millimeter throttle body and, more importantly, better cylinder heads. They were actually a back-pedal to the truck-sourced E7TE castings used on the 1985 5.0 HO, but combined with fuel injection, they provided a noticeable power boost up to 225 horsepower and 300 lb-ft, even with a dip in compression ratio to 9:1.

Ford's engine dyno figures were obviously reduced once the engines were installed in vehicles with full accessories and exhausts, but power was further mitigated by the placement of an air silencer before the air filter, and, on automatic cars, quieter, more restrictive mufflers.

The always inadequate brakes got a minor boost to help corral the extra power; front brakes grew to 10.84 inches in diameter, but the antiquated rear drums still measured 9 inches around.

Inside, a completely revised interior featured a much improved dash with a distinct gauge pod and package shelf. GTs also received sport seats, with lumbar and side supports, plus standard tilt wheels.

1988

Nothing new happened in 1988—at least in 49 states. However, Cal-

ifornia, with its tight emissions standards, forced Ford to improve the Mustang's fuel injection in a way that opened the Pandora's Box of 5.0 performance. Mustangs equipped with 5.0-liters and destined for California were equipped with a revised form of EEC-IV fuel injection incorporating a mass airflow sensor. Unlike the speed density on all other 1986–88 5.0s, the mass-air system in the 1988 California cars actually measured the incoming air, rather than inferring it. While improving drivability and emissions, this system also allowed the fuel injection to compensate for improved airflow.

1989

In 1989 all 5.0-equipped Mustangs were equipped with a 55-millimeter mass airflow sensor, and Ford Racing Performance Parts (formerly Ford Motorsport SVO) released a

After the addition of driver-side airbags in 1990, 5.0 Mustangs changed little from 1990 to 1993. Ford did upgrade the exterior package in 1991 with the attractive five-spoke pony wheels and in 1992 5.0s, such as this convertible, received body-colored side moldings. *Ford Motor Company*

conversion kit to update 1986–88 Mustangs to the new standard. These two events were the catalyst for the explosion in popularity of the Mustang, as the disappointing performance of the 1986 5.0 coupled with fear of new technology had 5.0 owners adding performance by removing the fuel injection and replacing with carburetion. Mass air meant having one's performance cake—and not eating shabby fuel economy and emissions.

After two years of steady sales of 5.0-equipped LXs, Ford also reacted to the market and released the 5.0 LX Sport model. These cars were like previous 5.0 LXs, because they had all the GT performance, including 75-amp alternators, 10-hole wheels, Traction-Lok differentials, and 14.7:1 power steering rack ratios, without the frills and extra cost. Hatchback and convertible 5.0 LXs were also fitted with the same sport seats as the GTs.

1990

Most of the changes were inside the 1990 Mustang. Black joined gray, tan, and red as an interior color option. Map pockets were added to the door panels. A dead pedal gave the driver a place to rest a lazy left foot, and smaller, more modern heating ventilation and cooling controls were added.

To improve its Corporate Average Fuel Economy, Ford removed the center console to reduce weight. The deletion proved unpopular, and the console was revived as a running production change. Ford also added safety in the form of rear-passenger shoulder belts and a driver-side air bag, which eliminated tilt steering.

Additionally, Ford built 4,103

5.0 LX convertibles with Emerald Green paint, GT wheels, and white leather interior.

1991

After 1990, all the upgrades were minor. The cars were almost exactly the same in 1991, save that they looked much better. This was due to the addition of Ford's best-looking Fox Mustang wheel. These 16-inch, five-spoke wheels are known as "Pony" wheels in deference to the running horse on their center caps. The wheels and their 225x55ZRx16 tires mandated widened fender openings, but the minor change was certainly worth the dividend. In this model year, sports seats became standard in all 5.0 LXs, including coupes, replacing forever the subpar "taxicab" seating found in 1987–88 5.0 LXs and 1989 5.0 LX coupes.

1992

Aside from aesthetically pleasing body-colored moldings and a larger interior dome light, 1992 5.0 Mustangs remained largely unchanged. They still carried the 225 horsepower and 300 lb-ft of torque originated in 1987. Ford did sell 2,109 limited-edition 5.0 LX convertibles with Vibrant Red paint, rear spoilers, white wheels,

Ford closed out the Fox-bodied 5.0 in shameful fashion, installing weak hypereutectic pistons and down-rating the engine's horsepower to 205. *Ford Motor Company*

Though the standard 5.0 Mustang went out with a whimper, the birth of Ford's Special Vehicle Team in 1993 spawned a new era of performance Fords. The 1993 Mustang Cobra packed a 235-horsepower engine, a beefed T-5 transmission, and a refined suspension. SVT also built 109 stripped-down Cobra Rs designed for road racing. *Ford Motor Company*

and white leather interior. These cars looked great but packed no extra performance.

1993

As the last year of the Fox-bodied Mustang, the 1993s received little respect. Ford said it changed the way its engineers measured horsepower, which caused the 5.0's horsepower ratings to drop to 205 horsepower at 4,200 rpm and 275 lb-ft of torque at 3,000 rpm. Though the new numbers were said to be merely a product of the measuring process, the numbers may also have decreased due to camshaft and electronics changes made over the years.

Not only did the 5.0 lose power in 1993, it grew less tolerant. To gain tighter piston-to-cylinder-wall clearance for improved efficiency and emissions, Ford started using new high-silicone cast pistons known as "hypereutectics." Though they made good sense for

Ford, performance enthusiasts found them less resistant to detonation and, thus, frequent casualties of forced induction.

Mustang Cobra

All news was not bad in 1993, however. Ford introduced the ultimate iteration of the Fox-bodied Mustang—the Special Vehicle Team's 1993 Mustang Cobra. This car was no sticker upgrade. It packed numerous performance and aesthetic improvements.

Adding performance to the Cobra 5.0 were high-flow cast-iron cylinder heads similar to the GT-40 heads sold by Ford Racing Performance Parts. The Cobra heads were specially machined to work with the car's unique camshaft. A cast aluminum intake featuring the same staggered-round-port layout as Ford Racing's GT-40 intake improved airflow with the help of a 65-millimeter throttle body. Plus, a specially calibrated EEC-IV

processor controlled larger 24-pound/hour injectors with the help of a 70-millimeter mass air meter. All told, the Cobra produced 235 horsepower and 280 lb-ft of torque.

A revised, heavy-duty T-5 transmission handled the extra power, and a new running horse grille insert, rocker panel side spats, rear wing, revised rear valance, rear disc brakes, and SVT Cobra badges set the black, red, and teal Mustang Cobras apart from run-of-the-mill GTs.

Ford also produced some other limited-edition Mustangs in 1993, including 5.0 LX convertible "feature cars" and Mustang Cobra Rs. White and yellow feature cars were sold. The white cars were fitted with white tops, white or black interiors, white Pony wheels, unique rear spoilers, and unique floor mats with embroidered black horses. Yellow feature cars were similarly equipped with white or

In 1994, Ford offered up a new, greatly improved Mustang design based on a revised Fox platform, the Fox-4. Internally coded as the SN95, these Mustangs met early skepticism for their styling, but rapidly became among the most popular 5.0 Mustangs. *Ford Motor Company*

black tops, white leather interior with ponies embroidered on seats, chrome wheels, unique rear spoilers, and unique floor mats with embroidered yellow horses.

While the feature cars included no performance enhancements, the 109 racer-only Mustang Cobra Rs were stripped of all unnecessary weight and equipped with numerous durability upgrades aimed at road racing longevity. Among the 60-plus changes, the major additions included larger disc brakes, 13-inch front and 11-inch rear, 17-inch wheels that would end up on the 1994 GT, plus oil coolers and coolant degas systems.

1994

It was time again to revamp the Mustang's looks. Ford spent a great deal of time developing new designs and market testing their Mustang worthiness. The result of the process was the 1994 Mustang, internally code-named SN95. Though radically improved, with a

Fox Mustangs went through three different interiors. The 1979–1985 cars utilized a flat, Fairmont-based dash; 1987–1993 Mustangs received a unique dash and console plus revised seating; and the 1994–1995 cars received this attractive, retro-styled interior. *Ford Motor Company*

stiffer platform, longer wheelbase, wider track, and revised K-member (which improved caster from 1.5 to 4 degrees), the SN95 was still built on a version of venerable Fox platform, though the upgrade deserved

SVT continued on in the SN95 era with a new Mustang Cobra. They came packing 240 horsepower, bigger wheels and tires, larger brakes, unique front fascias, and Cobra-specific rear wings. These cars and their 351-powered Cobra R cousins became the visual measuring stick for SN95 modifications. *Ford Motor Company*

a new name, Fox-4. Other improvements included four-wheel disc brakes on all Mustangs. They measured 10.9 inches in the front and 10.5 inches in the back and were available with an optional anti-lock braking system. The brakes slowed the optional six-spoke, 17-inch wheels wearing 245/45ZR-17 Goodyear Eagle GTs.

Riding on the new platform was a wildly different Mustang body. Upon its introduction, many people, including those in the automotive press, likened the SN95 Mustang to the Toyota Celica; not exactly shining praise for a car that had previously represented pure Americana. Still, the Mustang did include many styling cues from earlier Mustangs, including a twin-arch dash design and tri-bar taillights. The new body style aged well, and many Mustang fans grew to like it more than the much-adored Fox-body cars.

Though Ford was readying a

new 4.6-liter version of its modular engine family for the new Mustang, it wisely allowed a transition period with the beloved 5.0-liter. However, the engine had to be modified to fit the new bodywork. Most obvious of the shoe-horn changes was a new version of the in-line oval intake manifold. It wasn't really new (it had been used on 5.0-liter Thunderbirds), but it was new to the Mustang. Along with the new intake was a new throttle linkage and throttle body design, featuring a longer body and horizontal throttle shaft. An external tube from the passenger-side header handled exhaust gas recirculation to the revised intake, and a stainless-steel exhaust system, featuring six catalytic converters, pushed the 5.0 begrudgingly past tighter emissions standards. The same standards were the likely driving force behind the SN95 EEC-IV computer's less aggressive calibration.

Despite the more restrictive intake, exhaust system, and computer programming, the SN95 Mustang registered a horsepower boost from 205 to 215 horsepower at 4,200 rpm. Torque also jumped 10 lb-ft to 285 at 3,400 rpm.

Perhaps in response to the power renaissance, the SN95 T-5 manual transmission received bonded-carbon-fiber synchronizer rings. This was also the first year the aged AOD four-speed automatic transmission gave up some control to the EEC-IV transmission. It became the AODE.

Besides the new dash design, the SN95's interior was leaps and bounds ahead of any previous 5.0 Mustang, thanks to better seats and overall fit and finish. The best factory stereo ever offered to Mustangers was optional as well. Ford's Mach 460 stereo packed three amplifiers, one four-channel and two subwoofer amps, and eight speakers into the Mustang, keeping all but serious audiophiles out of car stereo shops.

Mustang Cobra
Other than the refined chassis and interior, SVT's 1994 Mustang Cobra really wasn't much different from the Fox-bodied Cobra. Externally, it benefited from a sexier front fascia with molded-in driving lights, Cobra badging, a new rear spoiler with built-in LED third brake light, and new 17x8-inch wheels replete with five spokes and 255x45ZRx17 Goodyear Eagle GS-C tires.

Inside, SVT buyers were welcomed by white gauge faces, Cobra-lettered floor mats, and leather-wrapped parking handles and shift knobs.

Naturally, the engine was the real story. The GT-40-equipped Cobra 5.0 was essentially a carryover of the 1993 SVT product, but it wore a revamped cast upper intake designed to clear the hood line. Plus, engineers gave it a bit more plenum area to better suit it for 351 Windsor duty, as it was slated to pull in the 1995 Mustang Cobra R. The throttle body, however, shrunk down to 60 millimeters from the previous 65-millimeter 1993 Cobra measurement.

Despite the EEC-IV calibrations growing more conservative in the SN95 era, the 1994 Cobra 5.0 garnered 5 more horsepower and five more lb-ft of torque, rising to 240 horsepower and 285 lb-ft.

1995
There were no remarkable performance changes worth noting in 1995. The 5.0 Mustang was in its final year before giving way to Ford's powertrain-consolidation line-up of modular engines.

Though few changes occurred, 1995 did bring out two Mustangs worth noting. One, known as the GTS, hearkened back to the price/performance heyday of the 5.0 LX. The other, the 1995 Mustang Cobra R, was a car Mustang enthusiasts had begged for, one fitted with the 5.0's big brother—the 351 Windsor.

Born of customer and dealer requests for a budget 5.0 Mustang, the Mustang GTS offered buyers power without padding. Ordering a Mustang GTS meant you missed out on driving lights, the leather-wrapped steering wheel, sport seats, illuminated side mirror, and, most noticeably, a rear wing. You did get the coveted 5.0-liter V-8, and almost all the optional equipment was available upon order, save the sport seats and leather interior.

While the undermarketed GTS made up only 7 percent of Mustang production in 1995, the overmarketed Mustang Cobra R only numbered 250 units. Though they don't really fit into this book, because they were fitted with 351Ws, the road race-prepped cars were overhyped only because their limited production was only available to licensed racers at a hefty price.

The Cobra R proved one of the most influential SN95 Mustangs this side of Steve Saleen's small-volume rockets. Cobra Rs featured bulging, two-staged fiberglass hoods and beautiful five-spoke wheels, the best factory Mustang wheel to date. Both became *de rigueur* on modified SN95s, and the wheels became popular additions to all manner of modified Fords, especially those stepping up to larger brakes.

It was a long, grand haul for the 5.0 Mustang. All the model years and hot rodding that happened before this book was written make the 5.0-liter Mustang the best car you can buy to tune and modify.

Induction

2

Like any other engine, Ford's 5.0-liter V-8 is simply an air pump. The easier you make it for the engine to move air, the more power it will produce. Unfortunately, there is no single assembly restricting airflow on a stock engine. Ford faced many obstacles in mass-producing the 5.0-liter, including emissions regulations, fuel economy regulations, safety regulations, and profitability. As a result, many of the engine's systems were compromised, particularly the systems charged with handling inlet airflow and exhaust flow.

When modifying a 5.0 for performance duty, you must think of the entire powertrain. In other words, to get maximum performance you must improve airflow from before the air filter to the tip of the tailpipe. This chapter will cover the 5.0 inlet system, including the numerous aftermarket solutions for increasing airflow.

Air Filters
Clean air is a requirement for engine durability. Many race cars operate without air filters, but their engines are subject to frequent rebuilds and replacements. To get the most from your 5.0-liter and maintain durability, a high-flow aftermarket air filter is the easiest and wisest initial modification.

There are several aftermarket filters on the market, but by far the most universally accepted is the K&N Filtercharger. All K&N filters are constructed of a woven cotton surgical gauze filter media captured by a durable wire mesh. By treating the gauze with a special oil solution, K&N meets the necessary filter requirements and retains superb airflow characteristics. In fact, a

properly sized K&N or similar filter will often improve performance versus no filter by straightening airflow and reducing turbulence.

A new K&N outflows a new paper filter and, according to K&N, a dirty K&N maintains a distinct advantage over a dirty paper filter. This, they say, is because the K&N doesn't have to rely on dense, thick media to filter. So as the paper element gathers air, the dense media becomes clogged, while the K&N still allows pathways for the air to travel through.

K&N Filterchargers are cleanable and reusable up to 25 times and come with a warranty that extends for 1,000,000-miles or 10 years.

I don't have much experience with oiled foam filters, but K&N claims they suffer the same restriction problems as paper filters. There is another viable option for 5.0 filtration. Filters marketed by S&B and Kenne Bell are strikingly similar to K&N Filterchargers, but feature a polyester gauze rather than cotton. Like K&Ns, these filters are treated with oil to achieve proper filtration. Their flow characteristics are on par with K&Ns and they are often cheaper.

Carbureted
A high-flow air filter is obviously a good addition to any carbureted engine. However, the manifestation of this filter must be chosen to

The first step to improving airflow and power on a fuel-injected 5.0 is removing the factory air silencer. This greatly enhances airflow to the factory filter box. Some people choose to gut the silencer and plumb homemade ram air hose into it. These crude modifications are of negligible benefit, especially when you consider that the path of least resistance for ambient air cramming into the inner fender is the silencer-free air filter. The 1994–95 5.0s have a similar silencer device, but it is less restrictive than the earlier piece.

Removing the air silencer usually goes hand-in-hand with installing a factory replacement K&N panel air filter. This is a great one-two combo for bolt-on 5.0s. It outperformed every 5.0 ram air kit in tests performed.

best suit your 5.0's intended duty. While street, street/strip, and pure race 5.0s can all benefit from more airflow, they all operate in different environments.

The dual-snorkel air cleaners on 1982–85 Mustangs aren't really that bad. They duct in ambient air from the inner fenders, and it becomes slightly pressured when the car is at speed. So for a street 5.0, simply replacing a paper with a high-flow aftermarket replacement filter is the best way to go, because the filter is shielded from hot underhood air and receives a slight boost from the air piling up in the inner fender.

Of course, depending on the level of modifications your 5.0 has received, a stock size filter may no longer be large enough, meaning a switch to an open-element filter is a necessity. A highly modified engine is more likely to spend time on the drag strip, where brief spurts make it less susceptible to underhood heat, so an open-element filter is more acceptable. According to K&N, a shorter, larger-diameter filter will outflow a taller, smaller-diameter filter, so keep that in mind when choosing an open-element aftermarket air cleaner and filter.

Fuel-Injected

Fuel-injected 1986–93 5.0-liter Mustangs feature a fairly restrictive air path compared to their carbureted brethren. The stock air box is bolted to the inner fender. This seems a logical setup, although Ford deemed it necessary to install an air silencer inside the fender to reduce the sound of the air rushing into the air box.

One limitation of a K&N panel filter is its surface area. The way to increase surface area is by clamping a conical air filter onto the end of the mass air meter. K&N's Filtercharger Injection Performance Kits are a great way to add a conical filter and maintain emissions legality. They really don't provide maximum benefit until the engine has been modified with aftermarket cylinder heads, intakes, and the like. They also serve up a few negatives. All open-element conicals breathe hot underhood air and lose the slight pressurization available to a panel filter sealed to the inner fender. Open filters are also open to accepting stray air pulses from the engine fan, which can upset the mass air meter and cause drivability problems in some cars. When installing an FIPK or other conical, consider building an air box or shield around the filter as a barrier to hot air and fan wash.

Removing this performance nuisance should be first on your list of modifications, although it's likely many of the 5.0 Mustangs on the road today have already been relieved of their silencers. The later 1994–95 SN95 5.0s have a similar, less-restrictive air horn in their fender wells too.

Inside the factory 1987–93 air box is a flat panel paper air filter. Removing the silencer and replacing the paper filter with a direct-replacement K&N Filtercharger is one of the more effective one-two punches of 5.0 tuning. The K&N frees up airflow and receives unfettered and, at speed, slightly pressurized air from the inner fender. In fact, removing the silencer can be worth over four horsepower when tested on a Dynojet, while the K&N becomes more important when coupled with other airflow modifications. Of course a moving car would receive even more airflow and, thus, power.

Conical Filters

Unlike the Fox-bodied cars, the SN95s feature a conical paper air filter and low-restriction air box from the factory. So the question of converting to a conical only pertains to the earlier EFI 5.0s. There are numerous variations of K&N conical filters that clamp right onto the end of the stock mass-air meter or air hose, in the case of speed-density 5.0s, but the only emissions-legal conical is marketed by K&N as part of their Filtercharger Injection Performance Kit. The kit includes the filter, plus all the necessary hardware to bolt it in place of the stock air box.

Of course K&N has a stock replacement filter and FIPK for SN95 Mustangs too. The replacement filter is worth a few horses, while the FIPK becomes beneficial after the engine's airflow demands are increased.

Ram Air

There is another alternative to simply adding a high-flow panel or conical air filter. Several aftermarket

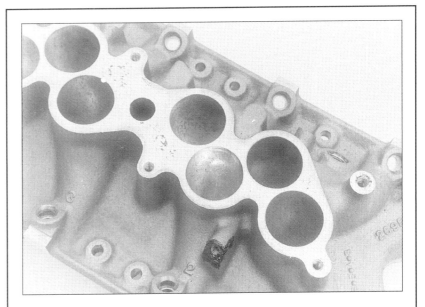

Porting for Power

Although bolting on an aftermarket intake will give you a performance improvement, that improvement can be maximized with porting. The easiest way to gain power is to port match the intake to the cylinder head's ports. This is easily achieved by using a marker to shade in the discrepancies between the intake-to-cylinder head gasket. Then you simply use a die grinder or rotary tool to grind away the excess intake meat, providing a smooth transition from intake to cylinder head.

Smoothing and enlarging the ports on a carbureted intake or fuel-injected lowers requires the proper flexible grinding tips, a great deal of patience, and care not to break through the casting. Many shops will weld material onto the runners to allow maximum porting for improved line of sight from port entrance to exit, but this is something best left to an experienced porter.

Something also best left to a porter is the fuel-injected upper intake. To properly port one of these with a grinder requires band sawing the intake in half to gain access to the runners. Once the runners are ported, the intake must be welded back together. This is a time-consuming, and usually expensive, methodology. Only the Edelbrock intakes offer a removable plenum cover allowing access to the upper runners.

For all other EFI intakes, the best option is the Extrude Hone Powerflow service. By pressure-feeding a part with carbide-laden putty, the Extrude Hone Powerflow can remove as little as .010 of an inch and as much as .040 of an inch in one treatment. This process removes material and smoothes the casting in such a way that improves airflow without a large reduction in velocity. The process can also improve an intake's runner balance, reducing the chance of random lean or rich cylinders.

Both these methods are useful for improving airflow, and they are not mutually exclusive. A hand-ported part can be Extrude Honed afterward to provide a smooth blended surface for maximum airflow.

manufacturers, including Hypertech, March Performance, Kenne Bell, and F.A.S.T. manufacture ram-air kits for 5.0-liter Mustangs. These kits place scoops under the front fascia of a Mustang. The scoops are designed to deliver air, via ducting, to the air filter. F.A.S.T.'s kit ducts air to the stock air box or an open conical, while the other kits provide new air box housings that enclose conical air filters.

In theory these kits are designed to force-feed the air filter

A great way to add the surface area of a conical filter and maintain the pressure and temperature benefits of a conical is Moroso's Cold Air Kit. Whether the incoming air is cold or not depends on the weather, but the air in the fender is certainly colder than the air under the hood. The Moroso kit is cost effective and looks great. The only knock on it is that its K&N filter might be a bit small for heavily modified 5.0s. BBK Performance offers a similar arrangement featuring chrome tubing.

The grandaddy of all aftermarket mass air meters is Pro-M's 77-millimeter unit, which is also available bored out to 83-millimeter. These larger meters are simply high-flowing castings fitted with reworked factory hot-wire sensors. The sensors are recalibrated for larger fuel injector flow rates by sandblasting the electronics to change their voltage output. This system works great for street applications but when used with huge injectors, the low-rpm drivability can be affected because the EEC-IV computer looks at other factors, such as throttle position and rpm, to help determine how long to spray the injectors. Changing the voltage enough to compensate for really larger injectors' flow rates like 72-pound/hour can cause the computer to load the table with data that is inappropriate for true engine demand.

with "cold" air when the car is at speed. In practice, the temperature of the air, while it might be cooler than the air under the hood, is simply ambient air. So, on a 95-degree day in Florida, the temperature of the inlet air is still going to be hot, especially after it travels through the hot intake. Additionally, testing a K&N panel filter with no air silencer showed it outflowed every ram-air kit in a 0–85 mph on-car test I performed, using mass air-flow sensor readings captured by a Crane Interceptor. (See Chapter 10 for more on the Interceptor's modern brother, the PMS.)

The ideal scenario is likely to place a conical air filter in the fender well. This allows a much larger filter surface area, which is also exposed to a constant influx of fresh ambient air.

Installing a high-flow air filter is a straightforward operation, but in the case of panel air filters, it's a good idea to apply some of K&N's filter grease to the edge of the factory air box. This grease will take up any slack caused by deformities in the stock air box and provide an airtight seal.

Mass Air Meters

Obviously, this section only applies to the fuel-injected 5.0 owners in the audience, more specifically those with 1989–95 cars and the 1988 California minority. The mass air meter is designed to measure the mass of the incoming air. It does its job via a hot wire. Keeping the hot wire at a constant temperature means the wire requires less voltage for low airflow and more voltage for more airflow. A second wire measures the incoming air's temperature.

Once the meter determines the mass of the air, it sends this data to the EEC-IV computer, which compares it and other input from the oxygen sensors, throttle position sensor, air-charge temperature sensor, and manifold absolute pressure sensor to numbers in its memory known as look-up tables. This is how the computer calculates fuel

injector pulse width, or the duration the injectors spray, and timing advance.

The reason mass air is so important to 5.0-liter Mustangs is that it allows the computer to respond to increased engine airflow caused by high-performance parts. The downside of the mass airflow sensor, which early 5.0 hot rodders discovered, is that it places

yet one more restriction in the engine's air path. This is true of the stock 55-millimeter 1989–93 sensor and the 70-millimeter sensor found on 1994–95 Mustangs. Though the later sensor is larger, a backflow inhibitor running down its center reduces its flow to near that of the smaller 55-millimeter unit.

For street-going 5.0s, there is no better EFI setup. Ford Motor-

Pro-M meters are also available in a low-cost Bullet version with a 75-millimeter diameter. The Bullet meter is built on thin-wall tubing, while the 77 and 83 are large cast pieces. According to Pro-M, the Bullet meter is capable of supporting 600 horsepower when coupled with the proper fuel injectors. Pro-M also offers a race-oriented meter constructed of thin-wall tubing and measuring over 100 millimeters.

sport, Best Products, and a few other aftermarket outlets offer mass air conversion kits for speed-density 1986–88 Mustangs.

Naturally, the stock mass air meters are only designed for the minimum airflow necessary to achieve the factory's horsepower goal. Increasing the airflow on the engine requires a larger mass air meter.

The original high-performance mass air meter for 5.0s was developed by Bob Atwood at Best Products. His line of Pro-M mass air meters are market favorites, thanks to customized calibrations for larger fuel injector flow rates. Best Products technicians tweak the resistance of the air meter's electronics with a precision sand blaster and verify the results by comparing airflow to output voltage to achieve the revised calibration.

Capitalizing on the high price point of the original Pro-M 77-millimeter meters, Lee Bender of C&L Performance developed the C&L mass air meter. Rather than recalibrating the electronics, this meter comes with a replaceable sampling tube—the small tunnel surrounding the hot-wire sensor. By increasing the size of the tube, more air flows over the sensor, requiring it to use more voltage. This is how the C&L, now marketed by Vortech Engineering, approximates for larger fuel injectors. In general, these meters work just fine on street 5.0s, but have been known on occasion to give up a bit of drivability. On race cars, only the size of the orifice matters anyway, because the EEC-IV relies less on the mass air sensor and more on

C&L Performance developed its mass air meter as a market response to the expensive 77-millimeter Pro-M meter. The C&L meter alters the voltage output of stock hot-wire sensors by installing larger sampling tubes around the sensor. The C&L meter flows nicely and allows easy injector changes, but, like the Pro-M, gives up some accuracy to the Ford's method of injector calibration inside the EEC-IV.

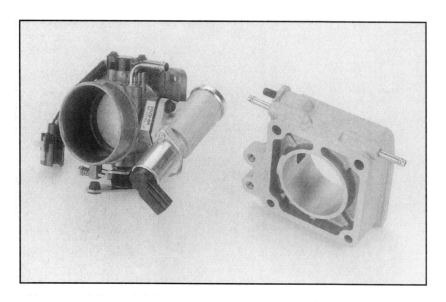

Ford Racing Performance Parts was the first on the market with its 65-millimeter throttle body, and it is still a viable bolt-on for street 5.0s. To install this unit, you must also use Ford Racing's 67-millimeter EGR spacer, unless you are installing it on a Cobra intake. If you are installing it on a stock intake, you must also port match the intake. Ford Racing also offers a giant 86-millimeter throttle body for serious racing applications.

Carburetors

The gateway into your 5.0 is probably the first place you think of modifying. The easiest way to get more air into the engine is to install a bigger entryway, right? Well, bigger is not always better, especially in the case of carburetors.

While mass air restriction and injector calibration aren't concerns for a carbureted 5.0, just putting on the biggest carburetor you can buy isn't the answer. Since carburetors provide the engine with air and fuel, an oversized carb can kill air velocity and drown the engine with fuel.

I'm ignoring the small two-barrel carbs on 1979 and 1982 5.0s,

programmed strategies at wide-open throttle (WOT)—at least in 1986–93 5.0s.

Ford Racing Performance Parts first made mass air noise with its conversion kit for 1988 and earlier 5.0s. With the advent of the Mustang Cobra in 1993, Ford Racing got into the hi-po mass air market with a 70-millimeter meter, 24 pound/hour injectors, and a computer. Known as the Cobra mass air kit, it was initially big with Mustangers, as it offered an affordable way to step injector flow rate and maintain factory drivability. Unfortunately, tuners soon learned the Cobra's EEC-IV featured a less aggressive calibration, including an rpm-triggered timing retard and a speed limiter.

Despite its limitations, the Cobra mass air kit delivers such good drivability characteristics, because it handled the mass air/injector calibration inside the computer. This is the optimum way to perform calibrations, although Ford eventually offered a 70-millimeter meter calibrated for 30 pound/hour injectors, much like the Pro-M units, only with a laser rather than a sand blaster.

Perhaps the best combination of factory-style calibration and aftermarket responsiveness comes in a meter marketed by Kenne Bell.

It combines an 80-millimeter Ford air meter and with a computer chip, which overrides the EEC programming with the new injector size, plus power-making timing and air-fuel calculations.

We'll get into the pros and cons of computer chips in Chapter 10, but picking a mass air meter comes down to how big an injector you need to run, how large a meter you need, and how much you want to spend.

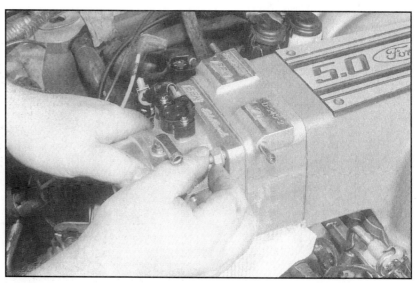

Port matching a stock intake for a larger throttle body is easily achieved by stuffing a rag into the intake, to prevent contaminating the engine, and port matching the inlet to the larger throttle body gasket. After porting is complete, vacuum out the metal chips, remove the rag, and install the new throttle body and EGR.

Though it is still viable, the 65-millimeter throttle body essentially has been made obsolete by the 70-millimeter units on the market, like this BBK throttle body. The 70-millimeter throttle bodies leave room to grow and don't hurt low-end performance. Because many of the aftermarket intakes, such as the Cobra and Edelbrock Performer 5.0, feature 70-millimeter inlets, the 70-millimeter throttle body is a good choice for most street-going 5.0s. BBK throttle bodies are available in 65-, 70-, 75-, and 80-millimeter diameters. *BBK Performance*

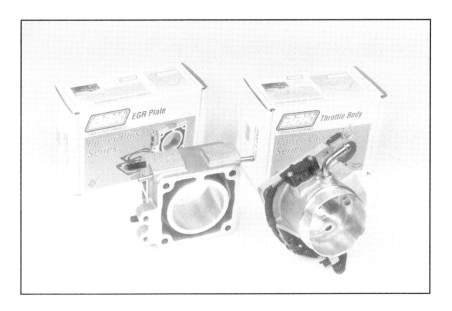

because the first most sensible modification is installing an aftermarket intake manifold and four-barrel carburetor. Not only does a four-barrel offer more airflow potential, it provides better air/fuel distribution by bringing the number of venturis (four) closer to the number of cylinders (eight).

Most out-of-the-box carbs from the likes of Holley and Edelbrock will offer a nice performance increase over the stock Holley 4180. The stock Holley and aftermarket Holleys offer a distinct advantage, because they feature a modular assembly that can be tweaked with parts from Holley and aftermarket Holley modifiers like Barry Grant and the Carb Shop. Of course, there are whole books dedicated to this subject, so I won't belabor the issue here.

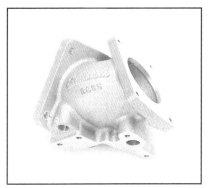

To install SN95 throttle bodies on intakes originally intended for use on 1986–93 Mustangs, one of these elbow-shaped adapters is required. Only the 1994–95 Cobra intake features the elbow cast as part of the intake. Ford Motorsport and Edelbrock are the only sources for these adapters, and the adapters are manufactured to match the respective companies' intake manifolds. *Edelbrock Corporation*

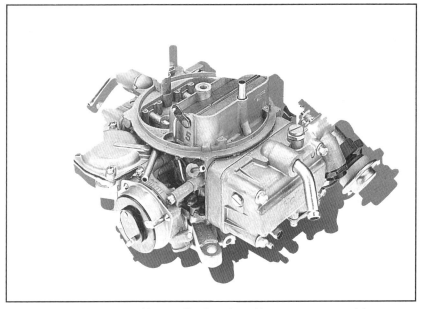

An aftermarket carburetor like a Holley four-barrel is an easy way to add extra performance. Because these carburetors are built for performance, they increase power, even over an equal cfm rating stock carburetor. Depending on how much bolt-on performance you have added to your 5.0, a larger-than-stock carb might be in order. Some people who don't mind trading some low-end torque—made up for by steep rear-end gears—for high-rpm power go as large as a 750 on the street, but a 650 should handle all but the most extreme airflow needs on the street. *Holley Performance Products*

To get even more performance from an aftermarket carb, you can buy a tweaked Holley-style carb from a number of aftermarket builders, like Barry Grant. Most of the BG line, like this Demon carb, is directed toward the racing market. The Demon differs from the CNC-modified BGs because it features a removable venturi, which may be substituted to tune the carb to your engine. Tuner carbs, like tuner cars, perform better than stock carbs. *Barry Grant Fuels*

Whichever brand you choose, you can ballpark the size of carburetor you need by plugging your engine's specifics into a mathematical formula, but most carburetor manufacturers recommend you purchase a carb larger than your theoretical needs to achieve the engine's maximum performance.

Running a typical warmed-over 302 up to 6,000 rpm at 90 percent volumetric efficiency through one of the typical cfm calculations shows its airflow needs are theoretically well under 600 cubic feet per minute (cfm), so the stock 600-cfm Holley four-barrel is well matched to getting good power from the 302-inch 5.0. However, you can run a larger carb in the neighborhood of 750 cfm, if it has

been properly tuned to deliver good mileage and performance.

There is, however, more to selecting your 5.0's carb than cfm. You may want such niceties as an electric choke for easy start-up, a kick-down lever for your automatic transmission, etc. One big choice will be between vacuum and mechanical secondaries. The sec-

ondaries allow the carb to act like two carbs by restricting airflow at low rpm, for good torque, and opening up at higher rpm, for good power. Vacuum secondaries engage in response to engine vacuum, while mechanical secondaries open with a direct linkage, whose ratios may be tuned for your engine. A safe bet for the street is a vacuum

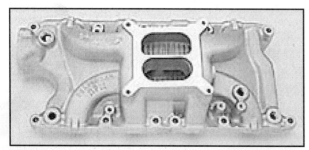

Dual-plane intake manifolds are the choice for street performance. Traditional dual-planes offer good performance off idle to just above 500 rpm. While these intakes are plentiful, a new breed of dual-plane intakes, like this Edelbrock Performer RPM, offers good performance just off idle and extends the powerband into the 6,500-rpm comfort zone dominated by single-plane manifolds. These are a good choice for geared up 5.0s that frequently make it to the strip or the top of the tach. However, if snappy off-idle performance and street legality are your concerns, stick with smaller dual-planes, like the Edelbrock Performer. *Edelbrock Corporation*

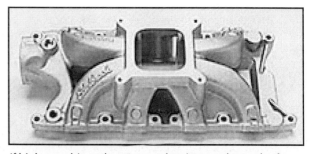

If high rpm, big carburetors and racing are the goals of your carbureted 5.0, single-plane manifolds, like this Edelbrock Victor Jr., offer performance all the way up to 8,000 rpm. These intakes will support all but the raciest engines and some 5.0s with steep rear axle ratios even get away with running these on the street. Most, however, are not street legal. *Edelbrock Corporation*

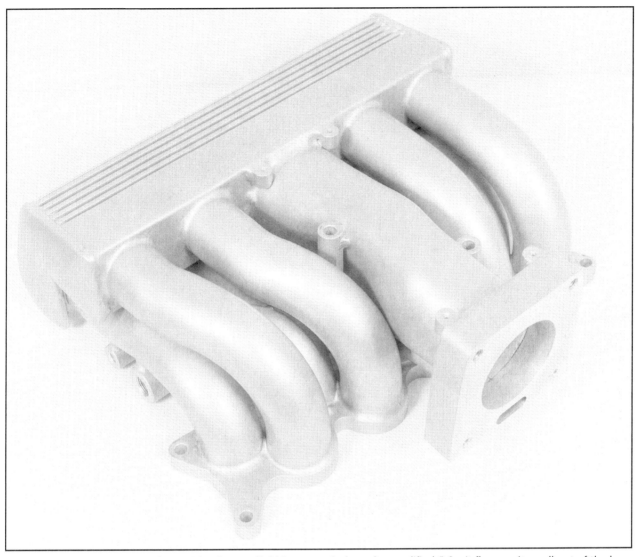

Ford Racing Peformance Parts' GT-40 intake manifold is a great bolt-on for modified 5.0s. It flows quite well out of the box, thanks to its smooth tubular upper intake and really shines once the lower intake is ported. However, when displacement, rpm, or boost is increased, the upper architecture becomes a limit, as it cannot be ported. One popular modification for GT-40 intakes is shortening the two bolts on either side of the air inlet, then heating and straightening the inlet tube. *Ford Racing Performance Parts*

secondary carb, while the driver-oriented mechanical secondary is better suited to racing.

Throttle Bodies

Unlike a carburetor, the throttle bodies found on 1986–95 5.0-liters only deliver air to the engine. Fuel injection separates the tasks of air and fuel flow to gain a far more efficient air/fuel distribution, but while the stock carburetor may be tweaked for

better fuel delivery, the stock throttle body just gets in the way.

In the early days of 5.0-liters, there was no choice but to enlarge the stock throttle body by machining out a few millimeters from 60 to 63 millimeters; 1986s had even smaller 58-millimeter units. Ford Racing, naturally, was the first outfit to release a larger throttle body. It introduced a 65-millimeter unit for street 5.0s, and, later, an 86-millimeter unit for all-out racing.

The 65-millimeter unit is a nice bolt-on for a stock car, supports well over 300 horsepower, and gives up no torque to the stocker.

When changing throttle bodies, a larger exhaust gas recirculation spacer is required. Some people choose to machine the stock spacer, but Ford Racing offers a 67-millimeter spacer. Installing both means enlarging the opening on the stock intake, while other Ford Racing and aftermarket

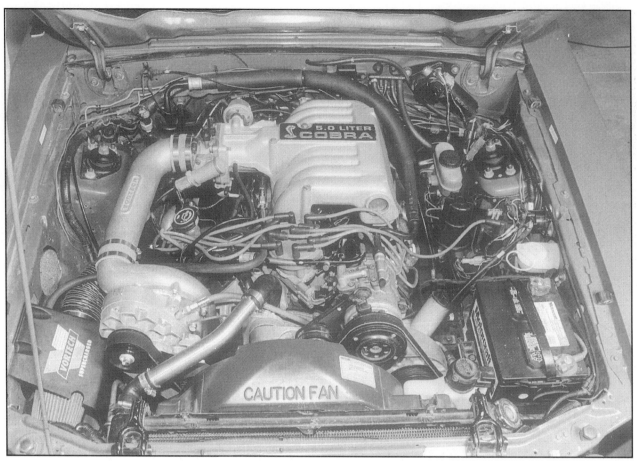

A cost-effective, cast alternative to the GT-40, the Cobra intake flows as well as the GT-40 intake and offers the additional benefit of allowing for porting or Extrude Honing. The Cobra intake also eliminates coolant traveling around the exhaust gas recirculation passages, which means you don't have to buy an EGR spacer to go with a larger throttle body. The Cobra's inner two bolts, at 7 inches, are longer than those used by the GT-40 intake. Be sure to have Cobra bolts on hand before installing this intake. Naturally, installing a phenolic intake spacer will require even longer bolts.

The Saleen/Vortech intake is a popular choice for supercharged street/strip Mustangs, thanks to its large ports. However, to gain maximum performance from this intake, the truck lower intake it sits on must be ported. The later versions of this intake feature eight cast-in bungs for additional fuel injectors. Installing secondary injectors in the intake is a good supplemental fueling option for high-horsepower supercharged cars, but this is a do-it-yourself proposition, as Vortech doesn't offer a kit to plumb or control the secondary injectors. *Vortech Engineering*

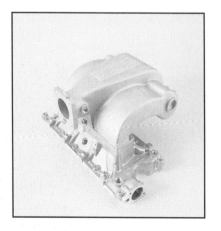

intakes usually have 70-millimeter inlets. Motorsport also has a 65-millimeter throttle body for 1994–95 5.0s, but rather than an

EGR spacer, it requires a special adapter elbow to fit on aftermarket intakes originally designed for Fox Mustangs.

Naturally, the typical bigger-is-better philosophy translated to the throttle body aftermarket, with vendors like BBK Performance and Accufab producing high-quality throttle bodies in 70-, 75-, 80-, and, in the case of Accufab, 90-millimeter varieties. BBK also offers 65-, 70-, and 75-millimeter throttle bodies for 1994–95 Mustangs.

Though these units all have their place, installing too large an oversized throttle body can hurt performance, particularly torque, as will installing too large a carburetor. This is mostly true regarding

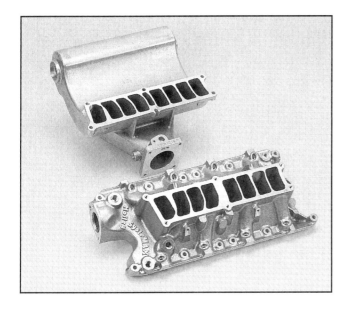

Holley's SysteMAX II intake is a kissing cousin of the Saleen/Vortech intake. Holley took the same basic design and improved it, primarily by casting up a new lower intake with enlarged ports designed to match its companion cylinder heads. This intake is good for blowers and high rpm, and the lower intake seems a natural for box and aftercooler upper intakes on all-out race cars. Trick Flow also offers three similarly-styled intake manifolds, with unique lower intakes. *Holley Performance Products*

naturally aspirated 5.0s, as supercharged and turbocharged engines will make up for the torque loss and capitalize on high-rpm airflow.

The last thing to remember about choosing a throttle body is it shouldn't be larger than your mass air meter. You want to create a funnel for the air, so the mass air meter and air filter should be large, necking down to the throttle body. Typically, a 70-millimeter throttle body coupled with a 73–75-millimeter mass air meter makes for a nice all-around street combination,

while racy 5.0s will want 75-millimeter and larger throttle bodies with 77-millimeter and larger mass air sensors.

Carbureted Intake Manifolds
A quick way to add extra power to a 1979–85 5.0 Mustang is to swap the factory intake for an aftermarket intake. This is particularly true of the 1979 and 1982 two-barrel carbs, as a new intake and four-barrel carb are obvious power builders. However, even the 1983–85 cars

with factory four-barrel Holleys can add performance with a new intake. First, however, you've got to consider the operating rpm range of your engine. Generally, dual-plane intakes are designed to improve performance from off-idle to around 6,000 rpm, while single-plane intakes shift the powerband up to 3,000 to 8,000 rpm.

It would be easy to differentiate the dual-plane as a pure street intake and a single-plane as a pure race intake, but it's not quite that simple. Many horsepower-crazed

Edelbrock's Performer 5.0 intake fuses value, flow, and airflow balance into one package. The 70-millimeter throttle inlet and runner accessibility make this intake a natural for street 5.0s with more power in their future. To extract maximum flow from this intake, without hurting its airflow balance, concentrate on heightening the individual runners and leave the main, T-shaped runner alone. *Edelbrock Corporation*

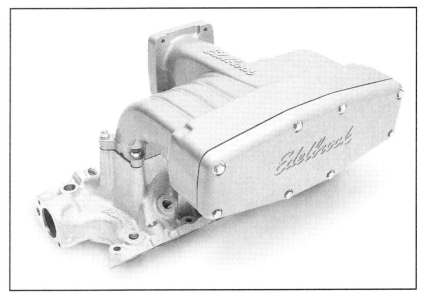

The one weakness of all the long-runnered 5.0 intakes is that they maximize low-end torque at the expense of high-rpm power. Well, Edelbrock offers a direct intake upgrade path in the form of their Performer RPM 5.0 intake. It features shorter runners and a larger cross-sectional area than the Performer 5.0. It is designed to offer increased power above 5,000 rpm, with a small loss of torque. This intake is the answer for high-rpm, big-boost or large-displacement engines with racetrack personalities and street pretensions. *Edelbrock Corporation*

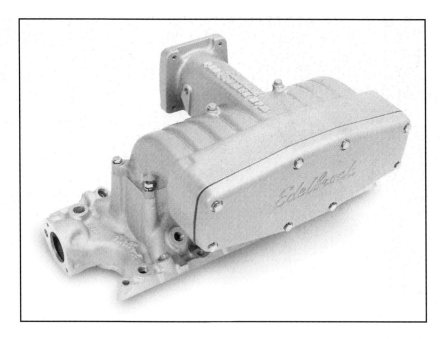

street pilots are more than willing to give up a little low-end torque for rip-roaring top-end power. They simply throw some steeper gears in the rear end and aim for the top of the tach.

Single-plane intakes used to run so much better than dual-planes on the top end, so it was an easy choice. These days the bigger dual-planes like the Edelbrock Performer RPM and Weiand Stealth run almost as well as single-planes up top and still preserve bottom-end torque.

It's important to remember street cars don't spend a lot of time at 6,500 rpm, so a dual-plane is the best choice for pure street cars. Street/strip cars should jump to one of the big dual-planes or, perhaps, a single-plane. Drag racers can go straight for single-plane induction.

Fuel-Injected Intake Manifolds

Where carbureted intakes must deal with fuel and air, fuel-injected intakes must only route air. Ford engineers began taking advantage of this with the 1986 5.0 Mustang. By lengthening the intake's runners, they were able to produce superb torque figures so beneficial in a rear-wheel-drive performance car. Of course, the factory induction is a compromise wedged between packaging, cost, and emissions. As such, the factory manifold is a primary restriction to power, just like the factory carbureted intakes. However, the manifold choices are bit more complex, thanks to different designs and materials.

Though some will likely throw in steep gears and rough it with this one on the street, the Edelbrock Victor 5.0 has no street pretensions, or emissions connections for that matter. This intake features a tall, tunnel-ram lower intake with an air-charge-insulating air gap between the runners. The upper intake is a small plenum with stubby 45-degree runners, which promote high-rpm power. *Edelbrock Corporation*

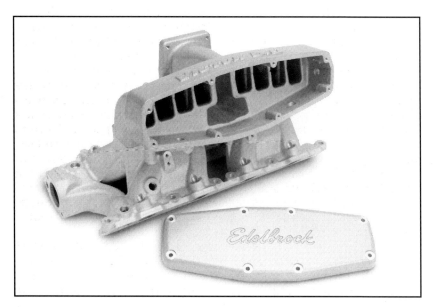

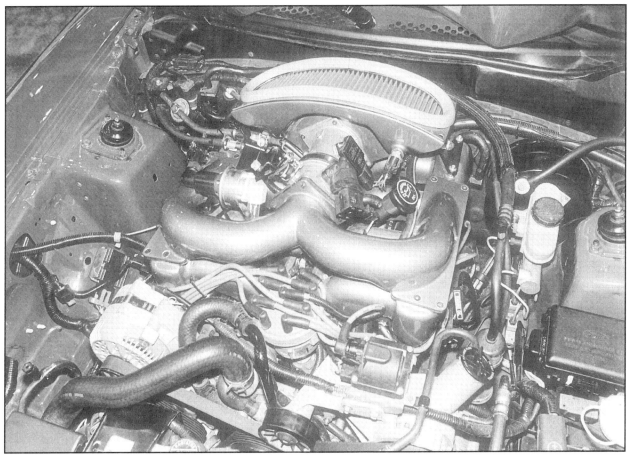

Using a unique tuned-runner design and complicated rear-inlet throttle body, the Roush Performance Parts intake is designed to really wake up a naturally aspirated 5.0. It works best when coupled with Roush's cowl-induction hood for SN95 Mustangs, although it can be run on Fox 5.0s equipped with non-Roush cowl-induction hoods. The Roush piece performs well and offers the whooshing induction sound originally lost with EFI. The downside of the Roush intake is expense, but it will set your 5.0 apart. Additionally, despite its reverse inlet layout, it can be supercharged.

Ford Racing Performance Parts

In the early days, 5.0 racers would cut the intake's plenum from its runners with a band saw to gain access to the runners. After hand-porting the intake, they would weld it back together. This labor-intensive process became nearly extinct when Ford Racing introduced the GT-40 intake.

Rather than using oval-shaped ports positioned in a line, the GT-40 gained room for larger runners by adopting round ports arranged in a staggered fashion. This allowed for bigger runners in practically the same space. Like the stock intake, the GT-40 is a two-piece manifold. The lower intake is cast aluminum, just like the stocker, while the upper features unique hot-formed metal tubes.

The smooth upper runners reduce airflow resistance and contribute to the GT-40 flowing an average of 60 cfm more air than the stock intake. This upper architecture also limits the intake's usefulness in truly high-output venues, as the upper is too thin for porting.

Despite its limitations and status as the first true performance 5.0 intake, the GT-40 remains the benchmark to which all 5.0 intakes are compared.

In 1993 Ford's new Special Vehicle Team introduced two new vehicles: the Lightning pickup and the first of their continuing line of Mustang Cobras. The Lightning received the GT-40 intake, while the Cobra got its first cousin, now dubbed the Cobra intake.

To bring GT-40 performance to the Cobra at a price point that made sense for the larger production run of Cobras, Ford built a cast-aluminum upper designed to fit the existing GT-40 lower intake. Though the Cobra intake has slightly smaller, rougher runners, it actually performs on par with the GT-40, plus the cast upper can be ported for performance exceeding that of the GT-40.

With the debut of the SN95 Mustangs in 1994, Ford revised the Cobra upper to fit under the Mustang's sleek new hood. The

Taking the tuned runner length, optimized port line of sight, and big airflow capacity to the nth degree, the BXR, or balanced cross ram, intake ignores most all factory packaging considerations to provide stunning performance. Adding one to a stock 5.0 long block with open exhaust resulted in over 400 horsepower. This intake really thunders on a modified engine. It can be supercharged, but that overshadows its runner tuning. The BXR intake is complex—with many must-have "options"—and expensive, but once in place, it shames factory-style aftermarket intakes. Plus, its Hi-Torque and Open plenum covers offer an easy powerband shift at the track. *BXR Manifolds, Inc.*

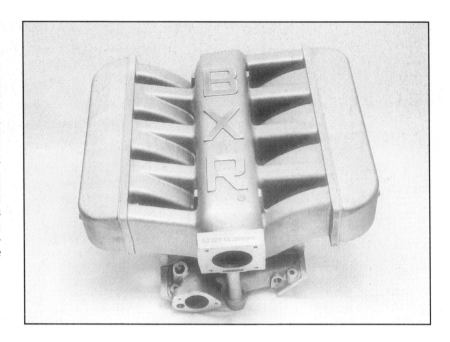

changes included reduced height, a curved throttle body inlet, and, for its use on the 1995 Cobra R, a larger plenum area. Despite these changes, the 1994–95 Cobra intake flows right with its sibling and the GT-40. However, it too can be ported and, thanks to its larger plenum, is happier on large-displacement engines.

Saleen/Vortech

Developed by Saleen for its 1989 Saleen SSC, which featured an optional Vortech supercharger, this intake was eventually licensed by Vortech Engineering as well, hence the dual identification. This intake used Ford's EFI 5.0-liter truck lower intake because of its generous runner dimensions and improved port locations. To this base Saleen bolted a unique upper intake which, as Edelbrock would later, placed the upper-to-lower fasteners out of the air stream. It also made the exhaust gas recirculation mechanism integral to the intake, eliminating the need for an EGR spacer. This intake is a favorite for use with centrifugal superchargers, but the truck lower intake must be ported or Extrude Honed to achieve its potential.

Edelbrock

Though it took a while to react to the 5.0 market, Edelbrock eventually put it and the GT-40 intake in its sights. To do so, its engineers started from scratch, building a completely new intake. The Edelbrock Performer 5.0 incorporates a taller lower intake, which eases the turns air must make, thereby increasing airflow. It also yields superb airflow balance between runners, thanks to ports shifted as far forward as possible.

To improve the upper intake's airflow, Edelbrock's designers moved all the upper-to-lower fasteners out of the air stream. They also enlarged both the throttle body opening (to 70 millimeters) and plenum volume, as compared to the GT-40. All told, the Performer 5.0 was the hands-down best all-around street manifold. And, thanks to Edelbrock's economies of scale, it is affordable as well.

Not willing to rest on its street laurels, Edelbrock later released two racier 5.0 intake manifolds: the Performer RPM 5.0 and Victor 5.0. The Performer RPM is an upper intake manifold designed to retrofit to the Performer lower. It incorporates shorter runners and larger cross-

sectional area for more power above 5,000 rpm.

While the Performer RPM 5.0 makes a lot of sense, especially for supercharged street 5.0s, the Victor 5.0 is cast for the drag strip. Thanks to a tunnel ram-style lower intake and a small upper plenum, the Victor 5.0 is meant for high-rpm power to 500 horsepower and beyond. Its lower intake offers the unique bonus of an air gap between the runners and the hot oil in the valley, which should enhance performance, thanks to cooler air-charge temperature. There is no fence-walking with the Victor 5.0, however, as it accepts no emissions equipment.

Holley

One intake that does walk the fence is Holley's SysteMAX II. It offers a streetable powerband of 2,000 to 6,500 rpm, but at the time of its release, the SysteMAX II intake was not street legal. For racers, the SysteMAX II should prove a formidable performer at the track. It may look familiar, as it is built on the same basic design as the track-friendly Saleen/Vortech intake.

There are, however, some key differences between the two. While

Downs Ford Motorsport's upper intake is designed for use on a GT-40 lower intake and is a popular choice for supercharged 5.0s with lots of boost and lots of displacement, or both. It does its best work at 7,000 rpm, so the electronic and reciprocating components must be upgraded. It also offers easy access to valve covers for between round rocker arm adjustments.

Holley removed some minor obstructions in the upper architecture, the big improvements are found down south. Whereas the Saleen/Vortech upper is mounted on a stock Ford truck lower intake with restrictive port exits, the Holley lower is a new piece with expanded ports designed to match the port entrances of Holley's SysteMAX II cylinder heads. The result

is an intake that should outperform the Saleen/Vortech in out-of-the-box form.

Box Intakes

The final, most specialized form of fuel-injected 5.0 induction is the box intake, as represented by Bennett Racing, Comp Composites, Downs Ford, and Cartech. These intakes are so named

because they place a small, empty plenum atop one of the common EFI lower intakes. By eliminating the complex, tuned runners found in most EFI intakes, the boxes trade low-end torque for high-rpm horsepower. Because of this characteristic, these intakes are best suited for high-rpm forced-induction and naturally aspirated applications.

Cylinder Heads

3

If eyes are the windows to the soul, cylinder heads are the windows to performance. These are the big ones. The bolt-ons of bolt-ons. They are the most important modification for a 5.0-liter Mustang. This is because the stock cylinder heads are so restrictive. Because of this the other common bolt-ons like intakes and exhaust systems will only deliver minor horsepower boost on 5.0s with stock cylinder heads.

Ford gradually improved the cylinder heads on the 5.0-liter engine during its lifespan in the Fox and SN95 Mustang, except for the step backward in 1986. The heads on the last series of Mustangs with HO 5.0-liters were derived from Ford's E7TE truck casting, featuring 1.78 intake valves and 1.45 exhaust valves.

Alas, the stock Ford cylinder heads have their shades half drawn. They provided impressive performance in a stock vehicle, but even the best factory 5.0-liter heads were reined in by emissions and fuel economy limitations. These constraints resulted in the aforementioned small valves and restrictive ports. At a pedestrian .500-inch lift, the stock head's intake flow signs off at only 155 cfm, while, in true Ford fashion, the exhaust ports were the most severe performance limiter, restricting .500-inch exhaust flow to only 122 cfm.

Dimensions

Aftermarket cylinder heads typically increase performance by casting their heads with larger ports, revised combustion chamber volumes, and larger valve openings. While these may seem like basic concepts, they have an influence on your engine combination and its operating range.

Larger ports, especially exhaust ports, are a quick way to increase performance versus stock castings. The stock E7TE intake port is 124 cc

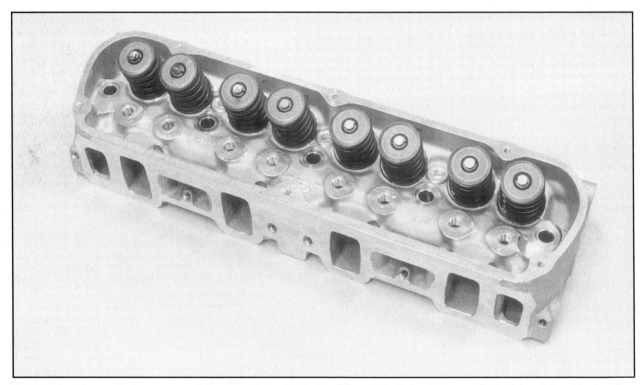

You aren't going to find too many of these heads in circulation. The original aluminum small-block head, Ford Racing Performance Parts J302, offers performance on par with many of the modern, streetable 5.0 cylinder heads. Unfortunately, they lack emissions provisions. The 2.02/1.60 valve package and 58-cc combustion chambers make the J302 a good choice for naturally aspirated and nitrous-equipped 5.0 strip cars. If you find a cheap set at a swap meet, don't turn up your nose.

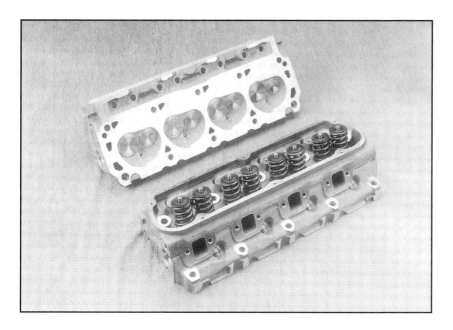

Ford Racing Performance Parts' featherweight GT-40X heads are the alpha cylinder heads in the Ford Racing Performance Parts GT-40 line-up. These 22-pound power makers are fitted with 1.94/1.54 valves and flow right there with most any street-legal 5.0 head. Plus, the GT-40X heads are offered assembled with good Ford Racing Performance Parts hardware compatible with Ford Racing Performance Parts camshafts. The assembled heads even come with CNC-machined exhaust runners. Naturally, all the Ford Racing Performance Parts parts bolt on like stock parts.

and performance heads usually range from 165 to 210 cc. Heads with intake ports exceeding 180 cc are aimed at high-rpm or increased-displacement engines that will gladly trade a decrease in airflow velocity, which usually hurts torque, for bigger lungs.

Bigger combustion chamber volumes in the neighborhood of 65 cc are desirable for supercharged and turbocharged engines, because the air forced into the engine artificially raises the engine's compression ratio. For naturally aspirated and nitrous engines, the reduction in compression ratio actually hurts performance. A combustion chamber volume like 58 cc is ideal for nonsupercharged street engines, while some of the racier heads are offered with chambers as small as 47 cc.

Like larger ports, larger valves can also slow airflow velocity, but the biggest concern when considering a valve size package is piston-to-valve clearance. Factory 1.78 intake/1.45 exhaust valves don't come anywhere near hitting the piston. The common aftermarket heads increase the valves up to 1.94/1.60 inches. These will clear stock dished pistons with all but the most outrageous camshafts; owners of 1986 5.0s must be extra

careful, however, as that model came equipped with lift-limiting flat-top pistons. The next step up in valve size moves the intake valve to 2.02-inch valves and leaves the

exhaust valve at 1.60. Stepping up to the 2.02 intake valves mandates moving to aftermarket pistons notched for proper valve clearance; this is easily accommodated at

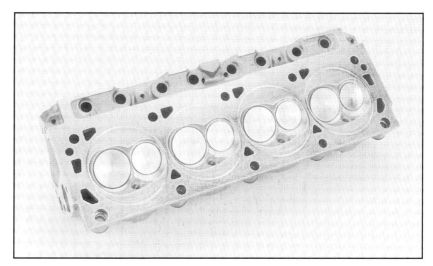

Many Mustang drag racers run eight-second elapsed times using Trick Flow Street Heat aluminum heads, so it's safe to say they provide ample airflow for any street/strip 5.0. Unfortunately, these heads are no longer available new, as Trick Flow is now pursuing the Twisted Wedge, and Will-Burt, who always manufactured the head, is no longer authorized to market the heads. Street Heat heads do mandate the use of stud-mounted rocker arms and, in some cases, special headers to obtain proper exhaust-to-floor pan clearance due to the heads' raised exhaust ports. If you are running short-tube headers, you can get by without a special header, especially when employing a two-cat high-flow H-pipe, but you will need a special long-tube header. These heads offer the best performance when ported, but they remain a benchmark in 5.0 performance. Street Heat heads were available in cast iron and aluminum and with or without emissions plumbing.

rebuild time, but bolting such heads onto a stock short block precludes such inconveniences.

Materials

This is a simple matter of cost. Cast-iron heads are cheap and readily available on the new and used market. Aluminum heads are a bit more expensive, but these days the economies of scale make aluminum an affordable choice for the 5.0.

Though they cost a bit more than cast-iron, aluminum heads offer a number of advantages. They shave weight off the front of the car, and they allow running more ignition timing because of their excellent heat conducting properties. Aluminum is also easier to repair via welding, should you have a catastrophic mishap.

Conversely, cast-iron heads will make a bit more power on naturally-aspirated engines by holding heat energy in the cylinders.

Street Heads

Most people who spend their hard-earned money on this book are driving their 5.0s on the street. While there is still plenty of room for improved cylinder head performance on the street, there are also a number of important considerations: emissions, fitment, and range of performance.

Though the Twisted Wedge is an impressive performer, it is still a street head. To service the all-out race market while maintaining affordable valvetrain architecture, Trick Flow offers the Twisted Wedge R head. While it retains the twisted 61-cc combustion chamber, it adds raised exhaust ports and huge intake valves and ports. On the exhaust side, Twisted Wedge Rs offer horizontal and diagonal header-bolt flanges to allow maximum exhaust porting. Some racers have reported as much as 150 horsepower gains by switching to the R over some of the more common inline heads. These heads are a great racing value below the canted-valve Yates radar. *Trick Flow*

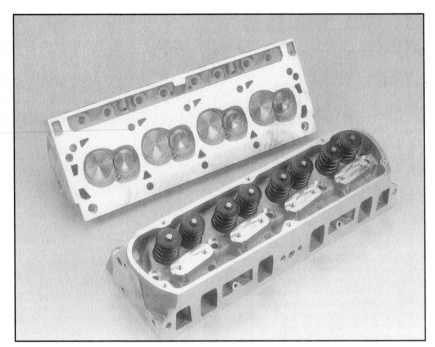

Successors to the Street Heat heads are Trick Flow's Twisted Wedge heads. These heads employ unique 61-cc combustion chambers, which are rotated to unshroud the valves and increase flow. The chamber is the source of the Twisted moniker, and some radical valve angles decreed short valve guide life, a problem Trick Flow attributes to poor valvetrain hardware choices by enthusiasts. In any event, Twisted Wedges are formidable performers in a street-legal package. It's tough to overlook them, especially when they require less specialized hardware than their raised-port predecessor. If you can't resist, plan to buy unassembled heads and fill them with good hardware, as the budget assembled heads skimp a bit on valvetrain pieces. While you're at it, you might be tempted to port the heads too. If you decide to do so, make sure to use a porter who specializes in Twisted Wedges, as these heads flow so well out-of-the-box, big airflow gains are tough to achieve.

The primary concern is that the heads are deemed street legal as outfitted with a California Air Resources Board Executive Order or as a direct replacement part. Key to a cylinder head achieving street-

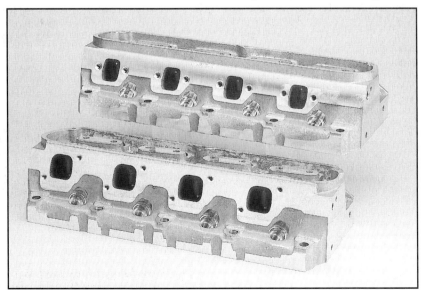

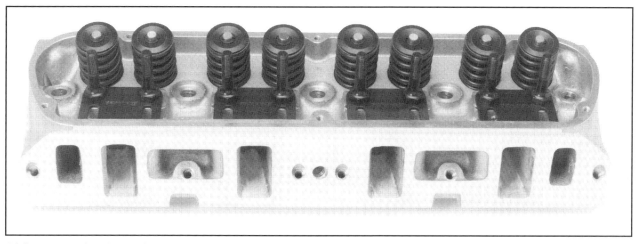

Of the non-Ford Racing Performance Parts offerings, the nicest, bolt-it-on-and-forget-it cylinder head is Edelbrock's Performer 5.0. This street-legal head is available with 1.94- or 2.02-inch intake valves matched with large but velocity-promoting intake runners and ambidextrous 60-cc combustion chambers, which work well in natural and forced induction environments. While they will never be race heads, Edelbrocks really thunder after porting the exhaust side. These heads are only available in aluminum. *Edelbrock Corporation*

legal status is the presence of exhaust crossover passages to recirculate exhaust gases via the exhaust gas recirculation system. This system bleeds off a bit of the exhaust gas and mixes it with intake air to reduce combustion temperatures, as combustion temperatures above 1,300 degrees cause the formation of oxides of nitrogen, or NO_2, a primary culprit in the formation of smog.

Another key component keeping your aftermarket heads green is the presence of Thermactor air passages. During warm start-up, these passages direct air from the belt-driven Thermactor pump, commonly referred to as a smog pump, to lean out the typically rich mixtures exiting the head during the warm-start cycle. Two vacuum-controlled solenoids, the Thermactor Air Bypass and Thermactor Air

Diverter, route the Thermactor air. During cold start and wide-open throttle, the TAD vents the pumped air to atmosphere. The TAD either sends air to the catalytic converters during warm cruise or to the aforementioned cylinder head passages.

While these features are important in keeping our air breathable, a subject of more immediate concern is fitment. Key to a cylinder

Attacking the vibrant but not too radical race market is the Edelbrock Victor Jr. head. This aluminum offering is not street legal and offers a considerable boost in performance without moving to radical valvetrain hardware. These heads feature huge intake ports, raised exhaust ports, and 62-cc combustion chambers. They are ripe for high-rpm or stroker 5.0s, especially after porting. *Edelbrock Corporation*

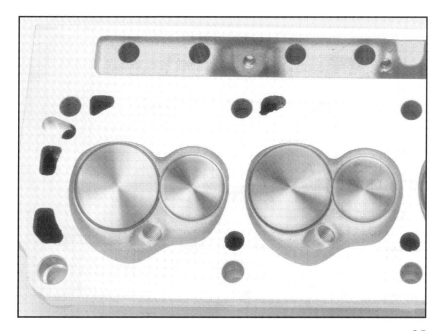

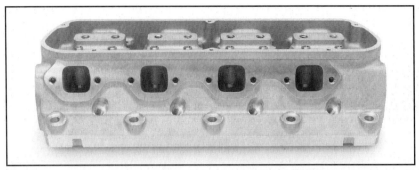

Pulling out all the stops on a budget are Edelbrock's Victor cylinder heads. With big valves, big ports, thimble-sized combustion chambers, and raised exhaust ports, there is no mistaking that these are racing cylinder heads. Add to that the required shaft-mounted rockers, custom headers, and manifold spacers—they are essentially Chevy heads with Ford ports—so you had better be serious. Still, when fully ported, these heads can approach Yates power levels for less money. *Edelbrock Corporation*

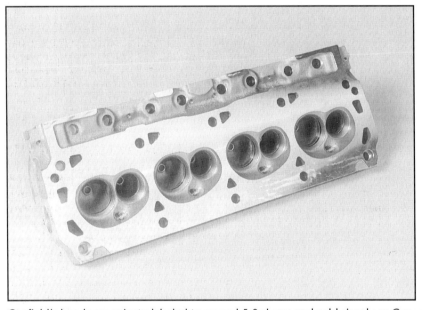

Canfield's heads are private-labeled to several 5.0 shops and sold simply as Canfield heads. They are similar in style and mission to the Trick Flow Street Heat head and offer excellent performance for the dollar. Unfortunately, none of the Canfields are street legal. These heads are equipped with large runners and thick decks and are often sold fully ported and fitted with large 2.08-inch intake valves. Panhandle Performance even offers a version with a large, 1.69-inch exhaust valve to help evacuate exhaust in forced induction applications. In any form, these heads are best suited for displacement or rpm, or both.

head's streetability is its compatibility with your existing hardware. The primary culprits here are raised ports, larger valves, and relocated spark plug locations. Raised ports, typically exhaust, sometimes require application-specific headers, as they might raise the exhaust

system too close to the floor pan with standard headers.

As mentioned before, 1.94 intake valves and 1.60 exhaust valves are typically the largest valves you can employ without flycutting the pistons for clearance. However, this is also dependent on

how much valve lift your camshaft delivers. As a result, it's a good idea to place Play Doh on the piston eyebrow, then install the heads and manually reciprocate the engine with a wrench on the crankshaft. Then remove the head and measure the Play Doh to make sure the clearance is within spec. This is usually too much work for the average home hot rodder, so the easy way out is to stick with proven valve/cam combinations.

It is also best to stick with smaller heads on the street. As detailed earlier in this chapter, huge valves and intake ports are meant for increased rpm and displacement. If you are dealing with 302 cubic inches and a 6,250 rpm rev limiter, going beyond 1.94/1.60 valves and port volumes above 170 cc will likely hurt naturally aspirated performance. Combining bigger ports with a power adder, however, can mitigate those concerns.

Before the 5.0-liter Mustang exploded as an aftermarket darling, things were far less complicated. Ford enthusiasts hopping up a 302 would simply scour the junkyards looking for 351 Windsor cylinder heads with casting numbers C90 sport the favorable combination of 1.84/1.54 valves and 60-cc chambers. Porting these heads and fitting them with larger 1.90/1.60 valves can yield performance on a par with unported aftermarket heads.

These days there is really no reason to go with old 351 castings, other than penny-pinching. If cheapskating it is your way, Aerohead Industries in Indianapolis, Indiana, specializes in reworking 302 and 351 heads with new valves, springs, seals, locks, and retainers. Replete with a three-angle valve job, these heads typically retail under $400—a cheap gearhead's dream.

However, the amount you spend usually reflects the performance you are buying. Ported factory heads can equal some unported aftermarket pieces, but if

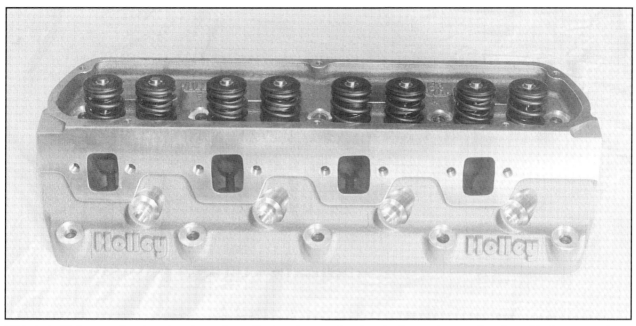

With their 62.5-cc combustion chambers, the Holley heads are uniquely suited to perform well on forced-induction and naturally aspirated 5.0s. Only available assembled, the SysteMAX II heads are fitted with high-quality stainless-steel valves, phosphor-bronze valve guides, and 7-degree steel keepers. They do mandate stud-mounted rocker arms and special care in selecting headers, thanks to the raised exhaust ports. When run as part of Holley's complete SysteMAX II package, these heads help add over 100 horsepower to a mildly modified 5.0.

you port the aftermarket pieces, the comparison ends. Additionally, aftermarket aluminum heads offer even more performance because they reduce weight.

Ford Racing Performance Parts

Ford's in-house aftermarket division naturally put forth the first street head for 5.0-liter Mustangs. Drawing inspiration from the 302 castings used to propel the Le Mans-winning GT-40 cars, Ford engineers created modern cylinder heads that nearly equal their racy namesake, while incorporating emissions compatibility. By today's standard's, the cast-iron GT-40s are downright pedestrian, with airflow peaking out at 196 cfm on the intake, and 140 cfm on the exhaust, at .550-inch valve lift.

One of the iron heads to better the Ford Racing Performance Parts GT-40 is the GTP-40. Despite this nomenclature, the P head is not a Ford Racing Performance Parts offering. It is the stock cylinder head on 5.0-powered Explorers. Ford engineers improved on the basic GT-40 design by reconfiguring the combustion chamber and centering the spark plug. Because of the increased combustion efficiency, Ford was able to equip the GTP-40s with 1.46-inch exhaust valves as opposed to the 1.54 valves present in the rest of the GT-40 family. These heads are an excellent choice for budget power building, thanks to assembled, valve-jobbed heads sold by Central Coast Mustang for around $700.

GT-40 was the only head on the block until Trick Flow introduced its Street Heat heads. Since then, each successive iteration of aftermarket Ford heads flowed more and more. In 1995 Ford Racing Performance Parts finally introduced an aluminum version of the GT-40, dubbed the Turbo Swirl head because of its high-swirl combustion chamber. This head flowed considerably more than the iron head, registering 217 intake cfm at .600-inch lift. Still, by 1995 these numbers weren't going to strike fear into anyone.

The upside of the streety GT-40 heads are price, compatibility, and emissions exemption. Either variant can be had for well under $1,000 fully assembled with good Ford Racing Performance Parts hardware. Given that they must meet Ford's standards for original equipment parts, they bolt right on and are also emissions legal. The price differential between the two makes the aluminum Turbo Swirls a good choice for a politely warmed-over street machine with no racing pretensions.

Trick Flow

Trick Flow Specialties set the standard by which all street-oriented small-block Ford cylinder heads would be judged back in 1988. Its Street Heat aluminum cylinder heads outperformed the prescient J302 heads and, unlike the racy J302, offered Thermactor and EGR passages. They flowed 228 intake cfm at a racy .700-inch lift and

Another streetable race head is Brodix's Track I Ford aluminum head. These heads follow the usual tradition of big valves, big ports, and big combustion chambers, making them adaptable to naturally aspirated or forced-induction small-blocks. Though Brodix played with the valve angle on these heads, they offer plenty of performance from standard valvetrain hardware. These heads are available with the N exhaust port bolt pattern spawned by Ford Racing Performance Parts' Sportsman head. Since they aren't street legal anyway, stepping up to the N port and header is worth the increase in exhaust flow, especially for strokers and forced 5.0s.

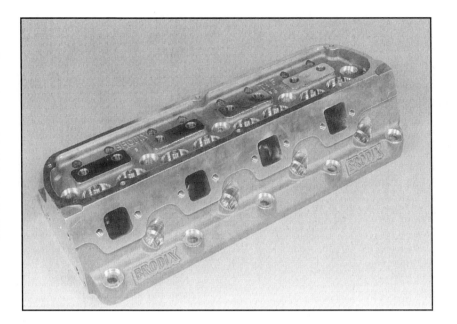

143.3 cfm at the same lift. Their intake numbers bested anything on the market at the time, giving them a special place in the hearts of head porters and engine tuners.

Because of their inherent intake flow and the potential flow lurking in its raised exhaust ports, these heads were the heads to race. They remained the head of choice until racier heads from Trick Flow and others flooded the market. Still these heads are a good choice for a hot street 5.0, especially if you can find a set on the used market. This is the only way to get them these days, as Trick Flow has moved on to a new design and Will-Burt, the company that manufactured Street Heats for Trick Flow, is no longer authorized to manufacture and market them.

Trick Flow's Twisted Wedge aluminum cylinder heads put the Street Heat in the history books. Unlike the Street Heats, these heads don't have raised ports requiring special headers. Trick Flow put all its magic into the twisted 61-cc combustion chamber, which packages 2.02/1.60 valves at a radical angle to unshroud the valves for improved flow.

These heads flow an impressive 251 intake cfm at .600-inch lift and an even more impressive

193 exhaust cfm at .600. Despite the impressive out-of-box performance, Twisted Wedge made the biggest noise because of its price. They retailed for under $900 for assembled heads, via Trick Flow's parent company, Summit Racing Equipment, which cut painfully into the rest of the aftermarket's beloved profit margin.

Twisted Wedges didn't get that cheap without cutting some corners, though. The hardware, especially the alloy guides and stamped steel valve locks, isn't going to win any durability contests. This is especially important because the radical Twisted Wedge valve angle is known to promote premature valve wear. According to Trick Flow, the guide problem can be traced to consumers straying from their recommended rocker arms and push rods, but they have since added durable bronze guides.

There is no doubt good valvetrain gear will slow the wear, but head builders say you can get part of the geometry right, but not all of it. Because of the heads' overwhelming out-of-the-box performance and low cost, it is still a viable street option. However, you should consider buying bare, stud-mount heads. By building them up with the best aftermarket hardware

and utilizing the valvetrain adjustment available with stud-mounted rocker arms, you should get the most performance and durability from Twisted Wedges. You also can't get much more radical than an E303 camshaft without notching your pistons or installing Twisted Wedge-specific pistons, which are available from many aftermarket suppliers.

Edelbrock

Though Edelbrock usually takes its time waiting for a market to develop before releasing a product, the resulting product almost always exceeds expectations. Such is the case with its Performer 5.0/5.8 aluminum cylinder heads. At the time of their release, these parts set a new standard for the affordability of small-block Ford cylinder heads, signaling parity with the Chevy aftermarket.

Besides being cost effective, the Edelbrock heads pack a number of attractive features, including emissions legality, large valves, 5/8-inch-thick decks, and Heli-Coiled inserts to prevent stripped threads. Performers are machined with 60-cc combustion chambers, which work well with naturally aspirated and forced-induction combinations and are available with 1.94- or 2.02-inch

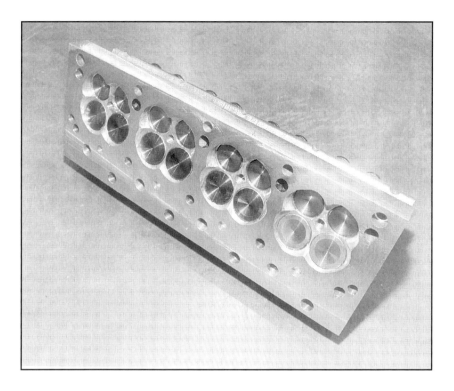

An expensive, but high-flowing option is Dominion Performance's four-valve-per-cylinder head. These heads feature a unique push-rod-driven shaft-rocker system that allows Dominion to cram four small valves into the combustion chamber. Though they seem a bit exotic for the street, the Dominion heads offer the burger stand appeal of no other head, thanks to the 32-valve demarcation on the valve covers. With a proper—read big—intake and exhaust system, these heads should shine.

intake valves—the latter necessitating notched pistons.

The Edelbrock Performers are never going to be race heads, but Edelbrock and others have plenty of parts directed at that market. These heads are potent street heads that bolt right on, without special headers or rockers, and offer good durability and performance. If you really want to step them up, concentrate your efforts on enlarging and smoothing their exhaust ports.

Airflow Research

Bringing its stellar Chevy reputation to the Ford small-block world was a long time coming, but Airflow Research's 165-cc aluminum heads are formidable out-of-the-box performers. These street-legal parts offer CNC-ported intake ports, exhaust ports, and combustion chambers right out of the box. A five-angle competition valve job is also part of the AFR package.

Most surprising, the AFR heads are emissions legal and require no special rocker arms or headers. Additionally, these heads rival the flow numbers of the top street head, the Twisted Wedge, without

any tricky valvetrain geometry. They clock in with peak intake airflow at 250 cfm at .500-inch lift and 191 exhaust cfm at .600-inch lift.

Knowing there is a great deal of difference between 5.0s and 351Ws, AFR also offers a street-legal 185-cc head for 351s. However, this head is also a natural for high-rpm and stroker 5.0s. It is machined for 1/2-inch fasteners, so reducers are required for all 5.0 blocks, save the Ford Racing Performance Parts A4. AFR also offers a nonemissions version of this head without an exhaust heat crossover. The exhaust ports on this head are unchanged, so the exhaust flow is equivalent to the 165-cc head. However, the 185-cc intake runners really step up the intake flow, registering 282 cfm at .600-inch lift, for a 32-cfm improvement.

World Products

Another company that made its name servicing the Chevy market jumped on the 5.0 fairly early with its Windsor cylinder heads. World Products big head was initially available in cast iron. These heads

are built with massive 200-cc intake ports fed by 2.02-inch intake valves. Both the intake valves and the 1.60-inch exhaust valves are high-quality Manley Street Flo parts. These heads are best for high-rpm or larger displacement engines and are forced-induction friendly, thanks to 64-cc combustion chambers. They flow 241 intake cfm at .600-inch lift and 150 exhaust cfm at the same valve lift.

With the jumbo-sized Windsor head aimed at the heavily modified 5.0 market, World Products eventually released a cylinder head aimed at the basic bolt-on crowd. Dubbed the Windsor Jr., this head debuted with stock-sized 58-cc combustion chambers, 351W-sized 1.94/1.60 valves, and modestly enlarged 170-cc intake runners. These heads are affordable power builders for mildly modified, naturally aspirated and nitrous 5.0s, but the valve springs in both the assembled World Products heads must be upgraded for compatibility with the roller cams found in 1986 and later 5.0s. Also, these heads mandate the use of stud-

Key to installing a new head gasket is a clean block surface. However, you don't want to abrade the block surface to the point you damage the finish. Also, make sure the tab that says front is closest to the front (closer to the radiator) of the car. A graphite gasket is the best choice for a street-going 5.0, while race engines require block O-rings, copper gaskets, or both.

mounted roller rockers, so you must purchase new rocker arms to use these heads.

Street/Strip Heads

This is the Jekyll and Hyde category. All of these cylinder heads lack the necessary CARB Executive Order for 50-state emissions legality—a few will likely get it in the future—but some of them do have the necessary Thermactor air passages and exhaust heat crossovers to have hope of passing emissions. The rest of the group are race heads in street clothing, meaning they bolt on without too many special parts and, more importantly, they won't break the bank of a weekend warrior.

Ford Racing Performance Parts

Since the release of Ford Racing Performance Parts J302 heads back in 1988, the number of perfor-

mance small-block Ford cylinder head choices went from embarrassingly few to an embarrassment of riches. The Ford Racing Performance Parts J302 heads kicked this party off in an unusual way. The aluminum heads proved hearty performers, flowing 210 cfm intake and 143.8 exhaust, but they lacked street-legal status.

They were soon usurped by the Trick Flow Street Heat heads and eventually replaced by the GT-40 line, but if you find them at a swap meet cheap, don't discount them, as they are a lot better than the stock 5.0 heads. Beware, however, of their compact 58-cc combustion chambers, which have likely shrunk after being machined. If you are running a supercharger, these might yield excessive compression, leading to detonation.

Topping the modern street/strip offerings from Ford Racing

Performance Parts are the GT-40X aluminum cylinder heads, the latest iteration of the GT-40 lineage. The X heads, as they are known, feature reworked intake and exhaust ports enlarged 12 cc and 8 cc respectively. This, coupled with a large 1.94-inch intake valve—the exhaust valve remains GT-40-spec 1.54—yields respectable out-of-the-box flows of 249 intake cfm at .600-inch lift and 175.2 exhaust cfm at .650-inch lift.

These heads really should be detailed in the "Street Heads" section; however, they lack the necessary emissions exemption. They do have the required Thermactor and exhaust heat passages, so they are completely streetable.

A wild card head in the street/strip deck is Ford Racing Performance Parts' cast-iron Sportsman head. These heavy castings sport raised intake and exhaust

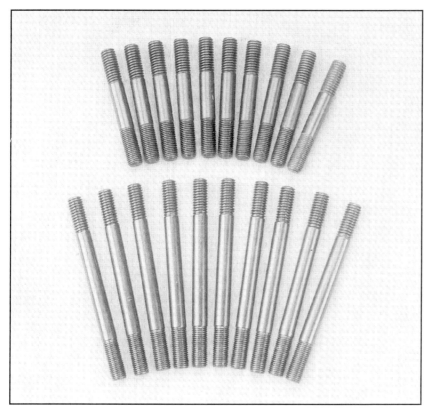

When installing new cylinder heads, it's a good idea to upgrade to stronger after-market fasteners like those sold by ARP and others. The main choice is bolts or studs. Bolts are likely fine for naturally aspirated and mild forced-induction 5.0s. Big boost or nitrous means considering studs, which deliver more clamping force—which might exceed the strength of the factory block. If you choose studs, use a non-hardening sealer like Permatex 2 to seal the lower studs, because they protrude into the water jacket.

ports, 64-cc combustion chambers, and a 2.02/1.60-inch valve package. While the N castings flow quite well, especially at high rpm, they require special rocker arms and headers, driving up the price of the cheap bare castings close to that of the racier aluminum heads. Still they make good power, particularly on stroker 5.0s, and make for a unique combination.

Canfield Cylinder Heads

Canfield burst onto the 5.0 cylinder head scene with its aluminum castings. These heads quickly filled the void left by the discontinuation of the Trick Flow Street Heat heads, which continued on for about a year under the Will-Burt banner. It seems the Canfields mimicked the Street Heats in more

than demographics, as the two companies went to court, but eventually reached a settlement.

That said, the Canfields are only similar to the Street Heats. In fact they are dimensionally larger in a number of areas. They have thicker decks and larger, 192-cc intake runners, but offer the same 1.94- or 2.02-inch intake and 1.60-inch exhaust valve choices. Also, Canfield did lean a bit toward the nitrous and naturally aspirated markets with its compact 54- or 58-cc combustion chambers. Perhaps the most striking similarity between the two heads is the Canfield's raised exhaust ports.

Still, Canfield makes no street pretensions, as its heads lack Thermactor and exhaust heat crossover plumbing. They deliver race-worthy

airflow rated at 272 cfm on the intake and 201 on the exhaust at an achievable .600-inch lift.

Brodix

Yet another company with a strong Chevy rep finally warmed up to the small-block Ford with its Track 1 Ford aluminum heads. These Brodix offerings are aimed at large-displacement and forced-induction engines. They feature voluminous 68-cc combustion chambers and 195-cc intake ports. In addition to the big architecture, Track 1 heads are fitted with big 2.08-inch intake valves.

Brodix relocated the center-lines of the big intake valves and standard-sized 1.60-inch exhaust valves to make room for the larger valves and improve flow. The trade-off is they require buying custom pistons or fly-cutting your existing pistons for valve clearance. It may well be worth it though, as out-of-the-box Track 1s flow 252.2 cfm on the intake side and 196.5 cfm on the exhaust. Though they are quite streetable, Track 1s don't have any emissions hook-ups.

Holley

Private labeled to Holley's specifications, the SysteMAX II cylinder heads are a big part of Holley's SysteMAX II performance package for 5.0 Mustangs. This package is a well-thought-out component set including an intake manifold, camshaft, heads, timing chain, and all the necessary fasteners. The SysteMAX II setup is meant to improve power at the higher rpm, but below the factory 6,250 rev limiter.

Thanks to Holley's aluminum heads, this package increases horsepower by 100 over a 5.0 with some minor bolt-on modifications. They feature raised exhaust ports, revised valve angles, 1.94-inch intake, and 1.60 exhaust valves. Though these heads are not emissions legal, they do include the required Thermactor and exhaust heat crossover architecture, but it doesn't hurt their flow. At .600-inch lift, the streetable 155.8-cc intake port flows 235 cfm, while the 70.9-cc exhaust port handles 185 cfm at the same lift.

Dominion

Providing the most unique after-market cylinder head upgrade path for a 5.0 is Dominion Performance. Dominion offers a four-valve-per-cylinder cylinder head hewn from a single chunk of billet aluminum. By incorporating four smaller valves, the Dominion heads are able to flow more air than a two-valve head. This is because more of the combustion chamber is consumed by valve area.

Don't be frightened away by the Dominion heads, though. Although they are more expensive than two-valve heads, they bolt right on because they combine the stock push rod arrangement with lightweight shaft-mounted rocker arms good for upward of 9,000 rpm. All told, the B version of the Dominion head, fitted with two 1.65-inch intake valves and two 1.40 exhaust valves, are said to flow an astounding 346.2 intake cfm and 261.5 exhaust cfm. These big numbers were achieved on a head fitted with the optional N exhaust port lifted from Ford Racing Performance Parts' Sportsman head. Since only long-tube headers are available for this port, these numbers are a bit optimistic for a street-going 5.0, but the flow potential still remains. Dominion also offers a smaller valve package, the A head, and a larger valve package for 351W applications, the C head.

If you have the money, this head really has the potential to shine with optimized intake and exhaust paths. High rpm is its strong suit, though forced induction and high-rpm promises a powerful racing combination.

Race Heads

If you really want to go racing there are more than a few choices to mull over. Long gone are the days of bolting on a set of ported stock Windsor heads or grafting

Many aftermarket cylinder heads are made to accommodate the larger 1/2-inch fasteners used on 351 Windsors. To properly fasten these heads with 7/16 bolts, buy a stud or bolt kit with reducer bushings to reduce the movement of the heads on the block. It is also important to install fresh dowels on the block. These are even more critical to maintain the heads' proper placement on the block.

on a pair of 351 Cleveland heads. The Ford aftermarket is teeming with racing cylinder heads. Big valves, big ports, raised ports, and small combustion chambers are the common characteristics, but each company takes a slightly different path to performance. Of course, to get the most out of these heads requires an engine built to handle high rpm and high compression, meaning the engine must be optimized for durability.

Ford Racing Performance Parts

The big dog of small-block racing heads is the Robert Yates Ford Racing Performance Parts High-Port head. Designed for the high-rpm world of NASCAR circle track racing, the Yates head, as it is known on the street, extracts maximum flow from a 5.0 by altering almost all the standard dimensions. Yates heads feature canted valves and voluminous, raised ports. On top of their already high entry fee, the Yates heads also require specialized induction, exhaust, valvetrain, and piston hardware.

These heads are well above the budget of the average weekend

warrior. When prepped to the max, however, these heads can flow over 380 intake cfm, making them big performers at any cost. This is largely thanks to 210-cc intake and 119-cc exhaust ports, gated by 2.10-inch intake and 1.60 exhaust valves. Small 47-cc and large 67-cc combustion chamber configurations are available to suit naturally aspirated and forced-induction applications.

Brodix

Packing 2.125 intake and 1.60 exhaust valves into a compact 46-cc combustion chamber, the Brodix Neal head is positioned to challenge the Yates cylinder head. The head mandates a Fel-Pro 1022 or 1023 head gasket meant for a 4.125 cylinder bore. It takes an Autolite 51 plug for alcohol or a 52 for gasoline and requires 100 lb-ft of torque to seal it with 1/2-inch studs.

The Neal's voluminous, 248-cc intake ports will flow air into the high 300 cfm range. The port dimensions are 1.350 x 2.20 inches and will accept either a Fel-Pro 1265 intake gasket or a

Torquing the cylinder heads properly means starting in the upper-middle head bolt and working inside out. Sneak up on the torque figures starting at 35 lb-ft, moving to 50 lb-ft, and finishing off with 70 lb-ft on the lower bolts. The upper bolts should go from 35 to 70 to 90 lb-ft. This is to offset the wedging effect the upper intake has on the upper head bolts. Once you torque all the bolts, go back and retorque the middle bolts, as the force exerted by the outer bolts can alter the clamping force of the middle bolts.

trimmed-to-fit Fel-Pro 1229. According to Brodix, you can employ a Yates-style intake manifold. However, the intake must be modified for something other than a 9.5-deck 351.

Edelbrock

The antecedents to Edelbrock's exotic Victor heads, its Victor Jr. offerings, bolt right to a stock short block and were redesigned with the weekend warrior crowd in mind. Sporting 210-cc intake runners and 80-cc exhaust runners, they are targeted for high-rpm power, but still use more affordable hardware. The exhaust ports are raised, so special headers are a consideration and the raised valve cover rail might cause valve cover clearance issues with some fuel-injected upper intakes.

Topping out at 291 intake cfm and 195 exhaust cfm, Victor Jr. heads are stout performers for those who want to stick with common valvetrain hardware. Their 62-cc combustion chambers make them accessible to naturally

aspirated and forced-induction environments.

For those looking for no-compromise racing performance at a practical bargain compared to Yates heads, Edelbrock offers the Victor aluminum heads. Victors come out of the mold with 47-cc combustion chambers and a 2.165-inch intake/1.165-inch exhaust valve package. While the combustion chambers are small, the Victor's 2.10 x 1.66-inch intake ports are deceptively large, clocking in at 240 cc, only 8 shy of the as-cast Brodix and a full 30 cc larger than the Yates intake port. Once ported, the volume swells to 265 cc. Intake airflow measures at 360 cfm range, plenty to meet Edelbrock's conservative horsepower goals of 600–700 horsepower. Compared to the 119-cc Yates exhaust port, 1.44 x 1.56-inch Victor exhaust ports clock in at fairly small 80 cc. You must use 1/2-inch manifold spacers, available from Edelbrock, to adapt intake manifolds to the Victor head.

Trick Flow

Like Edelbrock's Victor offerings, Trick Flow's Twisted Wedge R cylinder heads fill a performance void just under the costly Ford Racing Performance Parts Yates heads. Unlike the Victors, though, Twisted Wedge Rs use standard, stud-mount rocker arms and existing header applications. The R is simply an enlarged version of Trick Flow's popular Twisted Wedge street head.

While both Trick Flow offerings feature its signature twisted 61-cc combustion chamber, which unshrouds the valves by radically altering their angles, the R heads take the concept to a larger scale. They feature big 205-cc intake runners feeding 2.08-inch intake and 1.60-inch exhaust valves. Box stock, these passageways flow 305 intake cfm and 222 exhaust cfm. With baselines like these, the requisite race porting offers a tremendous upside on the R heads.

Twisted Wedge R heads aren't Trick Flow's first foray into all-out racing heads. In 1990 it debuted a cylinder head dubbed the Stage V Pro Stock Ford Cylinder Head. They were forever known among 5.0 fans as the Jr. Pro Stock heads. Initially advertised for $3,000 a pair, these heads reportedly flowed 368.5 cfm of intake flow and 293.2 cfm of exhaust flow after some porting. They were way ahead of their time, though, and never really caught on. Thus, only 20 sets were produced, and those that made it out of the foundry were equivalent to prototypes. As such, they needed a great deal of preparation before becoming usable. They might eventually see market again, given the number of racy 5.0s and 351Ws being built today.

Porting

Porting and polishing cylinder heads is as popular as airing up tires, but it isn't quite as easy. As such, it's a job best left to a professional, though many experienced enthusiasts are up to the chore. Still, die-grinder-wielding skills are

5.0 HEADS AT A GLANCE

Head	Part Numbers	Material	Combustion Chamber Volume	Intake Valve Diameter	Exhaust Valve Diameter	Intake Runner Volume	Rocker Arm Mounting	Head Bolt Diameter
Airflow Research 165-cc	1402, 1472, 1400, 1470	Aluminum	58 or 64 cc	1.90 inches	1.60 inches	165 cc	Pedestal or Stud	7/16 inch
Airflow Research 185-cc	1422, 1492, 1420, 1490	Aluminum	58 or 64	2.02	1.60	185	Pedestal or Stud	1/2
Brodix Neal	BF 200	Aluminum	46	2.125	1.60	248	Shaft	1/2
Brodix Track 1 Ford	T1 STD F	Aluminum	68	2.08	1.60	195	Stud	1/2
Canfield Avenger	20-450	Aluminum	54 or 58	1.94 or 2.02	1.60	192	Stud	1/2
Dominion	32VSF-A, 32VSF-8, 32VSF-C	Aluminum	62	1.60 or 1.65 (2)	1.45 (2)	218	n/a	1/2
Edelbrock Performer	6036, 6037, 6028, 6038, 6039, 6029	Aluminum	60	1.90 or 2.02	1.60	170	Pedestal	1/2
Edelbrock Performer RPM	6021, 6022, 6024, 6025, 6026	Aluminum	60	1.90 or 2.02	1.60	170	Stud	1/2
Edelbrock Victor Jr.	7716, 7717, 7718, 7719	Aluminum	n/a	2.05	1.60	210	Stud	1/2
Edelbrock Victor	7721	Aluminum	47	2.125	1.625	240	Shaft	1/2
Holley SysteMAX II	300-551	Aluminum	62.5	1.94	1.60	155.8	Stud	1/2
Stock 1987–95 5.0	E7TE	Cast-Iron	58	1.78	1.45	124	Pedestal	7/16
SVO GT-40	M-6049-L302, -L303	Cast-Iron	65.5	1.84	1.54	n/a	Pedestal	7/16
SVO GT-40 Turbo Swirl	M-6049-Y302, -Y303	Aluminum	64	1.94	1.54	160	Pedestal	1/2
SVO GT-40X	M-6049-X302, -X303, -X304, X-305	Aluminum	58 or 64	1.94	1.54	178	Pedestal	1/2
SVO J302	M-6049-J302	Aluminum	58	2.02	1.60	n/a	Stud	1/2
SVO Sportsman	M-6049-N351, -R351	Cast-Iron	64	2.02	1.60	195	Stud	1/2
Trick Flow Street Heat	n/a	Aluminum or Cast	64	1.94 or 2.02	1.60	187	Stud	1/2
Trick Flow Twisted Wedge	51400002, 51400003, 5141B002, 5141B003	Aluminum	61	2.02	1.60	170	Stud	7/16
Trick Flow Twisted Wedge R	52400001, 52400002, 524B0001, 524B0002	Aluminum	61	2.08	1.60	206	Stud	1/2
World Products Windsor Jr.	5303B, 2303B	Aluminum or Cast	58	1.94	1.60	170	Stud	1/2
World Products Windsor	5302A, 2302A	Aluminum or Cast	64	2.02	1.60	200	Stud	1/2

not the only porting requirement. Knowing where, how much, and how smooth to port is the black art of cylinder head porting.

There are whole books on the subject, so I won't belabor the how, but rather will give a brief idea of where. Most aftermarket small-block heads are pretty good out of the box. However, most can be improved considerably by gasket matching them—this goes for intakes as well. Simply affix a gasket to the head with a couple loose bolts, mark the metal inside the gasket with a permanent marker, remove the gasket, and grind away the excess material denoted by the marker. This will maximize the air path without too much work and isn't too difficult for the average enthusiast.

When it comes to full-on porting, 5.0s, particularly those employing forced induction, need most of their help on the exhaust ports. Naturally aspirated engines will see more benefit from intake porting, but the two ports generally differ on surface finish. Most porters like a glass-smooth exhaust port for minimum resistance and a slightly abrasive intake port to keep atomized fuel from sticking to the port walls. This is less critical in fuel-injected applications, though, as the injectors do a superb job of atomization. Because naturally aspirated and forced-induction engines often have different porting needs, you should supply your head porter with as much information about your combination as possible.

Besides porting, a quality three-angle valve job is also crucial to performance and best left to a pro. A proper three-angle valve job smoothes the air's transfer from the intake port to the combustion chamber and from the combustion chamber to the exhaust port. The three-angle name comes from the additional angles ground into the valve seat to ease the port-to-chamber transition. Typically, the stock 45-degree intake seat is modified with 30-degree angle at the combustion chamber and 60-degree angle at the runners (15-degree increments), while the 45-degree exhaust seat is ground with 38- and 52-degree angles (7-degree increments).

Sealing
The prevalence of forced induction and high compression in the modern 5.0 engine means that keeping the heads sealed to the block is an increasingly difficult task. Increased performance is only part of the equation. Marginal factory components are another culprit. Small-block Fords have always been at a sealing disadvantage to their Chevy counterparts. They only have four cylinder head bolts per cylinder, compared to the Chevy small-block's five. Compounding this problem is the fact

that the 5.0's head bolts are only 7/16 of an inch in diameter.

The 7/16 head bolts found in 5.0/302s apply 15 percent less load than the 1/2-inch bolts found on its big brother, the 351. This is reflected in the upper torque measurements recommend for the two engines by aftermarket suppliers. The max recommendation is 80 lb-ft for the upper bolts on a 5.0, while the upper bolts on a 351 can clamp all the way to 110 lb-ft.

Block strength is another factor. With limited, small fasteners threaded into a block that was continually lightened over its lifespan, the 5.0 block makes for a flexible sealing surface. While this problem is made worse by soft aluminum cylinder heads, the biggest problem is overtorquing aftermarket fasteners, which can distort the cylinder bores, promoting premature wear.

Fasteners

Since overtorquing can be a problem, many tuners recommend using a high-quality cylinder head bolt kit, like those offered by ARP. Though stronger aftermarket bolts offer more clamping force, the ultimate solution is using cylinder head studs. Because studs thread all the way into the block, they offer the ultimate in clamping force versus the same diameter bolt.

Using larger bolts would obviously be better, but doing so in a stock block is more trouble than it's worth. Sturdy aftermarket blocks, like Ford Racing Performance Parts' belated A4 block, are equipped with 1/2-inch bolt holes like a 351W. Additionally, many cylinder heads are drilled for 1/2-inch bolts, so you should select a head bolt or stud kit featuring reducers for the 5.0-spec 7/16 fasteners.

Gaskets

A variety of head gasket designs on the market are designed for a range of performance applications. Most feature steel cores covered in laminated paper or graphite, while others are built from dead-soft copper. Most 5.0 tuners recommend using a graphite gasket for good cylinder sealing, water retention, and all-around durability.

When getting serious, many racers will add an O-ring in the block for ultimate sealing. Additionally, some tuners have had success with Fel-Pro's Loc Wire head gaskets, but most stick with a graphite gasket for all but the raciest combos, which usually lend themselves toward a dead-soft copper gasket. Copper gaskets can be run with and without O-ringed blocks, but require using a high-temp sealant for coolant retention.

As always with any engine-building process, the proper surface finish is also critical. The block and heads should be smooth, but not too smooth, to provide appropriate grip on the gasket. This determination is usually made based on your machine shop's experience.

Valvetrain

4

Apart from the electronics on fuel-injected 5.0s, no other engine subsystem has as much influence over performance and drivability as the valvetrain. The camshaft, pushrods, rocker arms, valve springs, and associated hardware control how much the valves open, how long they stay open, and when they open and close. All this timing and movement determine the personality of your 5.0.

As such, it is important to choose a camshaft wisely. You must be realistic about your car's intended use. A big, lopey race camshaft might sound cool in your street 5.0, but it will likely slow it down, cause it to fail an emissions test, and make it jerky and no fun to drive. Likewise, a small, streetable cam in a race 5.0-liter will likely cost you some performance at the track. The trickiest 5.0s to cam are those dual-purpose street/strip Mustangs. Owners of these vehicles are usually willing to give up some streetability for an edge at the drag strip.

Operating Range

In all cases, it's important to consider the rpm range the engine will operate in. Most camshaft manufacturers list the working rpm range of their cams so you can make an informed selection. Depending on how radical a cam you select, you may need to swap rear-end gears to get the engine's rpm range to jibe with the operating rpm of the camshaft. For example, selecting a cam that works between 3,500 and 7,000 rpm is not a wise idea for a street car, as it usually operates from idle to around 5,000 rpm. Besides affecting the car's drivability, a street car likely doesn't have the durable internals and high-revving induction to make use of such a cam.

A street/strip 5.0 owner may put up with a lumpy idle and a bit less vacuum, but it's unlikely those who drive these 5.0s regularly will put up with the car lurching while trying to cruise down the interstate or the car feeling slow until 4,000 rpm. As such, it's important to make sure your 5.0's cruise rpm works within the camshaft's operating range, otherwise it would be wise to pick another cam or swap rear-end gears. You can determine the engine's rpm through the traps or cruising by multiplying the gear ratio by the miles per hour by 336 and dividing that result by the tire diameter. Remember that when you calculate the cruise rpm, it's necessary to multiply the final drive ratio by the overdrive ratio to come up with the appropriate gear

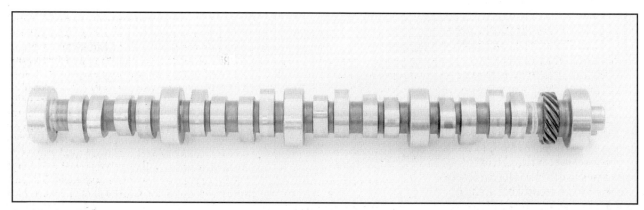

Ford Racing Performance Parts offers a veritable alphabet soup of camshafts for 5.0-liter Mustangs. As the factory source and original innovator of 5.0 speed parts, Ford Racing is an easy source for affordable 5.0 cams. Ford Racing offers the M-6250-B303, -E303, -F303, -X303, and -Z303 cams for hydraulic-roller 5.0s. The B cam was originally designed as an attempt to cam up a speed-density, fuel-injected 5.0 by using duration rather than lift, giving up some drivability in the process. Ford Racing's E303 cam blends lift and wide enough lobe separation to be an all-around cam for naturally aspirated and supercharged 5.0s. Emissions legality is also an E303 virtue. Ford Racing's F, X, and Z cams exceed the E303 by adding lift and narrowing the lobe separation, thus driving up the horsepower and rpm range. Ford Racing also offers two flat-tappet cams designed for streetability. *Ford Racing Performance Parts*

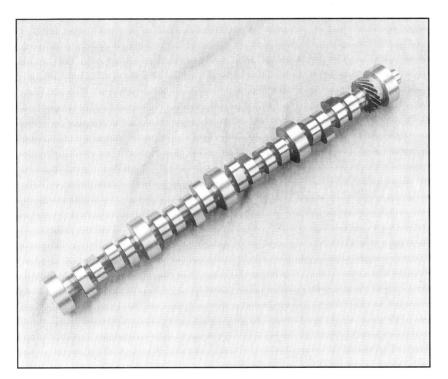

Stepping up to the 5.0 plate before many cam manufacturers jumped on the bandwagon, Crane Cams developed a complete line of computer-compatible, emissions-legal Compu-Cams for the fuel-injected, hydraulic-roller 5.0 Mustang: 2020, 2030, 2031 (designed for 1.7:1 rockers), and 2040 (equivalent to Ford Racing's E303). The numbers progress up the limits of streetability to the top-end 2040, but each cam provides excellent drivability, performance, and emissions. The latter three CompuCams also work nicely with superchargers, and all but the 2040 offer more duration on the exhaust side to compensate for notoriously lacking Ford exhaust ports. Crane also offers a slew of flat-tappet cams and more aggressive roller cams.

ratio value. By using these formulas you can come up with the working rpm of your combination.

Camshaft Characteristics

A camshaft, or bumpstick as it's known in the garage, is a metal shaft machined with distinct circular and semicircular facets. The cam usually features round bearing surfaces, oval-shaped lobes, and a distributor drive gear. Cams in carbureted cars also feature a fuel pump drive lobe. Each facet of the cam carries out a specific task.

The cam is driven by the crankshaft. In all stock 5.0s, this is done via a timing chain linking sprockets on the end of the crank and the end of the cam. Each of the bearing surfaces allows the cam to spin freely while the lobes move lifters, which move pushrods. The pushrods actuate the rocker arms which, in turn, open the valves. Meanwhile, the cam also acts as a transmission for the distributor and, on carbureted cars, the fuel pump.

Of course, what you are most interested in is how the camshaft affects performance. The way it does so is a result of the shape of its

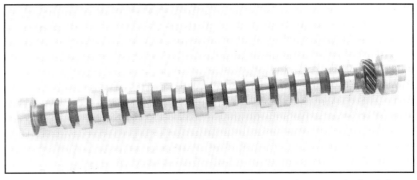

While major cam manufacturers obviously have the expertise to maximize 5.0 performance, these companies are too large to focus on the camshaft niches, like centrifugally supercharged engines. Well, Rick Anderson of Anderson Ford Motorsport, a respected supercharged-5.0 guru, decided to work with a major cam manufacturer to develop specialized supercharger cams for 5.0s. His only caveat was that he wanted to retain drivability and computer compatibility. As such, his B-series supercharger cams pull out all the stops using lift, ramp rate, and, especially, duration to create cams he calls the best-performing hydraulic roller cams. If you buy a cam from Anderson, you will get a cam card with its specs, but he advertises the cams by their recommended boost compatibility. The B-1 cam will work in a stock short block and support 8–14 pounds of boost. The B-2 is similar to the B-1, but it is designed to work with 1.7:1 roller rocker arms. The more aggressive B-3 cam is good for 8 to 15 pounds of boost and the top-of-the-line B-4 cam can work with 12 to 20 pounds of boost.

lobes. Lobe shape influences valve actuation in a number of ways.

Lift
There's no real mystery as to how

the cam works, but the way those lobes work is a bit more mysterious. The most straightforward job of each cam lobe is to (indirectly) lift a valve off its seat and allow air to

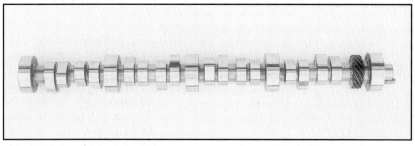

Working toward what most of their customers wanted, Steeda Autosports developed a pair of cams designed to improve naturally aspirated performance without sacrificing drivability. Respectively, the No. 18 and No. 19 cams service the 1985–93 and the 1994–95 5.0s respectively. While both cams will run in either application, the No. 18 cam proved aggressive enough to yield 11-second quarter-mile elapsed times in a naturally aspirated 5.0 drag car. The slightly more conservative No. 19 cam is designed specifically to work within the more restrictive EEC-IV confines of the 1994–95 5.0s. *Steeda Autosports*

enter the chamber or exhaust to escape. Lift is most often listed as gross lift, which is lobe lift after it is multiplied by the ratio of the rocker arm. (I'll get to that a bit later.) Lift is indicated in fractions of an inch. For example, the stock 5.0 HO hydraulic roller cam registers .444 inch of valve lift, while Ford Racing Performance Parts' radical, yet streetable hydraulic roller, the X303, lifts the valves .542 inch. All-out drag racing cams can often exceed .700 inch valve lift.

It's true that more lift means more flow, and lift has less impact on drivability than other lobe characteristics. However, more is only better to a point. Extreme valve lifts can be exceedingly rough on their valvetrain brethren, leading to worn or broken valve springs, push rods, and rocker arms. This is less critical in racing environments where parts are constantly replaced. On the street, all the valvetrain parts must yield long service life, so lift specs must be kept within reason.

Additionally, increasing lift too much can create piston-to-valve clearance problems. While a stock 5.0 can accept more, .480 inch is the practical limit for a 5.0 with stock pistons and cylinder heads with larger than stock valves. To fit a cam with more lift means fly-cutting the existing pistons, which can be done in the block with the proper tool, or installing custom pistons with premachined valve reliefs. No matter how much piston-to-valve clearance the cam should provide, it's always best to check the clearance by placing the clay or Play Doh on the piston, installing the head, and slowly rotating the crank. Then remove the head and measure the clay to determine the clearance. The prescribed minimum piston-to-valve clearance is .125 inch or more.

Duration

Cam lobes not only control how far the valves lift off the seats, but how long they stay off. This characteristic is known as duration, and is expressed in degrees of camshaft rotation. Like more lift, more duration means more airflow. More, however, is not always better. Increased duration reduces airflow velocity, which moves the powerband up. Increasing duration can also increase the amount of time the intake and exhaust valves are open simultaneously. This can enhance performance in some applications, but can also hurt emissions and fuel economy.

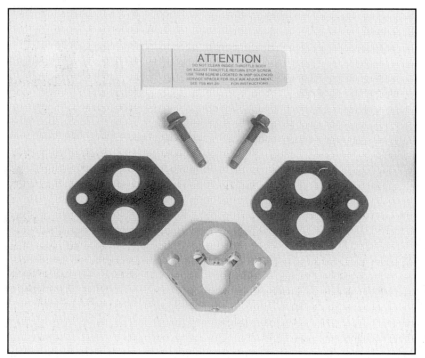

If you end up choosing a camshaft that initiates an unhappy idle in a fuel-injected 5.0, it might help to install this idle-air-bypass-solenoid service spacer (Ford Part No. F2PE-9F939-AA). This allows adjusting the amount of air bypassed around the throttle body at idle. If nothing else, it frees you from resetting the throttle-position sensor voltage every time you adjust the idle, as idle is altered by venting air rather than adjusting the idle set screw.

For those rebuilding early 5.0 blocks or adapting stronger 1960s 302 blocks, it is possible to convert to a hydraulic roller cam with special conversion roller lifters with vertical locking bars. These lifters simply drop in place of the flat-tappet lifters. They do require removing the cylinder heads for installation. They also mandate the use of custom-length push rods. This method allows use of any hydraulic roller cams, while Crane and Comp also offer hydraulic roller retrofit kits that must employ reduced-base-circle cams to compensate for the longer roller lifters. Converting to a hydraulic roller does allow for more aggressive cam profiles in a streetable package, but converting may be cost-prohibitive. *Crane Cams*

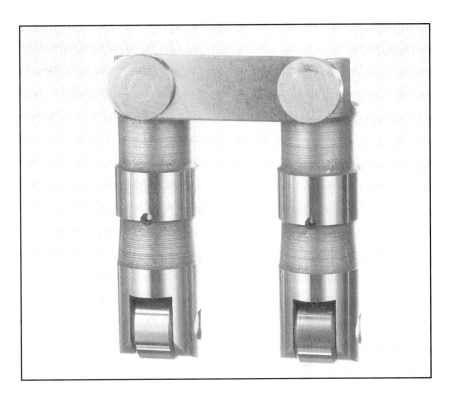

Most cam manufacturers list cams by advertised duration and duration at .050-inch valve lift. They calculate advertised duration by plugging in numbers to a formula. The problem is they don't tell you what numbers they are using, so it's impossible to compare cams from competing manufacturers using the advertised duration numbers. The .050 numbers are a much better way to compare cam durations between different manufacturers. The .050 spec was chosen as it's the true beginning point for airflow.

Advertised duration numbers aren't completely worthless, though. They can be used to ball-park a cam's drivability. In short, more duration means the power peak is higher, but it can also affect idle quality. According to Ford Racing Performance Parts' informative catalog, 270 to 290 degrees of duration provides a good idle quality and good low-end torque and works with a stock or mildly modified engine; 290 to 300 degrees delivers fair idle quality and good low and midrange power

and likely needs an increase in rear axle ratio; 300 to 320 degrees gives a rough idle and increased mid-range and top-end power and needs improved induction and exhaust; while cams with 320 to 340 degrees of duration yield a rougher idle and increased top-end power and mandate a race-prepped engine and rear axle.

Ramp Rate
Another influence of the cam lobe is the ramp rate, or how soon the valve is fully opened. To maximize

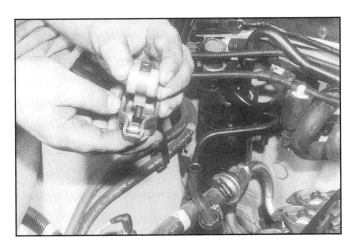

For budget-minded 5.0 owners, Crane offers die-formed roller-tip rockers, constructed of stronger material than stock, which ensure more accurate ratios, and roller tips for reduced friction. Crane also offers a needle-bearing conversion that can be used with stock or the aforementioned die-formed units, as pictured here. The needle-bearing conversion greatly reduces friction, which in turn increases horsepower, reduces oil temperature, and increases the rockers' load-bearing capacity. The latter conversion is only meant for hydraulic-roller cams.

49

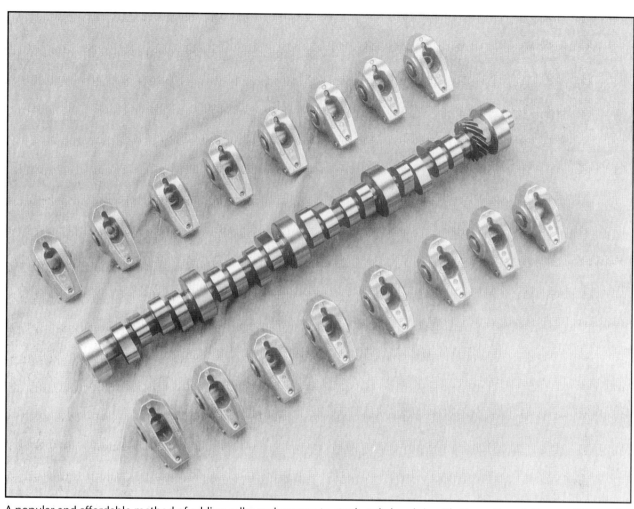

A popular and affordable method of adding roller rocker arms to stock-style heads is with Crane Cams' die-cast Cobra roller rocker arms. Affordable because they are die cast, these 1.7:1 roller rockers were originally designed for and used on the 1993–95 SVT Mustang Cobras. Naturally, these arms are equipped with needle-bearing fulcrums and roller tips, but their die-cast construction is not as durable as extruded-aluminum rockers. Still, they are plenty strong for all but the most radical 5.0s. By that point, shaft-mount rockers are the order of the day anyway.

flow and performance, the ideal ramp rate would be instantaneous, like the engagement of a solenoid. This would take something like a square lobe to pop the valve open immediately. Obviously, this is physically impossible and anything approaching it would be too rough on the surrounding valve-train components. It is possible to achieve higher than stock ramp rates, especially with an efficient roller camshaft, so keep this in mind when shopping for a cam. The sooner you get the valve open, the more it can flow over the course of its turn, as duration is

effectively increased. Most cam catalogs don't discuss ramp rate, but it's worth investigating, especially if you are attempting to squeeze more power from a street car.

Lobe Separation and Overlap
Duration is not the only factor determining a camshaft's personality. Lobe separation has a bearing on the cam's drivability and power characteristics as well. Simply put, lobe separation is the number of crankshaft degrees separating the time the intake is fully open to the time the exhaust valve is fully open. Wider lobe separations are

indicated by larger numbers, like the stock fuel-injected 5.0 H.O. cam's 116 degrees. Generally, performance cams with 112 degrees or more of lobe separation are considered to have wide lobe separation and deliver good idle quality and smooth broad powerbands. Conversely, those with narrower lobe separations, like the popular Ford Racing E303 cam's 110 degrees, trade some idle quality and torque for midrange and top-end power. This is because engines with compression ratios below 10:1 are more reliant on airflow velocity for low-end torque.

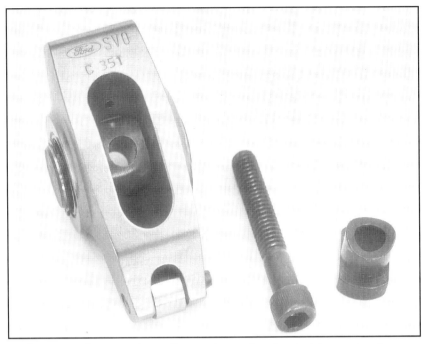

Ford Racing Performance Parts offers stud-mount and pedestal-mount rocker arms in extruded aluminum. These durable rocker arms are sturdy enough for virtually any 5.0 engine. The adjustable arms allow more latitude for achieving proper hydraulic lifter preload, but these, like most any roller rockers, are larger than stock rockers. This means clearancing the stock rocker arms or installing taller valve covers. The latter may also mean installing a phenolic spacer between the upper and lower intakes on EFI 5.0s to achieve clearance between the intake and valve cover. *Ford Racing Performance Parts*

Narrow lobe separation is also an indicator of increased valve overlap, which is the time the intake and exhaust valves are open simultaneously while the piston is at top-dead center. Overlap and narrow lobe separations are an after-effect of increased duration and can have positive or negative impact. For the positive, some valve overlap can aid power in high compression (above 10:1) naturally aspirated engines by creating a scavenging effect in the chamber, whereby the exiting exhaust helps suck in more intake air. Low-compression engines lose too much flow velocity to maximize the scavenging effect.

The downside of too much overlap in a street car is that some raw fuel and air will be leaked into the exhaust, giving the oxygen sensors a false reading and increasing emissions. In forced-induction engines, too much overlap will allow some boost or nitrous to escape into the exhaust system unused. As with any other cam specs, you should choose a cam with lobe separation and overlap dimensions befitting your combination; too much overlap or too little lobe separation can be detrimental.

Camshaft Designs
There are two basic cam designs found in 5.0-liter Mustangs. The early 1979 and 1982–84 designs feature hydraulic flat-tappet camshafts, while later 1985–95 5.0s sport hydraulic roller cams. Both cam designs push up on lifters and pushrods to lever the rocker arms against the valve stems. Friction is the factor that differentiates these two cam designs. Flat-tappet cams are so known because they are designed to work with short, cylinder-shaped lifters that slide on the cam lobes and transfer movement to the pushrods. This arrangement is quite workable, but the sliding motion creates friction, and the flat edge riding on the cam lobe limits how aggressive designers can get with profile design.

Conversely, the more modern roller-tappet camshafts utilize longer lifters fitted with a wheel that rolls on the cam lobe. This more efficient design cures the weaknesses of the flat-tappet cam by cutting down on friction and allowing more aggressive cam profiles. Because these cams are smoother and more efficient, they also allow streetable performance from a cam with specs that would be race-only if ground onto a flat-tappet cam. Those who choose to stick with flat-tappet cams can use variable-duration lifters, as pioneered by Rhoads, to run a more aggressive cam on the street. These lifters trade increased noise for improved drivability.

Because of the difference in lifter height, it is not possible to use 1985–95 roller lifters in earlier flat-tappet blocks. It is, despite the questionable logic of doing so, possible to use shorter flat-tappet lifters in a roller block. Crane Cams and Comp Cams both sell roller cam conversion kits which mandate the use of reduced-base-circle cams, and Crane offers drop-in lifters to convert a flat-tappet block to a roller cam. Given the age on most flat-tappet blocks, it's likely more cost effective to purchase a new or used roller lifter block for a rebuild than to perform a conversion on an older block. The only worthwhile conversion candidates are early Mexican or Boss 302 blocks, used because of their increased structural strength.

While a roller cam is the obvious choice for most any engine, there may come a time when a hydraulic cam is not enough. That usually means high-rpm racing and a mechanical cam. Mechanical, or solid-lifter, cams increase the rpm capabilities of an engine,

Changing a cam is much easier when the engine is out of the car, but it is possible in the car. If you have a friend to hold the air conditioning condenser out of the way, it's even possible to do so without discharging the A/C. Take care not to nick the cam bearings while sliding in the cam. Also, be sure you coat the new cam with assembly lube before sliding it home. Flat-tappet cams require installing new lifers and idling at around 2,000 rpm to break the two in. Hydraulic-roller cams require no break-in period and can reuse existing lifters.

provided it has the induction and reciprocating components to make the most of the cam. Mechanical cams use lifters that provide a direct connection between the push rod and the cam. Conversely, hydraulic lifters use engine oil to pressurize an internal mechanism that compensates for any slack in the valvetrain. As such, mechanical-lifter cams must have valve lash set to give them free range of movement, and hydraulic-lifter cams must have preload set to keep each lifter's hydraulic mechanism off its internal stop. Additionally, mechanical cams require adjustable rocker arms, while hydraulic cams can get away with stock-style nonadjustable rockers.

Rocker Arms

While the camshaft is the complex character of the valvetrain cast, the rocker arms have a decidedly simple role. Rocker arms just transfer the lift from the push rod to the valve stem in a see-saw motion. In the process these levers multiply the camshaft's lobe lift based on their angle. This is known as rocker ratio.

Perhaps because of their simple mission, Ford's rocker arms are downright basic. The stock pedestal-mount rockers have three weaknesses: they create friction because of their inefficient sled-fulcrum design and flat tip, they are not adjustable, and their minimalist construction delivers inconsistent ratios. Crane Cams offers

needle-bearing conversions and stock-style die-formed steel rockers with roller tips, but these are aimed at budget street applications.

Needle-bearing fulcrums and roller tips are the hallmarks of roller rocker arms, and they deliver increased performance by reducing friction and oil temperature. These benefits are yielded by the cheaper Crane conversion kits, but die-cast aluminum and, more specifically, extruded aluminum roller rocker arms also significantly reduce deflecting, thus delivering more consistent ratios. This characteristic yields more power and more rpm capability.

Roller rocker arms come in three basic configurations:

pedestal-mount, stud-mount, and shaft-mount. Pedestal-mount rocker arms offer the convenience and affordability of bolting to stock and stock-style cylinder heads, but they offer little adjustability. The only way to compensate for changes in valvetrain geometry is to install or remove shims beneath the pedestal mount. These rockers are an easy, cost-effective way to add roller rocker arms to a street or street/strip 5.0.

To install a stud-mount roller rocker on a 5.0 cylinder head, the head must be designed or machined to accept it. Stud-mount rockers offer increased strength, as the studs are usually larger than the bolts used to fasten pedestal-mount rockers. Beyond the added strength, stud-mount rocker arms are most advantageous because they allow adjustments to compensate for changes in valvetrain geometry. Stud-mount rockers do mandate the use of guideplates and hardened push rods for proper alignment and durability.

Stud-mount rocker arms provide plenty of durability for most performance applications, but all-out race 5.0s may need to step up shaft-mount rocker arms for ultimate rpm potential and durability. Rather than see-sawing on a fulcrum, shaft-mount rockers, naturally, carry out their appointed duty swiveling on a solidly mounted shaft. While this obviously enhances durability, it also ensures the most accurate ratios possible throughout the rpm range. Probe Industries manufactures shaft-mount rockers specifically for stock-style cylinder heads, while some heads like Edelbrock's Victors require shaft-mount rockers.

Push Rods

There isn't really any performance to be gained with push rods, but selecting the proper push rods will make your engine far more durable. If an engine is equipped with adjustable, stud-mounted rockers, hardened push rods are a necessity. These heat-treated push rods are designed to withstand wear from rubbing the guideplates. If standard push rods are used with guideplates, they will contaminate the oil with metal shavings and quickly damage the whole engine. It is, however, OK to use hardened push rods without adjustable rockers or guideplates.

Beside picking properly designed push rods for an application, picking the push rod length is critical. If you have adjustable rocker arms, you can make up for a push rod that is too long, but one that's too short is harder to work around. It's also possible to make minor adjustments to nonadjustable rockers using shims, but there is no substitute for a properly sized push rod.

An experienced engine builder will likely be able to select a push rod for a common application, but the best way is to measure each engine, as gasket thickness and cylinder head deck thickness will vary from engine to engine. The easiest way to do so is to use an adjustable "checking" pushrod and set it up to achieve proper preload or valve lash as measured by a feeler gauge. With this measurement assured, the checking push rod can be measured and the custom push rods ordered.

Valve Springs

For street applications, it's usually a safe bet to go with the cam manufacturer's valve-spring recommendation. A basic bolt-on engine won't be under the same stresses as a high-rpm race engine, which might require dual or triple valve springs. The basic rule of thumb is to install enough spring to take the engine beyond its redline, thus ensuring a bit of tolerance in case the engine is accidentally over-reved. The trick is to have enough spring pressure to do so without having too much pressure, which costs horsepower and causes premature wear.

If you are working with an engine builder, he may choose a valve spring that doesn't resemble the cam manufacturer's choice. This is because different engine combinations have unique requirements. For example, a supercharged or turbocharged engine needs as much intake valve spring as possible to help the valve open against the boost pressure. Meanwhile, the exhaust spring can be that recommended by the cam manufacturer, so as not to cause unnecessary frictional horsepower loss.

It's a familiar refrain, but like selecting all other engine components, valvetrain choices must be viewed as part of a system to maximize the total package. It's possible to achieve exceptional performance from a small camshaft, while installing a huge camshaft in a mild engine will only hurt performance. Bigger is not always better.

Exhaust

5

Like all mass-produced cars, the 5.0-liter Mustang is built with a number of compromises along the way. Absolute performance is sacrificed to the gods of penny-pinching, assembly line ease and wide customer appeal. So, like all systems, the exhaust must be cost effective, easy to install, and not too loud. Given those restraints, the 5.0 Mustang exhaust system isn't half bad from the factory—at least the 1986–95 version.

The 1979 and 1982–84 5.0s were bottled up with restrictive cast-iron exhaust manifolds and Y-piped single exhausts. In 1985 the Y-pipe was vented to a faux dual system. Finally in 1986, the EFI 5.0s received true-dual systems featuring tubular steel headers, two twin cat pipes joined with a balance tube, and twin 2 1/4-inch tailpipes with low-restriction mufflers. This is important to note when upgrading an exhaust system, as owners of pre-1986 5.0s must start from scratch. Owners of post-1986 5.0s can approach the upgrades piecemeal.

Exhaust upgrades are important, because no matter how you free up the intake tract—with air filters, intakes, superchargers, and the like—all that air and burned fuel still have to make it out of the engine. While the exhaust is only one piece of that puzzle, significant horsepower gains can be had on mildly modified and heavily modified vehicles. Such gains are usually achieved by upgrading the entire system, however, so don't expect mammoth gains from a single exhaust component.

Headers

There is no other word more closely associated with traditional

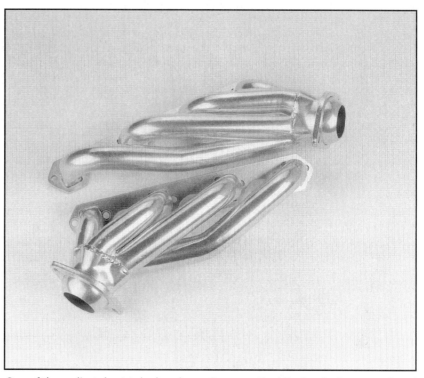

One of the earliest short-tube header options was Ford Racing Performance Parts' 1 5/8 unequal-lengths for 1986–93 5.0s. These headers are a sure bolt-on to any cylinder head with stock exhaust port location. They are stainless steel and available with optional Jet Hot ceramic coating. The coated version is all but indestructible and, as such, carries a limited lifetime warranty against rust-through. Ford Racing also offers SN95 headers and 1986–93 equal-length short-tubes and race long-tubes.

hot rodding than "headers." In basic terms these are a series of pipes that funnel exhaust from the cylinder head exhaust ports to the exhaust system. In the case of stock 1986-and-up 5.0 Mustang tubular headers, these are four short, crimped primary tubes with individual flanges at the cylinder head and a single collector with a ball fitting that bolts to the stock H-pipe. Unlike those lanky black headers you see hanging on the speed shop wall, stock headers give up a lot of flow in exchange

for assembly line fitment and chassis clearance.

Primary Tube Diameter

Obviously, installing headers with larger, mandrel-bent tubes will release more horsepower, but bigger is not always better. Headers are typically available in 1 1/2-, 1 5/8-, and 1 3/4-inch primary tube diameters. Primary tubes 2 inches and larger in diameter are often sold and custom built for racing applications. Larger tubes promote flow for increased horsepower, but

Equal-length short-tube headers, like these 1 5/8 units from BBK Performance, offer maximum performance in a short-tube package. Equal-length headers improve scavenging by separating the exhaust pulses and reducing reversion. Equal-lengths, however, only offer a few more horsepower than unequals, and in doing so they trade spark plug access and spark plug wire clearance. Depending on your perspective the trade can be worth it, especially on high-horsepower forced-induction engines. *BBK Performance*

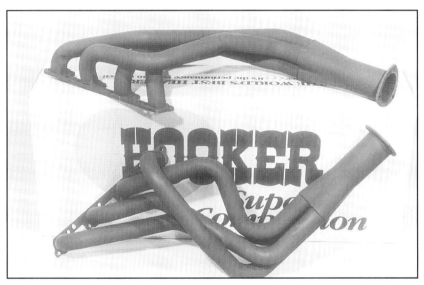

While short-tube headers offer emissions compliance and compatibility with the factory H-pipe, long-tube headers offer ultimate performance. Equal-length short tubes improve scavenging, but long-tubes maximize it. Many traditional exhaust vendors like Hooker offer long-tube headers for 5.0 Mustangs. Hooker offers 1 1/2-inch and 1 3/4-inch long-tubes and even produces a longer version for 5.0s equipped with raised-exhaust-port heads like Trick Flow Street Heat and Twisted Wedge R. The downside of these traditional long-tubes is that they require a custom H-pipe to join them to the mufflers and tailpipes. Since they are really meant for race cars running open headers, this isn't such a big deal. *Hooker Headers*

Header Length

Primary tube diameter is only one consideration. Header length is also an important issue. There are a wide variety of street-legal short-tube headers designed to bolt right in place of the factory headers. While short-tube headers are a compromise, it's still possible to make over 600 forced-induction horsepower through short-tubes. However, ultimate power is always found with long-tube headers.

Long-tube headers present challenges for street cars, though. Most of those old-school headers at the speed shop require a custom-welded H-pipe to funnel flow to the mufflers. A few long-tubes on the market are available with matching ball-fitting H-pipes. BBK, Basson, and MAC offer such packages with and without catalytic converters. Unfortunately none are emissions legal in all 50 states. This is because they relocate the heated exhaust gas oxygen sensor farther away from the exhaust port. Since oxygen sensors must be heated to work effectively, moving them can result in their running too cool and your failing an emissions test. This is not to say passing a tailpipe test with long-tubes is impossible. Some people have done so by running a stock 192-degree thermostat and making sure the car is at

larger tubes also reduce exhaust velocity and, consequently, torque. The smallest aftermarket headers are good for bolt-on 5.0s, but beyond that they are a restriction. For all but the porkiest, AOD-equipped convertibles (which seem to need the torque offered by 1 1/2-inch headers), 1 5/8-inch headers are ample for all but the most outrageous street applications. Beyond that, it's probably time to consult your engine builder for the appropriate header size.

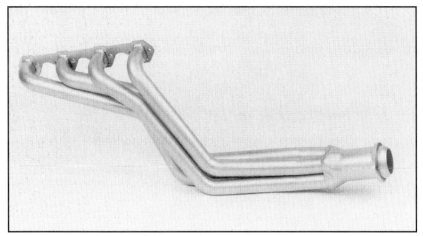

Those wanting to walk the street/strip line can get long-tube headers with ball-flange fitting and matching short 2 1/2-inch H-pipes from BBK. These 1 5/8-inch headers are available for Fox and SN95 Mustangs and are available with chrome or Jet Hot ceramic finishes. A 1 3/4-inch version is also available for deep-breathing Fox Mustangs. These bolt-on long-tube arrangements are great for street enthusiasts installing parts in home garages. Beware, however, that these long-tubes relocate the O2 sensor, which might make it difficult to pass an emissions test. Some people have had good luck passing emissions with long-tubes by retaining the stock 192-degree thermostat and making sure the engine is good and toasty before testing. *BBK Performance*

Whatever header you install, constantly tightening the bolts is an irritation worth avoiding. A simple aftermarket solution to this maintenance headache is available from Stage 8, which offers locking header bolts. These bolts utilize a washer that fits the bolt like a wrench and wedges against the header primary tube to keep the bolts from loosening. A C-clip holds the washer in place. You should put one heat cycle on the bolts before installing the locks and retaining clips. Depending on how the bolt heads line up with the primaries, the lock may require grinding to achieve a proper fit. In all, these are great for a street engine seeing infrequent teardowns. On a race engine, they would just get in the way. *Stage 8 Locking Fasteners*

operating temperature before taking the test.

Of course, using these bolt-on long-tube kits also negates the ability to play with primary tube and collector length. These tuning issues are largely a racing concern, as most racers run open headers or headers fitted with small racing mufflers, so they really shouldn't be an issue on the street anyway.

One issue of primary tube length is a concern for street cars. Most long-tube headers offer equal-length primaries to promote scavenging exhaust gases from the chamber by preventing the exhaust pulses from colliding in the collector. However, short-tube headers are available with unequal- and equal-length primaries. Unequal short-tubes are simply larger, uncrimped versions of the stock headers. Equal-length short-tubes use twisting, interwoven primaries to get the lengths equal while still fitting within the stock shock towers.

Materials and Design

Once you decide what primary tube diameter and header length your combination needs, the final consideration is how the headers are built. Most headers are available built from 14- or 16-gauge tubing. The thicker 14-gauge tubing is more resistant to warping and retains more exhaust heat and velocity in the header, while the thinner 16-gauge tubes are cheaper and offer slightly larger primary diameters. Your best bet is the thicker tubes if you want them to last. Thicker headers should also be easier to reinstall, as they are resistant to warping.

The header's flange design is another important consideration. Short-tube header manufacturers offer parts with one port flange or dedicated flanges for each exhaust. Proponents of the single flange say it adds structure, thus durability, to the header and reduces leaks, while individual-flange supporters say they allow more precise port and bolt location.

A final design consideration particular to short-tube headers is the fasteners used to join the ball flange and the H-pipe. Some headers offer studs or tack-welded bolts to facilitate one-man installations. However, if your H-pipe is heat set to your old headers, it might be difficult to get it aligned with the studs on the new headers. The other alternative is bolts. Headers supplied with bolts offer more installation flexibility, but mandate an assistant—which is not a bad idea anyway.

Paints and Coatings

Lest you want to replace your headers every few years, it's a good idea to consider a coating. Many headers are available with industrial nickel or chrome plating. This looks good before you install the headers and get heat in them. Then they turn blue and eventually rust. High-temperature paints are also an intermediate solution. They are usually black, so they don't immediately discolor like industrial plating, but they do eventually give way.

The ultimate solution is some manner of ceramic coating. These coatings are available from outfits like Jet Hot and HPC. (HPC even offers colors.) Ceramic coatings provide a long-lasting, attractive finish resistant to the elements, heat, and minor scrapes. Additionally, these coatings keep more heat in the exhaust for improved flow velocity and cooler underhood temperatures. The downside to ceramic coatings is increased cost, but they make headers a bolt-it-on-and-forget-it proposition.

H-pipes and X-pipes

No matter how good your headers are, trying to force high-performance levels of exhaust flow through the stock H-pipe won't yield maximum power. The stock 1986–95 5.0s are outfitted with 2 1/4-inch H-pipes fitted with two preconverters upstream of two more catalytic converters. This is not a bad system, especially when

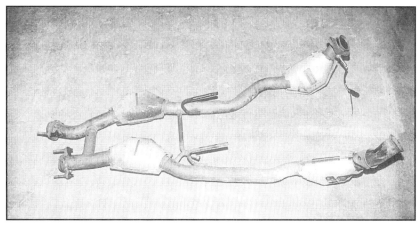

The stock H-pipe measures 2 1/4 inches in diameter and features two catalytic converters and two precats, which help warm up the exhaust systems, especially the O2 sensors, for proper emissions operation. Though it's not bad for a stock system, it definitely impedes performance. Many street 5.0 owners install off-road H-pipes, which lack catalytic converters. This offers a quick and dirty horsepower boost, but can hurt low-end torque on mildly modified 5.0s. While not great for street use, off-road H-pipes offer a way to maximize on-track performance without generating excessive under-car heat. In fact, they prove even more useful on open-track or road-race cars, due to the sheer duration those cars spend making power and heat.

The natural choice for hot street-going 5.0s is an H-pipe fitted with high-flow catalytic converters. Aftermarket H-pipes are usually offered in 2 1/2-inch diameter, rather than the stock 2 1/4-inch pipe diameter. The larger pipes combined two high-flow cats, rather than the four stock cats. This means that the high-flow catalytic H-pipes are a true performance alternative to the stock cats. High-flow cats also don't give up much power, compared to off-road pipes.

compared with the earlier 5.0 Y-pipe exhausts and the six-cat H-pipes found on later 4.6 liter Mustang GTs.

Naturally, enthusiasts aren't satisfied with a system configured for stock horsepower. So, removing the plug means replacing the stock

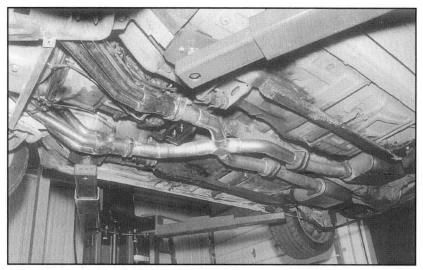

The first company to offer an alternative to the H-pipe was Dr. Gas. The good doctor proved its X-shaped crossover in NASCAR competition and quickly offered a kit for 5.0 Mustangs. The X allows the exhaust pulses to pick the tailpipe of least resistance. These pipes also give the car a unique sound and greatly reduce the cruise drone created by many aftermarket performance mufflers. The only downside to the Dr. Gas arrangement is that it is not premade. The kit is supplied in pieces and must be welded together. This does, however, allow a custom fit for each car and allows creative enthusiasts to add high-flow cats, as Dr. Gas doesn't offer a catalytic version.

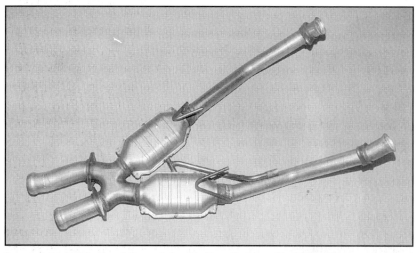

Bassani started in the 5.0 market with its equal-length short-tube headers and cat-back exhaust. It eventually complemented that line-up with a pair of premade X-pipes. Bassani offers 2 1/2-inch X-pipes with and without high-flow catalytic converters. Like the Dr. Gas pipes, Bassani's X-pipes tend to give up a little low-end torque in exchange for marked top-end horsepower improvements. X-pipes are best left to highly modified cars with plenty of torque and rear gear to compensate for any torque loss and maximize high-rpm gains. MAC offers a similar design dubbed the Power Chamber, but it is only available without catalytic converters.

H-pipe with an aftermarket version. Aftermarket H-pipes are available with and without catalytic converters. Ford Racing Performance Parts started this trend by offering the noncat export H-pipe in its catalog. Marketed as an at-the-track bolt-on, Ford Racing's off-road pipe eventually became so popular with street-going enthusiasts it was removed from the catalog.

Removing the catalytic converters has long been a quick easy method to gain horsepower. Despite being the cheaper method, there really is no excuse to remove the cats from a street car. H-pipes fitted with two high-flow catalytic converters offer power only 10 horses shy of off-road pipes. Surely 10 horsepower, which you won't even be able to feel, is worth cleaner air.

Part of the reason high-flow catalytic H-pipes come so close to open-pipe performance is they are usually offered in a larger diameter. BBK and MAC offer 2 1/2-inch H-pipes fitted with high-flow cats. Both companies offer 2 1/2-inch off-road pipes as well. In general, larger exhaust diameter will allow you to make more horsepower, but oversized tubing can reduce torque and drivability.

Besides H-pipes, there are also X-pipes. These systems join the dual exhaust system at an X-shaped crossover. This union allows exhaust pulses to select the tailpipe of least resistance without facing reversion, as in an H-configured system. These systems, available from Bassani and Dr. Gas, do trade some low-end torque for maximum high-rpm power, so they are not suited for mildly modified cars. Once you are making big power and have plenty of rear-end gear, these pipes will shine, especially with forced induction. They help you get the most from short-tube headers, though Dr. Gas does have a system designed for MAC long-tubes—the best of both worlds. Speaking of MAC, its Power Chamber H-pipe approximates the mission of an X-pipe.

Mufflers and Tailpipes

Just as your 5.0's inlet tract should be funnel shaped, it's not a bad idea to have tailpipes of equal or

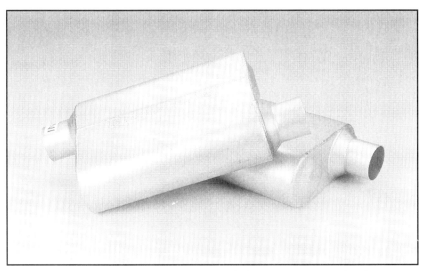

A proven power-builder and synonymous with the 5.0 Mustang is the Flowmaster muffler. These heavy, welded mufflers feature baffled chambers, which attempt to dampen sound without restricting flow. They are available with one, two, or three chambers. Two chambers are most closely associated with loud 5.0 Mustangs squealing out of parking lots everywhere. Three-chamber Flowmasters offer a quieter sound, but both versions, as is true with all mufflers, get much louder when the catalytic converters are removed.

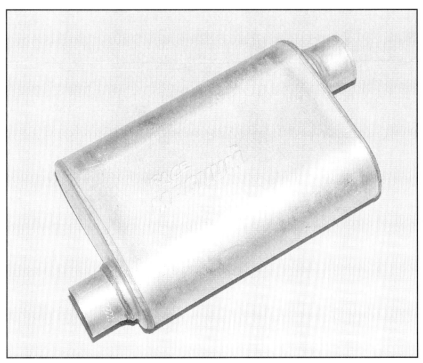

DynoMax offers a trio of popular mufflers for Mustangs. DynoMax sells Super Turbos, Ultra Flos, and Race Magnums (pictured). DynoMax also offers the best-fitting complete cat-back systems around. Those systems measure 2 1/2 inches, a de facto minimum for big-power street 5.0s, and feature stock-style stainless-steel tips. As for the mufflers, the Super Turbos and Ultra Flos offer similar performance, but the Super Turbos offer budget pricing. Ultra Flos cost a bit more and offer a polished stainless-steel case. The Race Magnum features a welded design, much like a Flowmaster, and is a favorite of Mustang tuners.

The Emissions Question

An overwhelming number of 5.0 Mustangs rumble around the streets without catalytic converters. Some do it simply for the sound, others do it for an easy horsepower boost. Removing the cats is illegal for street cars, and if you do so you are risking an expensive ticket. It is even illegal to remove the stock cats and replace them with high-flow aftermarket units unless the vehicle has over 50,000 miles and the cats are malfunctioning. With most 5.0 Mustangs clocking well beyond 50,000 miles, this really isn't an issue.

Though they are more expensive, high-flow cats are the way to go. They only surrender 10 or so horsepower to off-road pipes and don't give up streetable torque like the open pipes. Plus they allow you to pass emissions, avoid costly tickets, and preserve the atmosphere for your progeny. High-flow cats are only good so long as you have the rest of the emissions systems, like the exhaust gas recirculation valve and Thermactor (smog) pump, in place.

Long-tube headers can also complicate the issue. None are CARB exempted, as they relocate the oxygen sensor far enough from the exhaust port that it might not warm up to operating temperature. Short-tube headers, high-flow cats, 2 1/2-inch tailpipes, and performance mufflers are the definitive exhaust answer for street-bound 5.0s.

larger diameter than the H- or X-pipe. This is more critical on forced-induction engines running catalytic converters; the huge gas volume output by these engines will only expand further when superheated by the cats. As such, 2 1/2-inch cat-back exhaust systems are the defacto bolt-on standard, while 3-inch systems are usually custom built for all-out cars still running tailpipes.

While many racers run open headers or minimal header-mounted units, street and street/strip cars usually retain tailpipes. The factory tailpipes aren't that

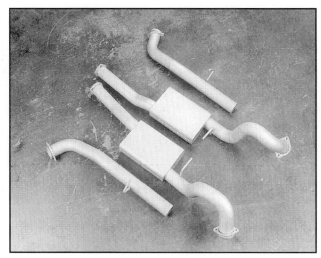

Flowtech's Warlock muffler offers a unique option in sound dampening. Its split personality delivers quiet streetable tones or loud full-on open exhaust growls. In street trim, the Warlock muffler is much like any other muffler. It routes exhaust flow through a traditional S-shaped path to reduce its sound energy before expelling it to the atmosphere via the tailpipe. However, when you remove its Flow Intensifier cap by twisting off three wing nuts, exhaust shoots straight through the muffler, bypassing most of the muffler and the tailpipe. It's a great muffler for 5.0s spending a lot of time at the drag strip.

Long-known as a header manufacturer, MAC Products eventually developed tailpipes and mufflers for 5.0 Mustangs. The Flow Path mufflers eschew the traditional single-path exhaust routing for a multiple path route. This design is said to reduce exhaust reversion and back pressure. Tuners have good things to say about these units and the complete cat-back system offers a unique installation. The flow tubes, mufflers, and the portion of the tailpipe that loops over the axle are welded together. The chrome tailpipes then join the system via the same ball-socket connections used at the header-to-H-pipe union.

Offering a vintage performance sound, Edelbrock's RPM and Victor series mufflers feature stainless-steel cases and cores filled with perforated ceramic packing designed to absorb sound without restricting flow. These mufflers are available in 2- to 4-inch diameters, but the Mustang cat-back system is a 2 1/2-inch system. These are high-quality systems and offer a unique musclecar sound. *Edelbrock Corporation*

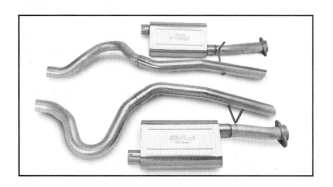

bad, but the stock mufflers are a restriction. Many aftermarket companies offer mufflers to fit 5.0 Mustangs, and many others offer complete cat-back exhaust systems with flow tubes (which bolt to the H-pipe and carry exhaust to the mufflers), mufflers, and tailpipes. DynoMax, Flowmaster and MAC all offer complete 2 1/2-inch cat-back systems for 5.0 Mustangs. The tailpipes are also available outside the kits, so they can be com-bined with other mufflers. Such systems will support plenty of horsepower, but some hardcore street/strip enthusiasts simply use turndowns to vent exhaust right after the muffler. This raspy arrangement likely trades torque for horsepower and looks silly on nonvalanced LXs.

The most important thing to consider when purchasing a cat-back system is the sound. Make sure you have heard the mufflers inside and outside the car while it is idling, cruising, and at wide-open throttle. Many of the systems sound great at idle, wide-open throttle, and out-side the car, but when you're cruis-ing at 2,000, they emit an irritating drone. Ford cured this problem by making one muffler longer than the other. Somehow this corrected the resonance on the stock system. However, to maximize profit, after-market vendors only make mufflers in one length.

Forced Induction

6

As the 5.0 engine made its transition from carbureted 302 to fuel-injected 5.0, it represented a microcosm of the auto industry. By taking a veteran, but relatively small, V-8 engine and gradually making it more fuel efficient and emissions friendly, it represented, for cars anyway, an end to gas-guzzling V-8s.

Fortunately, it didn't mean the end of performance. As the 5.0 added technology and increased efficiency, it actually made more torque and horsepower before plateauing in the early 1990s. Despite its impressive performance and positive response to traditional hot rodding—heads, cams, intakes, exhaust—there is only so much performance to be had from 302 cubic inches before you adversely affect economy, drivability and emissions.

Though adding more displacement via stroking or swapping in a 351 Windsor have been popular ways to make more naturally aspirated power, the prevalent way to have your power and not eat your street manners is forced induction. By artificially forcing air into a 5.0 with a supercharger, turbocharger, or nitrous oxide, an enthusiast can effectively add 100 or more horsepower.

Because this power isn't created by a lumpy camshaft or an open exhaust, it makes the perfect complement to a street or street/strip 5.0. Plus, forced induction also takes kindly to most traditional hot rodding techniques, so if you don't get too radical, you can build a streetable forced-induction 5.0 with outrageous horsepower.

This is true of all 5.0s, but the carbureted cars have fewer options. Nitrous is most easily adapted to the carbed 5.0s, but there are a few carbureted supercharger kits, most notably from Paxton and Accessible Technologies. When Ford divorced the intake air from the fuel delivery in 1986, forced induction became more adaptable to the 5.0. It's easy to plumb a blower, turbo, or nitrous into its throttle body and to compensate extra fuel through its fuel injectors. Therefore, a staggering number of forced-induction options are offered for the fuel-injected 5.0.

Superchargers

A supercharger, commonly called a blower, is the most popular forced induction available for the 5.0 Mustang. A supercharger is a belt-driven device that forces air into the engine. When this air is complemented with the appropriate amount of fuel, the engine produces far more power than it could naturally aspirate. Boost is simply pressure, which can be a byproduct of a restrictive air path. Airflow is the real power builder, so adding a free-flowing intake, heads, and exhaust will reduce boost but make more power.

Despite an entry fee around $3,000, a supercharger offers on-demand power that doesn't need to be replenished like nitrous.

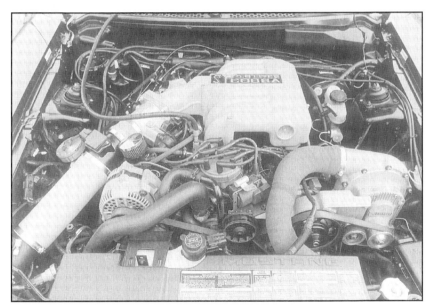

Accessible Technologies entered a hotly contested centrifugal supercharger market with intercooling as its real calling card. While the P600 unit pictured here is good for about 14 pounds of boost, the D-series of ProChargers offers from 15 to 40 pounds of boost. The D-series features a steep 4.4:1 step-up ratio, which promotes good low-end boost and improved belt grip, due to the ability to run larger pulleys. The D-1B and racer D-1 ProChargers offer plenty of performance for street and street/strip 5.0s and are available for fuel-injected and carbureted engines—the blow-through carbureted applications should only go to 12 pounds of boost before putting undue strain on the carburetor.

Only available for 1986–93 fuel-injected 5.0s, the BBK Instacharger offers a grin-inducing hint of low-end torque, while sacrificing high-rpm power. Based on the Eaton M90 Roots blower, BBK's 6- and 9-pound kits offer a wealth of essentials like larger fuel pumps, timing retards, and bypass valves, but these kits are best suited for pure-street 5.0s with moderate bolt-ons. In these applications, it offers a lot of value and performance.

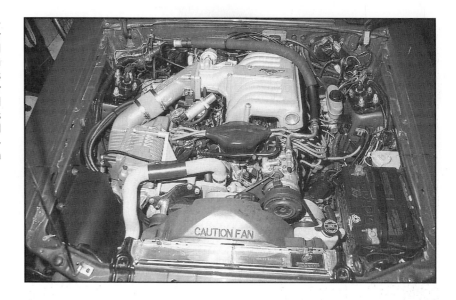

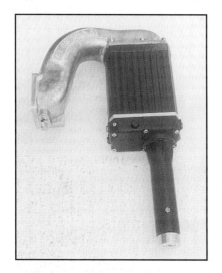

One of the easier superchargers to install, Kenne Bell's twin-screw supercharger mounts atop the factory lower intake and runs off the same belt as the stock accessories. In Blowzilla trim, the Kenne Bell blower can output 5 to 18 pounds of boost, which comes on at 2,000 rpm and stays on. In its original form, high-output Kenne Bell blowers were plagued by detonation due to heat soaking. However, Kenne Bell eventually introduced a bypass valve. It's best to pay the up-front money and buy a Kenne Bell designed for the GT-40 lower intake and equipped with the optional bypass. Then you can add more boost with smaller pulleys and step up to the free-flowing Flowzilla inlet. Another important consideration with the Kenne Bell blower is using one of their Switch Chip-calibrated mass air meters when installing larger injectors. Other meters can cause the computer to move to the improper timing table. This is not so critical on centrifugally supercharged 5.0s, but the instant boost delivered by the Kenne Bell blower can cause detonation when coupled with the artificially increased timing. *Kenne Bell*

Ball-drive Paxtons, such as the Novi GSS and its predecessors, the SN92 and SN93 superchargers, offer a nice, quiet hit of boost, which works well on the street. However, once spinning past 8 pounds of boost, their durability becomes questionable. At one time, Paxton offered the racy VR4 ball-drive blower, which was good for about 15 pounds of boost. The bottom line is the ball-drive Paxtons are street blowers, which require regular fluid changes and fluid coolers for maximum durability. If you only want 8 pounds of quiet boost, they fit the bill, but few people are satisfied with only 8 pounds. Paxton's blow-through carbureted kits are great because boost can only go so high before overwhelming the carb. *Paxton Automotive*

Superchargers also offer a relatively simple installation, which an experienced enthusiast can perform in his garage; turbochargers offer more complicated installation pitfalls.

Though they all fall under the same heading, there is a surprising variety of supercharger designs. Additionally, several companies are marketing superchargers for the 5.0. This makes choosing one fairly difficult. To make an appropriate decision, you should evaluate your

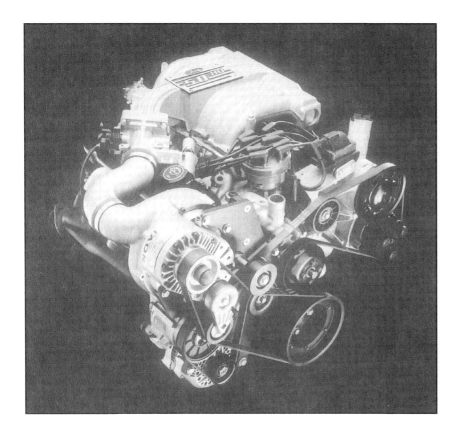

For those who must have more than 8 pounds of boost from a durable supercharger, Paxton offers the Novi family. These blowers have durable, relatively quiet helical geartrains and are good for up to 30 pounds of boost, depending on the engine. Novis are available with three impeller configurations: ST, 2000, and RX. The street-oriented ST is good for up to 19 pounds of boost, which should service any street strip 5.0s. Those wanting more can go with the 2000 or RX impellers. Whatever configuration you might choose, the Novi family of blowers has a street cred quite the opposite of its frail predecessors—it would take serious abuse to kill a Novi. Though they are capable of big boost, Novis are street legal up to 15 pounds of boost. The sturdy brackets for these kits are peerless. *Paxton Automotive*

budget, horsepower goals, and the primary use of your vehicle. Don't get hung up on boost, as a pound of boost is a pound of boost. You should consider durability, noise output, boost rpm range, and, if you plan to install it yourself, ease of installation.

BBK
A latecomer to the 5.0 blower party, BBK Performance is known for its throttle bodies and exhaust parts. Bidding for a slice of the mushrooming 5.0 blower market, BBK partnered with Eaton, a manufacturer of OEM-spec Roots superchargers, to develop its M90 supercharger for the 5.0 Mustang.

The idea of a quick-hitting Roots blower's powerful low-end torque boost on a street-driven 5.0 is appealing. To add to that appeal, BBK packaged the Instacharger with a number of features considered extras on most other kits. Aside from the blower and bracketry, BBK threw in a larger fuel pump, an adjustable fuel manage-

If you want a mild hit of street boost and you want to install it in your garage, the Powerdyne supercharger is a great choice. Though some people have reported durability problems with them, others love them. Whatever the case, Powerdynes are affordable and practically fall into place. Besides being easy to install, these blowers are quiet, thus providing a stealthy performance improvement. Do plan on adding a bypass, timing retard, and larger fuel pump with a Powerdyne, as they are not included in the basic kits.

Supercharger Accessories

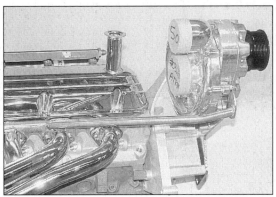

HP Motorsport

Braces

Supercharger manufacturers design their bracket kits to hold up to the rigors of street boost levels. When you start to get racy, however, the boost gets higher, thus the belt tension does too. While this obviously puts the blower and crank snouts on unfriendly ground, the most obvious byproduct of increased belt tension is bracket flex. When the bracket does flex, the blower is more likely to ditch its belt due to the improper alignment. Most standard-issue blower brackets are susceptible, so a brace is recommended for 10-pound-plus boost levels. The best examples are available from HP Motorsport and Vortech. Braces that affix the supercharger to the shock tower should only be used on cars with a motor plate or solid mounts, as the torquing engine can tug at the shock tower with the blower snout—not good for bearing life.

Paxton Automotive

Bypass Valves

Most supercharger kits designed for more than 5–6 pounds of boost come equipped with a bypass valve. These devices are critical for improving street drivability and decreasing the chance for detonation. Without a bypass, boost backs up against a closed throttle butterfly, creating heat and a surging idle. Then, when the throttle opens back up, the engine is hit with a gulp of superhot, detonation-ripe air. Obviously, this is an undesirable scenario, hence, standard bypass valves. Unfortunately, these valves are only good up to 8 to 10 pounds of boost. Beyond that they react too slowly and don't evacuate enough air. On mass air cars it's essential the air be routed back to the blower inlet as it has already been metered by the computer. Speed-density cars may vent bypass valves to atmosphere.

Injectors and Fuel Management Units

Moving to larger injectors is the new wave in blower tuning, brought about by low-cost aftermarket mass air meters and fuel injectors. The most common reason for stepping up injector sizes is for detonation protection, but there is also a tuning component. Larger injectors allow running less pressure, which is easier on pumps and injectors, and for ultimate power seekers, they allow you to remove the nonintuitive fuel management unit.

The common 5.0 injector flow rates are good for the following horsepower at 45/65 psi on a supercharged engine: 19 pound/hour supports 276/332 horsepower, 24 pound/hour supports 349/418 horsepower, 30 pound/hour supports 436/523, and 36 pound/hour supports 523/628.

Whether or not you decide to run big injectors with an FMU, you'll need to take special care when it comes to fuel regulation. FMU detractors suggest moving to boost-sensitive fuel pressure regulators like those offered by Kenne Bell, Kirban, and Paxton, while FMU fans simply suggest stepping down the FMU's pressure multiplication. If you choose the latter method, you can buy recalibration kits from Vortech and other supercharger manufacturers. These are the appropriate injector/FMU calibrations: 19 pound/hour=12:1, 24 pound/hour=10:1, 30 pound/hour=8:1, 36 and 38 pound/hour=6:1, and 42 pound/hour=4:1.

Besides FMUs and fuel pressure regulators, there are other ways to spike fuel demand under boost. Kenne Bell offers its Boost-a-Pump, which raises fuel pump voltage, thus flow, in response to boost, while Anderson Ford Motorsport and EFI Systems market a kind of electronic FMU called the Secondary Injector Driver, which activates a second set of fuel injectors in response to boost. All these methods allow you to add more fuel in response to boost, leaving idle fuel alone.

Power Pipe

Moving air is the supercharger's job, but the job of ducting air to the blower inlet is often left to flexible hose connected to the mass air meter and a small air filter. This works fine, but there is more boost, power, and efficiency to be had from a dedicated inlet system, larger air filter, and air from outside the hot engine compartment. All

three of these goals are met by the Power Pipe. This often-copied, but trademarked inlet system from Anderson Ford Motorsport ducts air to the blower from an inner-fender-mounted air filter through large-diameter mandrel-bent tubing. Depending on how restrictive the blower's inlet is and how fast you are spinning it, the Power Pipe can provide a 1- to 3-pound increase in peak boost, while aiding off-idle performance. These are highly recommended, especially above 10 pounds of boost.

Pulleys and Belts

Every pound of boost is equal to around 10 horsepower, so you can see the allure of smaller blower pulleys and grippier belts. Increasing boost via a pulley change is a semicontroversial subject, how-

Vortech Engineering

ever. Many people recommend it and several shops do it as a matter of course. The practice of removing the blower pulley and replacing it mandates a new blower belt, a sense of daring and a good sense of blower rpm. Do not overspeed the blower. Most blowers are damaged due to excessive impeller rpm. Faster is not always better. Therefore, it is wise to consult an experienced tuner or the blower manufacturer before speeding up the blower.

Vortech manufactures a wide array of pulley sizes and belt lengths for most 6-, 8-, and 10-rib serpentine belts. Upgrade pulley packages consist of the crank pulley, idler pulley, supercharger pulley, and belt. Auto Specialties and March Performance also offer pulley packages for centrifugal superchargers. Be sure the pulleys you pick are not smooth and slippery. They should have some grip.

It is also important to remember that changing the pulley will void the warranty. Select the highest-boost version of whatever brand of the kit you consider. The warranty is typically lost if the blower pulley is changed. The high-boost version may also include features not found in the standard kit. Sneaky types might be able to squeeze more boost by installing a smaller crank pulley to generate more boost and keep the warranty in place.

While you're stepping up the boost, you might be tempted to add cog belts for slip-free boost. People do run them on the street, but there are mixed opinions about their streetability—they are quite loud. At the least, be sure your blower has upgraded bearings and install an adequately sized bypass valve.

More boost is better so long as you have the proper support systems in place. A wider serpentine belt or cog belt is a must for boosting into the 15-pound range, but be mindful of the projected impeller speed and the status of your warranty before breaking out the impact gun.

Intercoolers and Aftercoolers

Compressing a gas creates heat. It's that simple. No matter how efficient a supercharger or turbocharger is, the inlet air will be heated by the process. Heat also expands the air, which might register as more boost. This goes to show that more boost is not always better. Since their inception, turbochargers have used air-to-air intercoolers to cool boost and regain efficiency. These devices are essentially radiators for boost. The other option is an air-to-water intercooler. Rather than using air as the heat-exchanging medium, these devices use water or a combination of water and ice to reduce inlet temperature.

Both of these methods can prove complex to install on the 5.0-liter Mustang, but both are well worth the effort, especially above 10 pounds of boost. Air-to-air units, however, are essentially maintenance free. Air-to-water units require you to activate the pump and replenish the reservoir with cool water. Adding ice to the air-to-water equation means you can achieve subambient air-charge temps in a drag-race environment.

Intercooling really becomes attractive after 8 pounds of boost and if you exceed 10 pounds, it really becomes a power adder. Consider adding a cooler as the final touch to a well-tuned supercharger setup.

The street blower to beat is Vortech's V-1 S-Trim. This street-legal blower can produce up to 20 pounds of boost, but offers a strong midrange hit, compared to the peakier output of its race-oriented Vortech brethren. Introduced after the A-, B-, and R-Trims, the S-Trim set a new standard for street blowers with more streetable performance and lower discharge temperatures. The S is standard in all Vortech street kits, which include all the fuel, bypass, and timing hardware you'll need to ensure their performance. Vortech also offers a popular T-Trim blower, which yields streetable low-end boost and racy top-end boost.

ment unit, underdrive accessory crank pulley, spring-loaded blower belt tensioner, plus integral bypass and throttle body assemblies. Its nine-pound kit even includes a piggyback inductive ignition/boost retard configured to allow users to delay the retard function until it is required—a key for making maximum power from the early boosting Roots.

If you plan to keep increasing your engine's power, however, the Instacharger is not a good choice, because you cannot simply swap pulleys for more boost. The Roots blower's boost potential is dictated by the size of its case, because it uses lobed rotors to compress the air in the case and push it out to the engine. Therefore it can only

gulp in as much as its case/rotor arrangement will allow; M90s gulp 90 cubic inches of air per rotation of their three epoxy-coated rotors.

Besides being boost limited, the Instacharger creates a hotter discharge than the other blowers on the market. This cause is aided by the built-in bypass, but Eaton claims only 65-percent adiabatic efficiency (measured efficiency with regard to discharge temperature) at 4,000 rpm. Most other superchargers are above 70 percent efficiency well beyond 4,000 rpm, while the Roots blower's efficiency degrades significantly with rpm and increased boost. Installing an air-to-water intercooler would certainly maximize the performance of the Instacharger, as less efficient

compressors naturally derive greater benefit from an intercooler.

Though the blower packs a massive torque wallop, it quickly runs out of boost at the top of the tach, particularly on modified engines. As such, the Instacharger is best suited to bolt-on street 5.0s with no racing pretensions. For these cars it offers a strong combination of performance and value. The best part of the early boost is not downshifting to pass on the open road. The engine just swells with power and gets you going—a great feeling.

Kenne Bell
Another purveyor of low-rpm boost and torque is Kenne Bell. It licensed the rights to the Whipplecharger,

exclusively for Ford applications, from Swedish manufacturer Autorotor. Though its design is similar to a Roots supercharger, the Whipplechargers use two close-tolerance, screw-shaped rotors, rather than the comparatively loose rotors found in a Roots blower. This design is said to improve flow and adiabatic efficiency.

Though it is more efficient, the Kenne Bell blower still suffers from the boost limitations set by its case/rotor configuration. So, to service the street and street/strip markets, Kenne Bell offers two blowers: the 1,500 and 2,200, or Blowzilla. These blowers are named for their displacement in liters of air, 1.5 and 2.2 liters respectively. The 1,500 is available pullied for 5, 8, and 11 pounds of boost, while the Blowzilla, thanks to redesigned deep-breathing screws, can pump out 6 to 18 pounds of boost from the same case as the 1,500.

Unlike the Instacharger, the Kenne Bell blowers offer upgradable boost along with a linear boost/torque curve. While these characteristics make it attractive, perhaps its best attribute is its top-of-the-engine mounting. The blower supplants the upper intake manifold and shares the accessory drive belt, making it one of the easiest superchargers to install. Because of its design, you needn't relocate or remove any vehicle accessories.

The Kenne Bell wasn't always so attractive. In its early days it was only compatible with the stock lower-intake manifold, a bypass valve was unavailable (detonation was common at high rpm/boost), and the blower inlet was somewhat restrictive. These days an optional bypass, GT-40-compatible manifold, and the enlarged and smoothed Flowzilla inlet make the Kenne Bell a serious contender to all but the raciest centrifugal. Though the Blowzilla is a bit more expensive, it's smart to start out with this unit so you can simply step up power with simple pulley changes—boost is addictive.

If the T-Trim doesn't offer enough performance for those who like to retain stock accessories, like air conditioning and power steering, the Vortech V-7 Y-Trim bolts into the standard V-1 street brackets. It offers performance approaching Mondo levels (1,000 horsepower). This blower needs a prepped engine, braced bracketry, a cogged belt, large bypass and serious fuel system to make that power. It is not street legal. *Vortech Engineering*

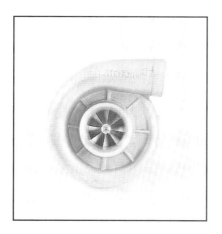

Though they have ended up on streetable vehicles, the Vortech V-3 and V-4 Mondos are pure racing superchargers. They offer huge boost numbers at the top the tach, but little boost down low. This of course is fine for drag racing, but does mandate all the usual engine, fuel system, ignition, and bypass hardware to operate to their fullest. These superchargers move so much air that racers often run two of Vortech's 600-cfm Racing Bypass Valves to vent enough air when the throttle closes at the end of a quarter-mile pass. *Vortech Engineering*

Accessible Technologies

Where the Roots and screw superchargers offer huge bottom-end performance increases, centrifugal superchargers provide little performance at low rpm. Instead, they start picking up steam in the midrange and offer a huge top-end rush. Accessible Technologies, Inc., commonly known as ATI, brought its ProCharger centrifugal supercharger into a marketplace already crowded by Paxton, Powerdyne, and Vortech, but it brought something new—*intercooling*. These systems are among the most difficult centrifugal superchargers to install, as they mount on the passenger-side, thus requiring a relocated battery, and have intercoolers, which must be installed forward of the air conditioning condenser or below the car. The SN95 kits require replac-ing the power steering pump bracket with an ATI bracket—an arduous task.

For marketing reasons, ATI is fond of rating boost as it comes out of the supercharger, rather than the pressure that actually enters the engine, so plan on at least three pounds less boost than advertised. There is a differential because of frictional losses to the intercooler hardware and contraction of the air due to the temperature drop from the intercooler. Still, it's simple to change the blower's pulley to make up for any perceived loss. Besides, less cool boost will make equal or greater power than more hot boost.

ATI builds three different superchargers, available with five different impellers. The original P600 supercharger services the street market with 6 to 14 pounds

Nitrous Accessories

No matter which nitrous system you choose, there are a number of accessories available to increase its performance and ease of operation. While the basic systems do a great job of increasing your 5.0's performance, nitrous requires some special considerations because of its instantaneous chemical nature. In other words, plan on spending more than the price of a nitrous system and bottle refills to extract max power from your combination.

Bottle Heater

Nitrous systems are tuned for maximum performance when the bottle is at 900 psi. This usually occurs around 80 degrees ambient. However, in cold climates, particularly in the fall and winter months, it rarely gets even close to 80. In these situations, the bottle pressure drops off, the mixture richens, and power drops off. Since consistency is the name of the game in many racing venues, some nitrous companies offer a nitrous bottle heater to keep the bottle warm and pressure consistent. NOS offers a thermostatically controlled unit that keeps bottle temp at about 85 degrees. Nitrous Express offers a transducer-controlled heater that maintains bottle pressure in the 900- to 1,050-psi range.

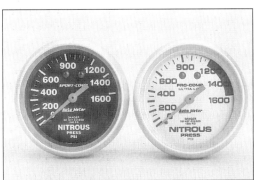

Auto Meter

Pressure Gauge

To make sure your bottle, heated or not, is in the proper pressure range, you will need a nitrous pressure gauge. Some companies offer gauges that fit right on the bottle, and others offer remote gauges for dash or A-pillar mounting. The remote gauges offer a more challenging installation, but yield greater accessibility, especially as you stage your 5.0 at the drag strip. When adding a nitrous pressure gauge you should certainly consider a fuel pressure gauge, because they go hand in hand.

Progressive Controllers

Nitrous is an abrupt power adder. It delivers its punch as soon as you push the button or trip the wide-open-throttle switch. If you are running a larger single stage of nitrous, say over 150 horsepower, or any amount on street tires, the kick can make traction a rare commodity.

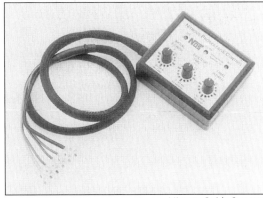

Nitrous Oxide Systems

Both NOS and Jacobs Electronics offer solutions in the form of their respective Progressive Nitrous Controller and Nitrous Mastermind products. Both of these products allow you to back off the percentage of the initial nitrous injection and gradually increase the level to a maximum you set. Obviously, this is a great way to promote starting line traction and add the nitrous once the run is under way. You could simply use a button and not engage your nitrous till second or third gear, but you'd be without nitrous until then.

Timing Retard

Common nitrous tuning practice is to run factory initial timing and a spark plug one heat range colder for the first 100 horses of nitrous, then retard the timing 1 degree for every 25 additional horses of nitrous, while changing to a colder plug for every 75 or so additional horses. Now it's easy enough to retard the timing and change the plugs at the track, but if you are running a street/strip 5.0, too cold a plug can foul on the street, and retarded initial timing will hurt your around-town power. Short of tunable electronic engine control on injected 5.0s, the easy timing answer for carbureted and EFI 5.0s is running an adjustable timing retard like those offered by MSD and Crane. These units allow you to run advanced initial timing off the bottle and retard it when you hit the button; naturally you'll also want to run the highest octane fuel you can.

Remote Bottle Switch

Though they are said to restrict nitrous flow a bit, the electrically activated remote bottle valves from NOS offer you the convenience of turning on your system without stopping and getting out of the vehicle. Short of mounting the bottle right behind your seat (a common street-racing practice), a remote bottle valve will come closest to simulating the on-demand power of a blower or turbo; you can't leave the bottle on all the time, as the nitrous will convert from liquid to gas in the line and eventually cause leaks in the system.

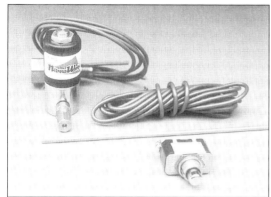

Purge Valve

Because nitrous will convert from liquid to gas after sitting in the system's line for a while, it's best to have a purge valve installed in applications where consistency is key, as some of the cooling effects of this change are lost. A purge kit also eliminates any delay of liquid nitrous reaching the solenoid, so you get power immediately after hitting the button. A purge valve should be engaged as close to the actual use of nitrous as possible, usually right before a drag racer stages.

Nitrous Works purge kit. *Nitrous Works*

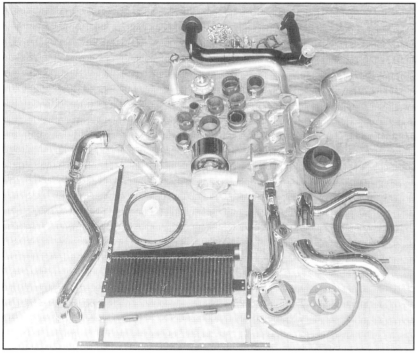

A complete single-turbo kit for fuel-injected 5.0s is available from Turbo Technology. The kits mount on the driver-side and requires relocating the battery to the trunk or the other side of the engine compartment. Depending on the turbo chosen, these kits can produce upward of 14 pounds of intercooled boost on a free-breathing 5.0 liter. They are fairly complicated to install, as they require custom exhaust work and fender well surgery, but they offer easily adjustable performance via a wastegate.

two race blowers share the same housing and both have straight-bladed impellers, the D-3 steps up to a huge 8-inch impeller for maximum performance. Some have been critical of the rough surface finish of their CNC-machined billet impellers, but ATI says there are more important factors at play inside the blower.

All the D-series blowers feature steep 4.4:1 step-up ratios in their reinforced transmissions. In these blowers, both the drive and impeller shafts ride on twin heavy-duty bearings, allowing them to reach 55,000 to 65,000 rpm. More importantly, the increased step-up ratio means running large serpentine pulleys, which allow more belt wrap, or surface contact, for increased grip. This means you can achieve big boost without running a cogged belt.

The biggest benefit of the ProCharger systems, however, is the intercooler. It cools the inlet charge, allowing you to run little or no ignition timing retard.

Combined with the cooler, denser air charge, this means these blowers have the potential to be the most powerful out-of-the-box kit. However, with the availability of the D-Series blowers, it makes little sense to opt for the P600 blower. The D-1 or D-1B should offer substantial street performance with room to grow.

of boost via a straight-bladed billet impeller. Stepping up to street/strip power levels, the D-1 and D-1B offer 17 to 20 and 25 pounds of boost respectively. The D-1 offers a curved impeller blade for better low-rpm performance, while the D-1B offers a straight impeller for increased top-end boost. For pure racing, the mammoth D-2 and D-3 superchargers offer up to 34 and 40 pounds of boost. Though these

Cartech offers single- and twin-turbo kits for fuel-injected 5.0s. These kits are designed for racing. The single-turbo kit allows for retention of the factory accessories, while the twin-turbo Street Outlaw system shown here sheds most of the accessories and any street pretenses for all-out racing. These kits offer performance from 10 to 20 pounds and require battery relocations and custom exhaust work just like the Turbo Tech kit.

Paxton

Paxton Automotive—formerly Paxton Products—started the centrifugal supercharger revolution, particularly on the street. The original Paxton blowers, as well as their SN-93, VR-4, and Novi GSS descendants, are spun by a gearless planetary ball drive. These blowers are used in industrial arenas, like submarines, to move air for ventilation. In the automotive world, we know them for ventilation engines with increased power; when pullied for 8 or so pounds of boost, these superchargers provide a quiet, fun boost in power.

As performance expectations, particularly in the 5.0 Mustang world, increasingly meant proving wares at the drag strip, Paxton's street-oriented, ball-driven supercharger developed a poor durability reputation. This was largely due to owners spinning the blower past its recommended impeller rpm, which wreaked havoc with the ball-drive mechanism. As such, Paxton had to consider a sturdier alternative for more aggressive customers while maintaining the quiet operation its mainstream customers expect.

The result of this market pressure was the Novi 2000. This helical-gear-driven supercharger is designed to push 1,700 cfm of air and 24 to 30 pounds of boost, depending on engine displacement and camshaft overlap. Although successfully resurrecting Paxton's reputation, the durable Novi was perceived as too racy for its intended marketplace—the street. This led Paxton to develop a street impeller, coded the ST, to increase low-rpm boost and better service the street market. The larger impeller, upgraded for extreme rpm with the RX impeller, found a home at the track and on big-boost street applications. Both Novis are street legal up to 15 pounds of boost.

If you thought the days of the ball-drive supercharger were over, think again. Paxton recently improved upon the ball-drive mechanism again and reverted to the Novi GSS moniker to denote the upgrade. The new Novi GSS has oil impregnated in the ball drive, so as the blower gets hotter the graphite in the oil actually comes out of the ball drive and keeps it lubricated. So if you were looking for a moderate 6- to 12-pound shot of boost in a dead-quiet package, Paxton would still recommend the Novi GSS. In fact,

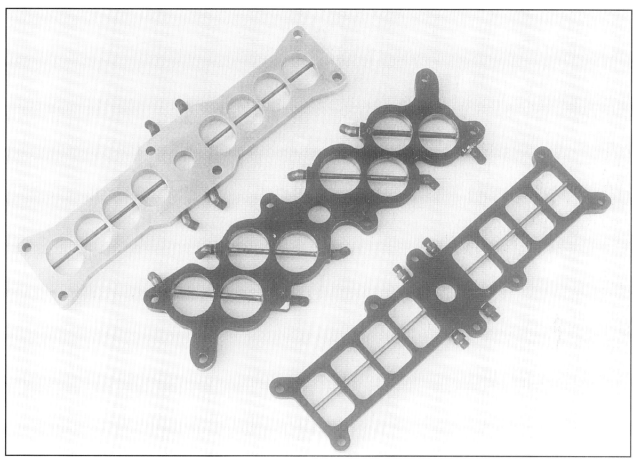

Nitrous Oxide Systems is the big name in nitrous, and it offers both versions of fuel-injected 5.0 nitrous kits. Two street-legal kits are available, which use one solenoid to spray nitrous into the throttle body and another to apply nitrous pressure to the fuel pressure regulator to compensate for the nitrous. Those kits are good for up to 150 horsepower with the stock fuel injectors, and two-stage versions are available. For boosts of 150 to 300 horsepower, NOS offers these Big Shot plates. These fit between the upper and lower stock, GT-40/Cobra and Edelbrock manifolds and spray nitrous and fuel. Because they apply the nitrous and fuel midway through the intake, puddling is said to be eliminated. NOS also offers custom-plumbed fogger setups for cast EFI manifolds and wet-plate systems for carbureted 5.0s.

the GSS should rival the off-idle performance of the Novi ST, thanks to its 4.4:1 step-up ratio.

Powerdyne

There are more 5.0 Mustangs, or any car model, on the street than on the racetrack, so Powerdyne's founder opted to build a blower specifically for the street. Rather than using a ball or gear drive, Powerdynes use an internal cogged belt to convert crankshaft into impeller rpm. Besides an internal belt, Powerdynes distinguish themselves because they are devoid of lubrication. The input and impeller shafts spin on spe-

cial ceramic bearings. All told, the Powerdyne is reportedly good for 40,000 impeller rpm.

Though the Powerdyne, also marketed by Ford Racing Performance Parts, is by far the easiest supercharger to install, it was plagued by internal belt failures. Powerdyne attributed these failures to a defective idler bearing, so they eliminated the bearing, lightened the internals, and swapped in a stronger belt. Despite these upgrades, Powerdynes are street blowers, period. Occasional trips to test 'n' tune night shouldn't bother them, but don't plan on going racing full

time with one. Also, the Powerdyne kits lack timing retards, bypass valves, and, save the 9-pound kit, fuel pumps. So, despite the value of the Powerdyne kits, plan on buying some extras if you don't already have them.

You should, however, be able to race with a forthcoming gear-driven, oil-lubricated Powerdyne, coded the XB-9000. Powerdyne says the new blower should be good for 70,000 impeller rpm and 17 pounds of boost. The promised 6:1 step-up ratio should allow running large pulleys, for improved belt wrap and grip, and nice bottom-end boost.

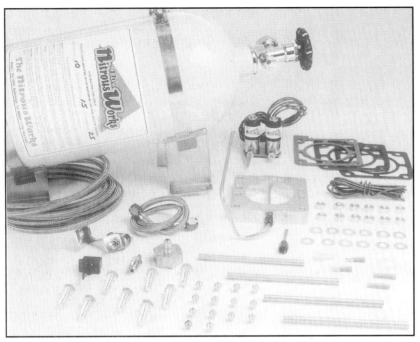

The other wet-plate nitrous system offered for fuel-injected 5.0s come from Nitrous Works. Rather than placing the plate between the upper and lower manifold, Nitrous Works installs its plates between the throttle body and EGR spacer. Like the other plates, the Nitrous Works kits use a centered spray bar to apply the fuel and nitrous. The bar in the air stream is said to promote better fuel atomization, which reduces puddling and backfires. Nitrous Works offers fixed and adjustable single-stage kits (up to 175 horsepower) and an adjustable dual-stage kit (up to 260 horsepower) for the 1986–93 5.0. With some ingenuity these can be adapted to the 1994–95 5.0 as well. *Nitrous Works*

Vortech

With the release of the A-Trim supercharger, Vortech quickly stole the thunder from Paxton's ball-drive supercharger. The straight-cut–gear-driven Vortech made more noise than the Paxton, but it also proved more durable in the high-rpm drag strip environment. Soon that reputation made Vortech's A-Trim the 5.0 supercharger of first resort.

Though it could have easily happened, Vortech refused to rest on its laurels. Rather than selling A-Trims until the competition bettered them, Vortech continued to offer upgraded impellers and upgraded compressor housings. This proved a savvy marketing strategy by giving news-hungry magazines and trendy 5.0 owners steady doses of new product.

Good for 10 pounds of boost and 480 horsepower, the A-Trim soon gave way to the B-Trim's 15-pound, 550-horse output. While the A- and B-Trim blowers serve the street market, Vortech developed the high-rpm R-Trim for racing applications. This impeller design allowed for 24 pounds of boost and 750 horsepower at the top of the tach.

These three blowers sold well, but with the advent of the S-Trim, they became less attractive. This street-legal blower supports 20 pounds of boost and 680 horsepower while delivering a more pronounced midrange power boost. The S also ran cooler and generally impressed 5.0 tuners. Before the S-Trim could even become old hat, Vortech released the T-Trim, which packs the midrange S-Trim punch and approaches the sparkling R-Trim top end. The T-Trim, like the S, is capable of producing 20 pounds of boost.

Between the introduction of the R- and S-Trim superchargers, which share the V-1 compressor housing, Vortech introduced the V-3 Mondo supercharger. This huge blower was intended for the marine market, but Vortech made no secret of its desire to get the big blower on drag-race 5.0s. It didn't take long and Mondos were on nearly every non-nitrous drag 5.0. Equipped with an R-Trim impeller, the Mondo can pump out 26 pounds of boost and 1,060 horsepower, while in J-Trim, Vortech says it's good for up to 1,100 horses and 28 pounds of boost.

Soon, even that wasn't enough. Pro 5.0 racers were heading for low-eight-second ETs and they wanted more. Vortech answered their need with the V-4 X-Trim. This huge supercharger is said to stir up to 29 pounds of boost, enough air for 1,300 horsepower. The XX-Trim features the same impeller and gear case as the X coupled with a larger volute, which helps it eke out a bit more boost and about 100 more horsepower.

Though the V-3 and V-4 are important race blowers, they are of little use on the street. S- and T-Trims do just fine on the highway. It is trendy, however, for bleeding-edge street 5.0s to run big boost. Because big race Vortech blowers mount in place of the air conditioning compressor, many such customers went elsewhere. To lure them back, Vortech created the V-7. This 'tweener supercharger can twirl the V-7-only Y-Trim impeller while fitting in the existing V-1 bracketry.

Vortech's S-Trim will handle all but the most radical street 5.0s. After exceeding 15 pounds of boost, you should consider an R- or T-Trim V-1 or a larger V-3, V-4, or V-7. Making this choice means you are ready to race. Most of these racy blowers produce peaky, high-rpm boost, which works great at the drags, but proves lazy on the street.

Turbochargers

Turbochargers never really caught on with 5.0 Mustang owners because they present more complicated installation challenges than belt-driven superchargers. This is largely due to the required exhaust plumbing and intercooler routing. However, the more difficult installation can yield more power than any other power adder, especially when two turbos are employed.

If you're not sure what differentiates a turbocharger and a supercharger, the division is simple. Superchargers are driven by the crankshaft via a belt. While turbochargers resemble many centrifugal superchargers, as both are snail shaped, turbos are driven by exhaust gases. A combination of exhaust flow and expansion from the heat spin an impeller on the turbo. This impeller is attached via a shaft to an impeller positioned in the engine's air inlet tract. As engine rpm increase, exhaust flow and temperature follow suit, so the turbo spins faster with more exhaust flow, which is fed by the turbo's boost on the inlet side.

While turbos are accused of adding heat to inlet air and backpressure to exhaust flow, it's easy to see how this self-sufficient strategy creates nearly free horsepower. Conversely, superchargers actually subtract some of the power they generate, because the more flow they create, the more power it takes to drive them.

Because turbochargers are completely controlled by engine rpm—you can't install a smaller pulley for more boost—it's critical to install the proper turbo/impeller combination. Once that is done, boost can be increased or diminished with an adjustable wastegate, which controls the amount of exhaust vented from the turbo to the exhaust system, thus the speed of the turbo. Bigger turbos provide more boost, but spool up slower, so

Turbo Sources

Cartech

Cartech offers single- and twin-turbo kits for 5.0s. Generally their kits include intercoolers, turbo headers, adjustable FMUs, adjustable wastegates, and all the tubing and small parts to get the job done. Cartech's Street Sleeper and Street Outlaw systems, single and twin respectively, both allow retention of the factory accessories, like power steering and air conditioning. The single- and twin-turbo systems place the turbos just above the frame rails, which means a trunk- or hatch-mounted battery is a necessity. The Outlaw system, however, is set up for all-out race vehicles with no accessories and prepped engines with aftermarket cylinder heads. Cartech also offers a complete line of fuel system components that complement high-power turbo, blower, and nitrous 5.0 Mustangs.

Incon Systems

Twin turbos are the name of the game with Incon Systems. They offer one kit for street/strip 5.0s and another for all-out race cars. These systems are designed to support 800 and 1,100 horsepower. Complete is an understatement with regard to these kits. Incon throws in two turbos, an air-to-air intercooler, cast-iron headers, high-temp spark plug wires, a 190-liter per hour in-tank fuel pump, 30 pound/hour fuel injectors, and an 80-millimeter mass air meter to make it all work properly. With an aftermarket intake, cylinder heads, and camshaft, this kit is said to produce 500 horsepower. More can be had, but it requires a prepped short block to withstand it. Both Incon kits permit retaining the factory accessories. While the turbos are mounted low and out of the way in this kit, they might cause interference issues with the shock towers, which must be modified.

Turbo Technology

Factory accessories aren't a problem with Turbo Technology's single-turbo kits. These systems offer up one turbo, an intercooler, an adjustable wastegate, a compressor bypass, and all the necessary hardware and tubing. These kits are good for 8 to 14 pounds of boost on a modified 5.0. These kits are complete, but like the Cartech kits, the high, passenger-side turbo mounting requires relocating the battery and shortening the power steering filler neck. Additionally, you must hole-saw the inner fender to route the inlet tubing from the inner-fender-mounted air filter to the turbo inlet. A boost retard is recommended, but not included with the kit.

two turbos are often used to maintain high boost, but hasten turbo acceleration. Turbos are often criticized for having turbo lag, but a streetable turbo on a V-8 offers little problem. The large displacement provides ample off-idle torque and turbos, particularly twins, build meaningful boost by 2,000 rpm.

Turbos do have special considerations though. They do introduce significant exhaust heat, which is especially rough on spark plug wires. For any turbo application, you should seriously consider adding a heat-retaining ceramic coating to the headers and some kind of heat-shielding wrap to the spark plug wires. The heat is also tough on engine oils, so plan on frequent changes of synthetic oil.

While turbo kits are often more expensive and complicated than supercharger kits, they also offer intercoolers and other parts not found in most blower kits. Kits typically range from $3,300 to $4,000. Beyond price, one big downside of most turbo systems is that they haven't achieved street-

73

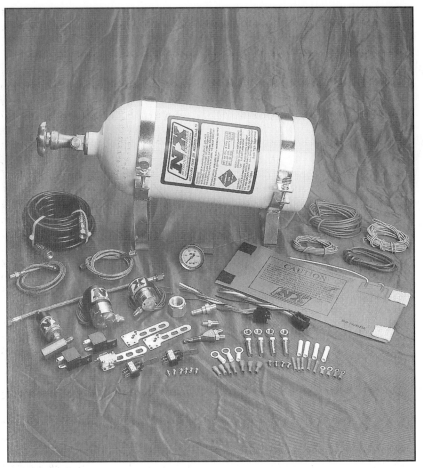

Simple nozzle systems like this one from Nitrous Express are easily adaptable to any fuel-injected 5.0. These kits place one or two nozzles in the air stream. The nozzles receive fuel and nitrous from the respective solenoids and use the oncoming air and the nitrous transformation from liquid to gas to atomize the fuel. These kits, which can add from 50 to 300 horsepower in one or two stages, are the most cost effective and easy to install. As with any high-power wet system, it's a good idea to consider a dedicated fuel system just for the nitrous system. Nitrous Works also offers several carbureted nitrous kits.

legal, CARB-exempted status like most streetable superchargers.

Buying a turbo is also a little more complicated than a supercharger, because the basic kits can be had with different turbo/impeller combination single or twin turbos, and a variety of accessories. Despite their complications, turbochargers are the most potent power adders available. Before choosing one, be sure to consult with a shop or tuner conversant in 5.0 Mustangs and turbos for a recommendation to suit your engine combination. There are three

major players catering to 5.0 Mustangs: Cartech, Incon Systems, and Turbo Technology.

Nitrous Oxide

Superchargers and turbochargers are mechanical devices that force more air into the engine. These devices are easily adapted to fuel-injected engines, but there is one power adder that goes on any engine with relative ease. Think of it as the chemical supercharger—nitrous oxide.

When first introduced to automobiles, nitrous gained the

reputation as a Pandora's bottle. Open its valve and your engine would either make tremendous horsepower or blow up. Well, thanks to modern nitrous system design and better knowledge of its requirements, nitrous is now a genie that dutifully performs horsepower wishes when released.

Nitrous oxide is saddled with a mystical aura, because you can't see what it does. However, the way it works is quite simple. Nitrous oxide is manufactured by chemically fusing two atoms of nitrogen with one atom of oxygen, hence its chemical designation, N2O. This is important because air only contains 21 percent oxygen at sea level, so nitrous carries more oxygen. This is how it creates more horsepower. When introduced into an engine, the additional oxygen requires more fuel, allowing the engine to burn more fuel and create more power. Because it allows the engine to consume more fuel in a given time period, nitrous systems richen the fuel mixture to compensate. If nitrous is introduced without fuel, detonation will occur, just like in the bad old days.

Besides carrying more oxygen than air, nitrous oxide provides a horsepower-enhancing side effect. It cools the inlet air. Nitrous is stored as a liquid in a pressurized aluminum bottle. When the bottle opens, the liquid travels through braided steel hoses to a solenoid. When an electric switch opens the solenoid, the nitrous hits air and transforms from a liquid to a gas by boiling. This isn't the boiling you do on your stove, however. The chemical reaction reduces the air temperature by up to 65 degrees, which increases the air-charge density for even more power.

Nitrous is obviously a powerful substance, but it will only do so much. Essentially, nitrous is like going on a diet and getting a makeover; it only accentuates the underlying qualities of the engine. If the engine likes to wind to 8,000 rpm, nitrous will make big power at high rpm. If the engine is a big thumpin' torque monster, nitrous will help it make more low-end torque. Nitrous is only good for minor miracles. You can't jet your nitrous kit for 800 horsepower, plumb it to a stock 5.0 and hope to make 1,025 horses. You'll just end up making a mess. A stock engine will take up to 150 horsepower of nitrous and like it. Beyond that you need to consider a built bottom end.

Wet versus Dry

At first, choosing a nitrous system appears complicated, but the first choice to make is quite basic. Do you want a wet or dry nitrous system? Naturally, you'll need to know the difference to make an educated choice. Wet systems employ separate solenoids for nitrous and fuel. When the solenoids are engaged, nitrous and fuel are sprayed into the engine's air path, just before or after the throttle body or carburetor. Dry systems are for fuel-injected engines only. They run a second nitrous line to the fuel pressure regulator and use nitrous bottle pressure to increase fuel pressure, which in turn enriches the air/fuel mixture.

Both system designs have their pluses and minuses, but the biggest plus for the dry-manifold systems, which are only marketed by Nitrous Oxide Systems for fuel-injected 5.0s, is emissions legality. Their Stage 1 and 2 systems for 5.0 Mustangs both come equipped with CARB Executive Orders and provide a power boost from 75 to 150 horses. The major knock on dry systems is that they cannot exceed these power levels. This is true given the factory fuel injectors. However, adding larger fuel injectors, as is common with supercharger applications, means dry performance can exceed 150 on a properly built engine. A dry system does place a greater emphasis on a high-performance fuel system due to its reliance on fuel via the injectors.

Conversely, wet systems supply their own fuel upstream of the fuel injectors, so they can support more horsepower without larger injectors. Oddly enough, this makes high-horsepower wet systems more emissions friendly, as they only add big fuel when it is absolutely needed. The downside of wet systems is that the EFI upper intake is not designed to carry fuel, so improper fuel atomization can cause fuel puddling and backfires. Over the years, manufacturers of wet systems have refined their delivery systems to make better use of the nitrous' chemical reaction to aid atomization. Wet systems don't rely on high fuel pressure, so they are more lenient with fuel system hardware. They are the only choice for carbureted cars and work exceedingly well on such applications.

While NOS is the only dry system marketer, wet systems are prevalent. You can purchase a wet nitrous kit for a carbureted or injected 5.0 from 10,000 RPM, Compucar, Nitrous Express, Nitrous Works, or NOS. Beyond that, it really comes down to the features and design you are most comfortable with. Compucar and Nitrous Express both place simple nozzles upstream of the throttle body, while 10,000 RPM, Nitrous Works, and NOS use plates and spray bars to distribute nitrous and fuel. The 10,000 RPM and NOS plates sandwich between the upper and lower intake manifold, while the Nitrous Works plate mounts between the throttle body and EGR spacer. All carbureted systems use plates mounted between the carb and manifold.

Of course most of these systems make power in the same general range, so the big choice comes down to price and ease of installation. The emissions-legal dry-manifold systems and wet-plate systems tend to be more expensive than those that simply place a pair of nozzles in the air stream. The cheaper systems also tend to be easier to install, but the installations can vary based on any extra components, such as oil-pressure cut-off switches or secondary and tertiary nitrous stages. Because of all the hoses and wiring, a nitrous system can sometimes be more complex to install than a comparable supercharger system.

Ignition

7

The goal of most performance modifications is to get more air and fuel into the cylinders. Once all that extra air and fuel are in the engine, the ignition system still has to light the fire to get maximum power. As is the case with stock parts, the factory Duraspark (carbureted) and Thick Film Ignition (fuel-injected) systems are designed to deal with stock air/fuel ratios, cylinder pressures, and rpm. To keep costs down, the factory installs the parts that will do the job on the street and not much more. As such, Ford equipped the Mustangs with modest timing curves, mediocre spark plug wires, and cost-effective inductive-storage ignition systems.

Timing

Ignition timing is the real key to getting maximum power out of any combination. You want to run as much timing advance as possible short of causing detonation or preignition. The earlier you can initiate the spark, the more time it has to act on the air/fuel mixture to create more complete combustion and more power. Advancing the timing also helps fuel economy but increases emissions.

You should buy a quality timing light—don't scrimp here— and reset the initial timing. Owning your own light ensures you are always working from the same baseline. Also remember to disconnect and plug the vacuum line to the distributor on a carbureted 5.0 or disconnect the spark output connector on an EFI 5.0 before adjusting the timing. Replace those connections when you are done.

You can go too far with the initial timing, as overadvanced

timing leads to detonation. Detonation, also known as preignition, occurs when the air/fuel mixture ignites on its own. This creates multiple flame fronts in the chamber. When these fronts collide, combustion pressure peaks swell (much higher than those occurring in normal combustion) and repeat in rapid succession. As such, detonation can cause, at the least, blown head gaskets. When combined with air/fuel mixtures enhanced by forced induction, high compression, or high rpm, detonation can

burn pistons, bend connecting rods, and generally cause expensive mayhem, so be careful.

To get to that edge, you have to keep advancing the initial timing in 1-degree increments until you encounter detonation; you'll need to develop an ear for the telltale rattle, knock, or ping announcing detonation. When you hear it, back off the timing until it goes away and you have optimum initial timing. If you have difficulty hearing minor detonation, it would be a good idea to pick up a knock sensor, as

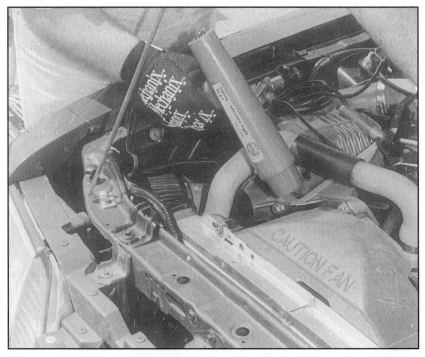

The most vital 5.0 tuning can be done with a timing light and a distributor wrench. Cranking the initial timing to 14 degrees is the most typical timing setting, but some vehicles, particularly those with manual transmissions, can go as high as 18 degrees initial. It's a good idea to clean off the crankshaft damper and mark the setting you will normally look for, especially if you plan to really advance the timing at the track and twist it back to a more conservative setting for the street. Be sure to run best fuel available to ward off detonation.

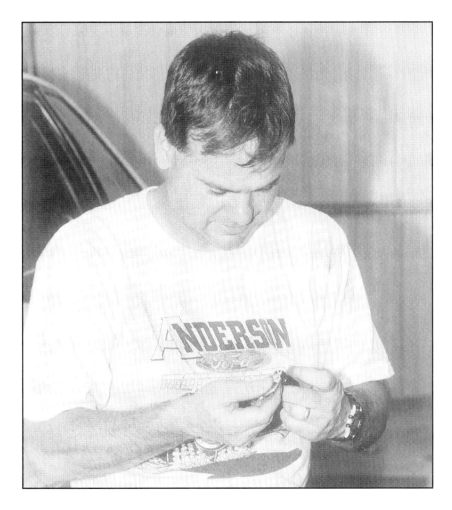

Frequent plug changes are the key to maximizing performance. When changing plugs, ensure the spark plug gap is set in accordance with your combination. In general, wider plug gaps help create a more complete burn and more horsepower, but it also puts greater pressure on the ignition system. Naturally aspirated 5.0s can utilize wider gaps, in the .45-inch range, while forced-induction 5.0s need more conservative gaps in the .30-inch range. Adding an aftermarket capacitive-discharge ignition will allow you to run wider gaps in both situations, but wider gaps mean the whole system, particularly the plug wires, must be in top shape.

offered by MSD, which senses detonation and emits an audible warning.

You'll also want to run the highest octane fuel available—usually 93 or 94 octane—to run with advanced timing. The octane rating signifies the fuel's resistance to detonation. As the octane number gets higher, the fuel burns more slowly. As such, running too high an octane fuel can actually hurt power because it takes so long to

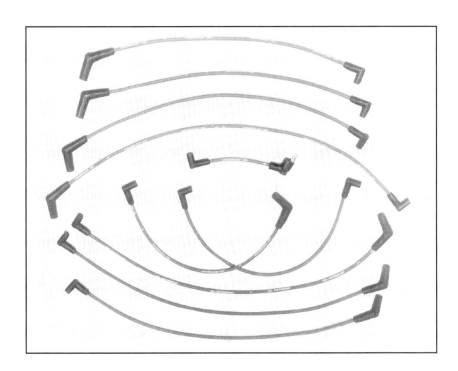

For those who don't want to mess with cutting universal plug wires down to 5.0 size, there are a number of premade plug wire sets on the market. One of the most obvious sources is Ford Racing Performance Parts. Ford Racing offers 8- and 9-millimeter custom sets for 5.0 Mustangs. These low-resistance, shielded wires are available in red, black, and blue and feature the nice touch of being numbered for the appropriate cylinder. It should be noted the Ford Racing wires are also designed to fit 351Ws as well, so they are a bit long. This makes them perfect for use with decorative wire looms. Crane, MSD, and Performance Distributors also offer high-quality premade 5.0 spark plug wire sets. *Ford Racing Performance Parts*

As the primary storage and discharge device in the stock system, the coil is probably one of the first things you'd think about changing. However, when combined with a capacitive-discharge ignition, the stock coil works quite well. Most ignition companies do offer high-output coils, but really the ones to consider are those designed to maximize output from capacitive-discharge ignitions. Also, if you can, run a more efficient E-core coil, rather than an old-school oil-cooled canister coil. MSD's Blaster TFI is a direct replacement for the stock EFI 5.0 E-core coil. MSD also offers a high-voltage Blaster coil meant for use with their ignition box.

burn. Most street cars don't need more octane, but 5.0s running high compression or forced induction can benefit from 100-plus-octane fuels, as it allows them to run more ignition timing. The advanced electronic tuning aids available to EFI 5.0s (see Chapter 10) allow far more fine tuning than simply twisting the distributor.

Spark Plug Wires

While advancing the timing is key to extracting more horsepower, it also places more stress on the ignition system. The stock system does surprisingly well, but the factory spark plug wires are the weakest links. According to MSD, the stock 5.0 spark plug wires serve up 74,700 ohms of resistance for the

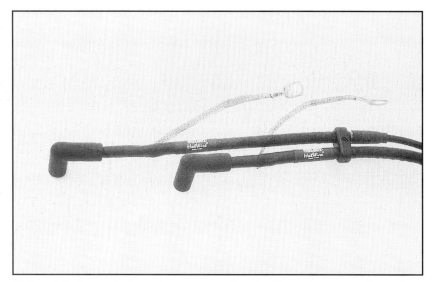

Nology bills its spark plug wires as a complete ignition system unto themselves. Rather than simple low-resistance wires, the Nology wires feature internal capacitors designed to store spark energy until the point of ionization, thus acting as a capacitive-discharge system for each plug. Nology says these wires deliver a single high-powered spark that does a good job of providing maximum combustion efficiency in a shorter period of time than more conventional systems. While these wires have been shown to make power, they do so partially by using non-resistor spark plugs. This might lead to EMI interference on some cars, necessitating a switch to resistor plugs and a small loss in spark energy. These wires are marketed as an alternative to a capacitive-discharge ignition box, but they are compatible with CD ignitions. *Nology Engineering, Inc.*

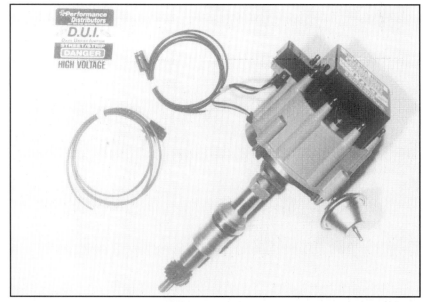

While high-tech distributors for EFI cars are a nicety for street 5.0s, an aftermarket distributor can be beneficial for carbureted cars. Where EFI cars can lean on electronic tuning, carbureted cars can benefit from a recurved distributor. A unique example of this is offered by Performance Distributors. In addition to a performance timing curve, their Davis Unified Ignition offers a trick one-wire installation because the coil is mounted atop the distributor. The coil discharges its voltage right at the distributor. This setup allows for wide spark plug gaps and high rpm from an inductive system. Street/Strip and Race DUI systems are available. *Performance Distributors*

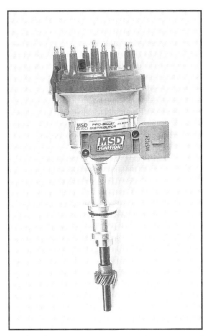

With the proper supporting cast of good wires, fresh spark plugs, and a capacitive-discharge ignition box, the stock distributor will go a long way. If you are trying to squeeze out every last drop of performance or you just want a high-tech look underhood, MSD offers billet distributors for fuel-injected and carbureted 5.0s. These CNC-machined beauties feature sealed ball bearings and oversized shafts coated for reduced friction, making them worthy of high-rpm operation. The carbureted distributors feature an adjustable mechanical timing advance curve, while the EFI distributors plug right in to the factory wiring harness. ACCEL and Mallory also have billet distributors for 1986–93 5.0s, but only MSD offers a billet unit for 1994–95 5.0s. *MSD Ignition*

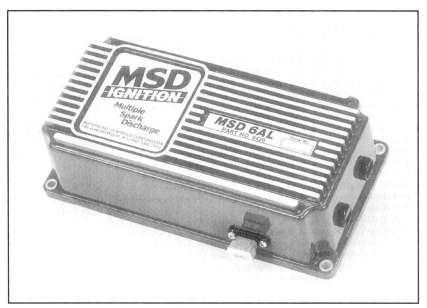

In the 1970s MSD revolutionized the ignition world with its Multiple Spark Discharge ignition system. This ignition used capacitors to store energy for instant dispatch to the coil, taking the load off the coil. Because the capacitors recharge so quickly, the MSD could provide a more powerful spark through a wide rpm range. The quick charging also allowed MSD engineers to employ multiple sparks to 3,000 rpm. While there is some controversy as to whether or not the multiple sparks help, according to MSD the multiple sparks down low help provide a more complete burn, which in turn delivers better drivabililty, emissions, fuel economy, and performance. MSD offers a wide range of ignitions servicing street and race vehicles. The weakness of these devices is they are wired up with complex analog circuitry, which can fail when exposed to the harsh underhood environment. These units are best installed inside the vehicle. A digital version of the popular MSD, dubbed the Digital-6 Plus, is also available. *MSD Ignition*

The best part of owning a 5.0 Mustang, particularly an EFI car, is the overriding aftermarket support. There are a number of parts designed just for the 5.0 Mustang. In the world of aftermarket ignitions, a number of plug-in wiring harnesses, like this one from MSD, allow you to install an aftermarket ignition system without cutting into the factory wiring. *MSD Ignition*

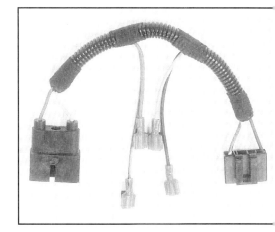

entire set, while MSD's 8.5-millimeter Super Conductor wires are said to only have 880 ohms of total resistance. For example, MSD says the stock No. 4 plug wire offers a staggering 10,000 ohms of resistance to the 125 ohms put up by their wire.

The scary part of MSD's numbers is that those are brand-new wires. As the plug wires get mileage on them and are exposed to underhood heat, they deteriorate and gain resistance. There aren't any

new 5.0 Mustangs anymore, but if you have doubts about how long it's been since the plug wires have been changed, change them. As pressures rise in the combustion chamber, the spark current is looking for the path of least resistance.

If the air/fuel mixture is dense and the spark plug wires are old, the spark will try an alternate route like arcing through the boot to the header or cylinder head.

Obviously it's a good idea to install low-resistance ignition

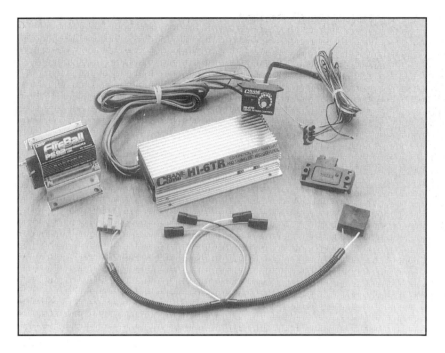

While MSD initiated the capacitive-discharge, multiple-spark craze, a number of companies have since produced similar products featuring more modern design. Crane Cams Fireball ignitions are among the more popular of MSD's competitors. Crane also offers ignitions servicing the street and race markets, but its ignitions utilize sophisticated and speedy computer controls in place of analog circuitry. The HI-6 TR (timing retard), PS92 coil, plug-in adapter harness, and optional MAP sensor (required for boost retard) are pictured here. Crane also offers a series of high-output coils, low-resistance spark plug wires, and add-on timing controllers; all offer plug-in compatibility with EFI 5.0 Mustangs, though they can easily be used on carbureted 5.0s as well.

wires, but you also want to make sure the wires are properly shielded against inductive crossfire and electromagnetic interference. Inductive crossfire occurs when two wires are run close to each other. When one wire fires, it will transfer some voltage to the neighboring wire. If the wires are not properly shielded, the voltage can cause the neighboring wire to fire and cause detonation-like damage.

EMI, on the other hand, creates a magnetic field that can interfere with other electronics, like the EEC-IV. Usually wires offering less resistance emit more EMI. So, it's important to buy quality, shielded aftermarket plug wires. Using dielectric grease around the inside of the boot will help cut down on crossfire and EMI.

Spark Plugs
The simplest and most important part of the ignition system is the spark plug. Spark plugs are the fuse lighting the internal combustion

bomb, but they have to light the fuse thousands of times in their lifetime. They can also be the only real indicator of what's going on inside the combustion chamber.

Reading spark plugs is a tuning black art, but the bottom line is pretty simple. You don't want the plug to be black. After a full throttle blast, cut the engine off and pull the plugs and look at the ceramic insulator around the electrode. If the plugs are black, the car is rich, and the plugs will foul. If

Better than any other ignitions, MSD's boxes are highly adaptable via modular add-ons that influence ignition timing. They offer a seemingly endless variety of timing retards and rev limiters. One of the most popular is MSD's Boost Timing Master. It allows you to retard the timing a number of degrees per pound of boost via a cockpit mountable knob. Thus, you can retard the timing more for pump gas, then retard it less for high-octane fuel on test-and-tune night. *MSD Ignition*

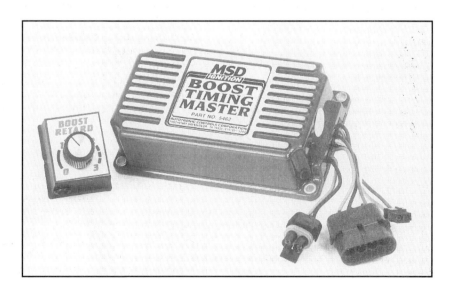

Most closely associated with its replacement carburetors, Holley made a big impact with the introduction of its Annihilator series of ignitions. Like most others on the market, Annihilators feature capacitive discharge and multiple sparks till 3,000 rpm. Unlike other systems on the market, Annihilators are not expandable via add-on modules. As such, you need to pick the right one for your application: HP Annihilator for street cars, Strip Annihilator for serious naturally aspirated performance, and the Pro Strip Annihilator for forced-induction engines. Annihilator ignitions feature computerized controls that allow you to adjust and store timing retard and rev limiter settings via a hand-held controller. This requires learning a short list of two-letter codes identifying each setting. Unfortunately, the processor used in the Annihilators is a bit slow, mandating that you adjust the distributor phasing to compensate. *Holley Performance Products*

the plugs are bright white and the electrode's edges rounded, the engine is running dangerously lean and prone to detonation. Signs of heat damage on the ground strap and specks (balls of aluminum from the piston) on the insulator also indicate a lean condition. The insulator should be an even brown and the edges of the electrode sharp.

Most tuners would like to see all the spark plugs reading alike, but because of airflow variations, particularly in EFI intakes, this is next to impossible on a street engine. Race engines with ported intakes and heads are more likely to have similar plug readings. The best you can do is pull the same plugs after each drag strip pass or chassis dyno pull.

Heat Ranges

Beyond getting the air/fuel ratio correct, you might need to select a special spark plug for your application. The most common plug decision is heat range. Spark plugs deemed hot have a long insulator nose, so they take longer to dissipate heat. This can be a problem in high-compression and forced-induction 5.0s, as it can add to detonation. Plugs considered cold have a short insulator nose, so they quickly dispense heat, thus warding off detonation.

Like advancing timing, picking the right heat range can be tricky. Some tuners will tell you to go one or two ranges colder for each step up in timing advance, boost or nitrous. The short answer is to run as cold a plug as you can

without fouling; using an aftermarket ignition helps reduce fouling, allowing you to go colder than you would with the stock system. You'll need to consult literature from your favorite plug manufacturer to determine how their part numbers reference heat range. Use the stock plug as a baseline and go colder from there.

Specialty Plugs

You might also need to consider a special spark plug design for a race 5.0. Ultra-high-compression and mega-boost 5.0s may need a retracted- or surface-gap plug to ward off detonation. Or you might want to go with a projected-nose plug so you can back off timing advance and avoid detonation. A fine-wire plug could also keep you from fouling plugs when your FMU floods the cylinder with fuel. Most street 5.0s can go with a colder version of a regular-gap plug.

You might be swayed to spend big money on spark plugs with special electrode materials, wacky ground strap designs, and exaggerated horsepower claims. Don't be fooled. While platinum-tipped plugs will give you extended plug life, that's not really what you're after. Frequent plug changes will give you the best performance, as a fresh plug will always perform better than any used plug, no matter how it's designed.

Gapping

Once you determine heat range and plug design, you need to set the gap in accordance with your combination. In general, naturally aspirated 5.0s can go with larger plug gaps, in the .045-inch range. Forced induction 5.0s must go with more conservative gaps in the .028 to .034-inch range. Running an aftermarket ignition will allow you to run wider gaps in most applications.

Distributors and Caps

The Ford distributor and cap are really pretty good. Ford's large-diameter cap was designed to

MSD offers a number of timing and rpm limiter add-ons. One of the most popular for drag racing is the Two Step. It allows you to set separate burnout and rpm limits. It is particularly useful on the starting line, where you can hold the throttle wide open, and the Two Step keeps the rpm at your preset limit until you release a switch. This photo shows setting MSD's adjustable rpm module, which is only good up to 3,000 rpm. MSD also offers nonadjustable resistor modules in 100-rpm increments. They can activate everything from rev limits to shift lights. The knock on these modules, or chips as they are known in the pits, is that they are inconsistent; they are, after all, only resistors.

reduce crossfire within the distributor, and these days even the stock-replacement Motorcraft caps feature rugged and conductive brass inserts. You can go to the edge of streetable power with these parts, given regular cap maintenance and changes.

When things get more serious, there are a number of aftermarket replacement caps and distributors. Most of the aftermarket caps offered brass inserts before Ford did, and some, like the MSD cap, are constructed of more durable polymers and special internal vanes said to reduce spark scatter. As for aftermarket distributors, there are a number on the market, and most are targeted at the EFI 5.0. These billet distributors are designed to ensure reliable timing at high rpm. They certainly won't hurt a street car, but mainly they just look cool; however, be sure to use a bronze distributor gear with flat-tappet cams and a steel gear with roller cams.

Coils

Coils step up battery voltage enough to jump the plug gap. Early carbureted 5.0s use less-efficient canister coils, which feature an open core design that must be surrounded by oil to cool it. New EFI 5.0s use an E-shaped core designed to work like a transformer. These E-core coils are more efficient and deliver more voltage to the spark plug. If you can, run an E-core coil.

As for selecting an aftermarket coil, that really depends on whether or not you plan to run a piggyback ignition of some kind. Many aftermarket coils increase the turn-in ratio of the coil to increase the ignition output at the plug. If, however, you are going to run an aftermarket ignition box of some kind, the coil needn't run such a high turn-in ratio, as the ignition box will ensure plenty of voltage. According to Crane Cams, engines running wide plug gaps work better with a more conservative turn-in ratio.

Ignition Systems

If you have the proper plugs, the right plug wires and an aftermarket coil, why would you need to install an aftermarket ignition box? Well, the stock 5.0 ignition systems operate under the inductive-storage principle. In this arrangement, the coil must step up battery voltage to create spark energy on its own. The coil must convert 12 volts from the charging system to 25,000-plus volts of spark energy. The problem is, this operation takes time, and the coil depletes its energy each time.

This might not sound so bad until you compare rpm with the fixed time it takes the coil to recharge. As rpm increases, the time available to the coil shrinks. Even this isn't so bad with a stock 5.0, but once you get a denser air/fuel mixture in the cylinder, the coil has less time and a harder job—not a good combination. This is why inductive-storage systems are only good for around 5,000 rpm, which is well below the stock 6,250-rpm rev limiter imposed on EFI 5.0s.

While they are too complex and expensive to even be considered by most auto manufacturers, capacitive-discharge ignitions are readily available in the aftermarket. These systems differ from the stock inductive setup, as they help take the load off the coil. Capacitive-discharge systems take the battery voltage, amplify it to over 400 volts, then quickly store it in a capacitor. The voltage is then fed to the coil, which steps it up to over 30,000 volts. Because the capacitor stores energy so quickly and the coil has less multiplication to do, it is able to fire lots of voltage in a short period of time. As such, most streetable capacitive systems can support at least 12,000 rpm—far beyond the capabilities of most engines.

Fuel System

8

If anybody ever kept score on oft-confused 5.0 subject matter, how to properly fuel a modified 5.0-liter Mustang would be near the top of the card. In many ways fuel injection simplified the way 5.0 owners interact with their vehicles, but by the time myriad aftermarket performance parts factor into the equation, the question of what to upgrade and when is clouded in black tailpipe smoke.

The overriding reason for the confusion is there is more than one part in a fuel system. Everyone understands replacing stock cylinder heads with aftermarket cylinder heads will give you more horsepower. However, replacing the factory fuel injectors with aftermarket injectors isn't necessarily a step in the right direction because you probably need a bigger fuel pump and a recalibrated mass air meter too.

Things don't get any easier when the market is flooded with a variety of fuel system components, all with different prices, installation requirements, and performance objectives. Well, it takes two to combust, so if you have started putting more air into the engine with hard parts, it's time to start thinking about feeding the fire with fuel. If you don't have enough fuel, the hard parts will melt, break, or come out the side of the block.

To keep you from running on the ragged edge, I talked to several experts in the aftermarket to come up with an overall picture of 5.0

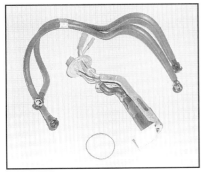

There are numerous in-tank replacement pumps available for the 5.0. These pumps come in 110-, 155-, 190, and 255 liter-per-hour configurations. Stock in-tank pumps are rated at 88 liters per hour and designed to support the factory-rated horsepower. Thus, pumping up your engine with bigger injectors or a fuel pressure regulator will only get you so far. In-tank pumps available from Ford Racing Performance Parts come complete and drop right in. The Ford Racing Performance Parts 190 even has larger outlet tubing to support the increased flow. This is important to consider when purchasing the cheaper aftermarket pumps, which replace the factory pump but retain the restrictive factory hardware. The 190 pump is a good first choice for a pump, as anything smaller will eventually be outmoded. *Ford Racing Performance Parts*

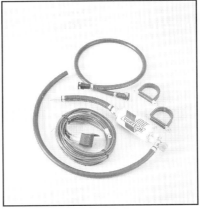

Though designed as a complement to Vortech's line of centrifugal superchargers, the T-Rex fuel pump is a popular add-on for many applications. The pump mounts inline between the in-tank pump and the fuel filter. T-Rexes are rated for up to 50 gallons per hour at 70 psi, or about 190 liters per hour at 70 psi. It's popular to combine the T-Rex with a 190-liter per hour in-tank pump. This works well because it's a one-to-one relationship. The in-tank pump feeds the inline pump, which pushes fuel upstream of atmospheric and boosted pressures. A 190/T-Rex arrangement will support over 500 natural, nitrous, or blown horsepower, making the pairing ideal for all but the most extreme street/strip 5.0s. *Vortech Engineering*

When the horsepower exceeds the capacity of in-tank pumps, even with inline helper pumps, it's time to step up to a big external pump. Several companies offer similarly designed pumps, some made by the same manufacturer, designed to meet this need. Paxton offers a series of such external EFI pumps. The Signature Series is purported to feed 1,100 horsepower with up to 90 gallons per hour at 70 psi. This pump is popular with both street and race enthusiasts employing superchargers or nitrous. Whichever external pump you choose, be sure to mount it below the pickup; they're gravity fed, and away from crumple zones, since a pump hit in an accident could fuel a fire. Wiring any aftermarket pump to the stock wiring is a good defense against fire, as the stock pump has an inertia cut-off switch to eliminate such incendiary tendencies. *Paxton Automotive*

If you're looking to make as much power as possible from a carbureted 5.0, a switch to an electric pump is the way to go. This Barry Grant Hot Rod pump is designed for bracket and drag cars that see occasional street time. It flows over 220 gallons per hour and only draws eight amps at 13.6 volts. More importantly, it includes a bypass regulator, because carburetors are designed for low pressure as compared to EFI. Holley, Paxton, and others manufacture electric pumps for carbureted applications. *Barry Grant Fuels*

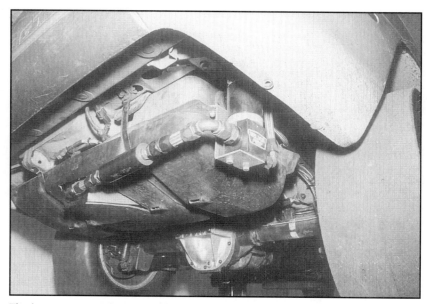

The last resort step for ultrapower 5.0 racers are the pumps from Weldon Racing Pumps. These aerospace-borne pumps are machined from billet aluminum and include top-drawer internals. Though these pumps sport an expensive entry fee, they are exceedingly durable. They also offer the flow/pressure ratings demanded by forced-induction racers. Weldon's 2025 pump, rated at a maximum of 150 gallons per hour and 1,300 horsepower, is popular with 5.0 racers. Though these pumps do require big current, some racers have even run them on the street occasionally.

fuel system requirements from mild to wild, naturally aspirated to blown/squeezed, and injected to carbureted. Obviously I can't address every combination in one chapter, but you should be able to get a basic idea of where to start. From there, find a guru, keep your horsepower goals in mind, and start pumping.

Pumps

The first fuel system part replaced

Mechanical fuel pumps, like this street performance unit from Holley, don't really have a problem delivering fuel. This pump provides up to 80 gallons per hour and shuts off at 7 1/2 psi. However, when moving beyond the street realm to high-flow street/strip and race pumps, the cam-driven pumps create parasitic horsepower loss. As pump volume increases, the power required to drive the pumps increases as well. Still, for pure street 5.0s a mechanical pump is just fine.

is invariably the fuel pump. This is smart because the factory in-tank fuel pump on fuel-injected 5.0s is supposed to be rated at 88 liters per hour, but the pumps vary a great deal, dipping well under 88. We know this, because the flow rating is stamped on the outside of the pump. So check yours out when you replace it. You might be surprised.

These pumps were set up to feed a stock engine, which they do well. However, performance

engines ask a lot more of the fuel pump than stock engines. Plus, the pumps don't get better with age. If you can hear your in-tank pump whining at idle, it's crying for help. It needs replacing anyway.

In the old days, people stepped up to 110-liter per hour pumps. Then the de facto in-tank pump was the 190-liter per hour, which gave way to the 255 in-tank pump. These help you make more power safely and more is better, right? Well, an oversized pump can be bad if you don't have the proper supporting cast.

"What you don't want to do is put too big a pump on," Kenne Bell's Jim Bell said. "Where's the fuel gonna go? It's gonna go back to the tank, then there's what you call frictional loss. Any time a fluid is flowing through a tube or a pipe, the only thing that creates loss or reduces pressure is friction of the fuel on the walls of the tube. Well you can't have friction without heat, right? If you have fuel going through a regulator and at idle you

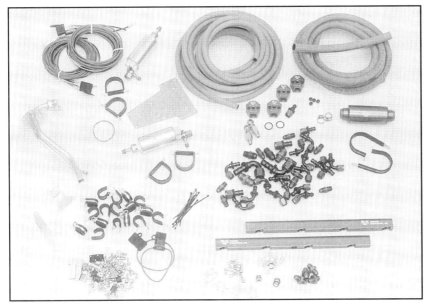

Plumbing your high-flow external fuel pump through stock fuel lines is pointless, so you have to invest in aftermarket fuel line. For street/strip applications, -8 feed and -6 return lines should be more than enough. When you get into racing, -10 is more like it, but you don't want to go too big, especially in a low-pressure carbureted system, as large fuel mass is likely to travel rearward on the launch, causing possible fuel starvation. Besides hose diameter, you have two main choices of hose material: braided steel and neoprene. Vortech offers both varieties in its complete EFI 5.0 fuel system. Braided steel hose is obviously more durable, but it also costs more, so the easy decision here is braided lines for racing and neoprene for the street. However, dual-purpose cars should just go with braided lines.

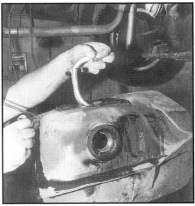

To install an external pump, especially on EFI cars, you need a nonrestrictive way of grabbing fuel from the bottom of the tank. Fortunately, several vendors, like Paxton (pictured), Cartech, and Vortech, offer in-tank pickups for 5.0 Mustangs. These mandrel-bent pickups feature .625-inch pickup tubes with -10 AN fittings and .75-inch return tubes with -6 fittings. They totally replace the factory in-tank pump and are a practical necessity over 500 horsepower.

only need 20 liters, so you're going to pump 280 liters back to the tank. It's got to go through the fittings and the regulator, so you heat the fuel.

"You'll also have a problem if you get too big a pump, and the regulator—the stock one, or ours, or anybody else's—can't flow enough fuel. Then the pressure starts rising, even on idle."

Of course, installing proper lines and stepping down pump voltage can help accommodate a big pump on the street. Choosing what size pump comes down to what kind of combination you are running. "Naturally aspirated is easy. A 190 in the tank with 36-pound injector naturally aspirated probably would support 500 horses if you could make it," Lidio Iacobelli of Alternative Auto Performance said.

When boost and, more importantly, high fuel pressure from a fuel management unit come into play, in-tank pumps, even the big ones, are quickly out their league.

"If you have a T-Rex, a 190 in the tank, and the stock lines, you can make 460 [horsepower] at the rear wheels, in a supercharged car with no problems," Rick Anderson of Anderson Ford Motorsport said. "If you try to start pushing it any

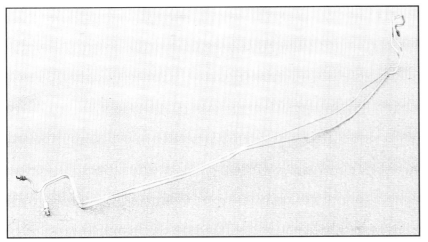

An intriguing alternative to braided or neoprene lines is steel tubing. Central Florida Motorsports partnered with prebent-tube vendor Classic Tube to develop a premade, tank-to-rails fuel line kit for 5.0 Mustangs. The kit features larger than stock tubing, which bolts right in in place of the factory lines. This kit is easy and durable, making it attractive for do-it-yourselfers. The number of sharp bends required to mimic the factory fuel lines present some flow restriction. This, however, is a minor consideration for the street/strip market these lines service.

Octane vs. Retard

A fuel's octane rating is related to how resistant it is to preignition, or detonation. If you are running high compression, forced induction, or a combination of the two, you certainly should be concerned about octane. You can get by with about 6 pounds of boost on high-octane pump gas, but beyond that you've got to retard the timing or step up the octane via additives or high-octane fuel.

As Kenne Bell's Jim Bell emphasizes, "A pound of boost is about 10 horsepower. There isn't one of those centrifugals or Kenne Bell cars with a retard knob that doesn't retard it 4 to 6 degrees. How much do you think 4 to 6 degrees is on the dyno? I'll tell you: 25 horsepower. They've lost what they gained with the boost. A guy can run an 8-pound kit, make 25 more horsepower, and all he's got to do is pour the octane booster in it."

Higher octane fuel isn't just a detonation suppressant. "Race gas burns slower, which makes the motor fatter," Rick Anderson of Anderson Ford Motorsport said. "So it doesn't need as much fuel, because it thinks it's richer." Because of this characteristic, Bell is able to eliminate the timing retard and lean out the mixture on the Shootout programs of his Switch Chips, which are meant for use with race gas. It also means that if you tune your car with race gas, it will be lean with pump gas.

If you can't get high-octane fuel where you live and don't have room for a 55-gallon drum in your garage, octane booster is a good way to step up. You can set your car on safe with a timing retard, then add the octane booster, put the timing back in, and get maximum power. Super 104 in the black bottle comes highly recommended by some of the people I queried. Bell said it's worth five octane.

In general, mass air 5.0s like to run at near stock fuel pressure, but it can be useful to adjust the fuel pressure up or down, depending on your engine's setup. Kenne Bell was first on the block with its billet aluminum fuel pressure regulator. This unit mounts on the stock 1986–93 rail, allows adjustments down to 30 or up to 100 psi and features a port for a fuel-pressure gauge. Furthermore, the Kenne Bell Regulator is built with good hardware and, if it does break, can be rebuilt. BBK, Paxton, Kirban, and several other vendors also offer adjustable fuel pressure regulators.

further than that, you need the better fuel pump and the better fuel lines."

The booster pump/190 in-tank combo seems the answer of choice for 90 percent of the street and street/strip 5.0s out there, but not everyone is a fan of the booster pump philosophy. "The disadvantage of an inline pump is they've got to suck like a vampire. They've got to suck the pump in the tank dry," Bell said. "If you put a gauge between the inline pump and the in-tank pump, it'll read zero. If the in-tank is too small or the inline pump is too big, then you'll actually get cavitation.

"If that pump in the tank is only an 88 and the one inline is 155, how could this ever work? Well the 88 is 88 at 45 pounds. At zero pressure that 88 is, let's say, 155. The 155 takes flow and it raises the pressure up," Bell explained. "In any event, what you always get with the inline pump when you activate it is a surge. It just whacks that in-tank pump and creates a surge on the inlet side. And, since every 10 pounds is .08 of an air/fuel ratio, it bounces up and down. That's why they lock 'em on. You eliminate that surge."

While companies like Barry Grant and Paxton offer inline regulators for use with large aftermarket fuel lines, Vortech offers a way to use a rail-mount regulator with these systems. This rail-mount regulator adapter is a great way to preserve your investment if you are incrementally improving your fuel system and already have a quality rail-mount regulator. It's equipped with -6 fittings, which is the only drawback to using it in an all-out system, but it should work fine in a street/strip application. *Vortech Engineering*

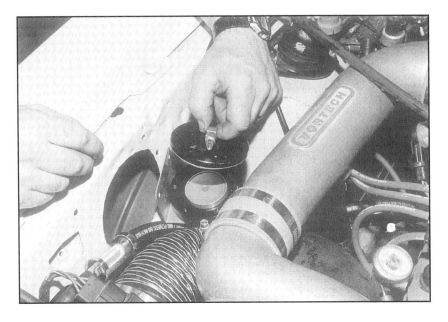

Key to making aftermarket superchargers street legal is the fuel management unit. Obviously, superchargers force more air into the engine, but air is only part of the story. It's necessary to add fuel in proportion to the air, or the engine will melt down. An FMU plumbs in between the fuel rail and the return line. As boost applies pressure to its diaphragm, the FMU pinches off the return line, effectively increasing fuel pressure at the injectors—a typical FMU is 12:1, meaning it pumps up fuel pressure 12 psi for every pound of boost. This causes more fuel to spray into the chamber during the injector's pulse. Because these only work under boost, they don't cause the engine to run rich while at idle or putting around town.

An easy cure for minor cavitation is likely a larger line between the in-tank and booster pumps. The Ford Racing Performance Parts 190 in-tank pump is sold with a larger pressure line, but many of the aftermarket in-tank pumps require you to reuse your stock hardware in exchange for a cost savings.

"What we find happens is when you've got a 302 car with good heads, milder cam, and in the neighborhood of 12 to 14 pounds, the fuel pressure will rise under boost (thanks to the FMU) until

Standard FMUs are adjustable by swapping out disks and adding bleeder screws, but for big-boost/horsepower applications, an adjustable FMU, like Vortech's Super FMU, is beneficial. SFMUs allow adjusting the lower and upper limits of the boost-on pressure spike, effectively allowing you to construct a fuel pressure curve to match your combination. The SFMU also allows you to set base fuel pressure, so you can eliminate a fuel pressure regulator and use it as a stand-alone fuel regulator. *Vortech Engineering*

Fueling Carbureted 5.0s

In some respects, carbureted engines are less complicated than EFI engines. While you don't have to worry about injector sizes, electronics, and return lines, dialing more horsepower into a carbed engine still requires upgrading the fuel system. You can't just slap on a bigger pump or a bigger carb by itself and expect to get the job done.

J.R. Granatelli advised, "On carbureted engines [the lines] are even more important than fuel-injected, because the fuel-injected engine carries the pressure, and with pressure comes flow. Carbureted engines are typically married to the 7- to 10-pound pressure ratio, so because you only get 10 pounds of pressure a larger fuel line is far more important. I would recommend for a guy trying to make over 500 horsepower carbureted, that he go to 1/2-inch line. It's a big step up from 3/8 and it's worth the extra $20 investment. It pays for itself."

Stepping up the pump is also important for carbureted engines, but not really for the same reason as on EFI cars. "Mechanical pumps are good up to about 650-700 horse-power, unless you start getting into blueprinted NASCAR pumps," Granatelli added. "The real reason why you want to abandon a mechanical pump and go to electric is not for horsepower support, but basically for manufacturing horsepower. Driving a mechanical pump off the camshaft takes a lot of horsepower, especially at pressure."

While conventional wisdom tells us a 600-cfm carb will do well on a street-driven 302, big carbs, like big fuel injectors, can be made to work on the street. This is especially true if you step up to one of the tweaked carbs from tuners like Barry Grant and the Carburetor Shop. And, many people will give up a little bottom end for the top-end charge of a bigger carb and a single-plane intake.

"The 750 [Holley double-pumper], you can make it drive, you can make it idle, you can make it get gas mileage, you can make it do everything," Rick Anderson said. "It's just like anything, if it's not tuned right, yeah, it's gonna get poor gas mileage. But you can tweak it, and performance-wise there is no comparison."

Regulators and FMUs certainly have their place, but the best way to match fuel delivery to your engine is with larger fuel injectors. Given stock pressure, the stock 19-pound/hour injectors will support just over 300 horsepower, while 24s feed about 380, 30s support around 480, and 38s (pictured here with a calibrated Pro-M Bullet) supply enough fuel for over 600 horsepower. With current mass air and electronics technology, there really is no reason not to step right up to a 30-, 36-, or 38-pound/hour injector on a modified 5.0. If you plan to add heads, cam, exhaust, and forced induction, you will eventually catch up with the extra capacity. Don't go too big on the street though, or you will run into idle and emissions problems.

you really start revving. It will shoot up to 70, maybe even 80, but then it drops, and it starts dropping a lot. It will drop from 80 back to 65 and that's totally unacceptable," Iacobelli said. "We've had really good luck using the 190 that you buy anywhere else for like $100, and we replace the rubber hose with just a clamp on high pressure 3/8-inch rubber fuel line, and it fixes a number of problems."

Beyond the in-tank/booster arrangement the next step is a large aftermarket external pump as offered by Cartech, Paxton, and SX. These pumps support huge horsepower but require adequate lines as well as a pickup in lieu of the in-tank pump. They are meant for serious street/strip cars and race cars and though they can support big power individually, racers often run two for peace of mind.

"I get to where I always recommend the customer run a two-pump arrangement. It's not because of the volume of fuel or the pressure or anything else. It strictly goes back to insurance," Central Florida Motorsports' Kevin Kelly said. "One pump will take the load off the other pump. If the guy drives the car around on the street, you wire the pumps independently. He runs one pump most of the time, goes to the track, and flips both pumps on. It's strictly insurance, and you prevent thousands and thousands of dollars of engine damage by spending $300 to $400 more on the fuel system."

In the pay-to-play world of ultra-high-horsepower race cars, the pricey but durable and muscu-

lar pumps from Weldon Racing Pumps are growing in popularity. "I run a Weldon pump on my yellow car because my car has to sustain 110 pounds of pressure to go down the track. That's the only way the 42s will feed that motor," Iacobelli said of his 700-horse street/strip car. "Usually the horsepower level to me is when they crack 550 plus. That's when we like to lean toward Weldons."

While blowers and turbos lean on fuel systems more than any other power adders, nitrous oxide has its own tricky nuances. As Anderson explains, "With nitrous, you don't need any extra fuel to help cool anything down, because it's not quite as demanding on it. With the standard kits, you could run a 125- to 150-horse on a 190 fuel pump. You need a T-Rex and a 190 above 150 horsepower. Now, if you get further than that, which is pretty radical really, then you need to go up with the bigger fuel systems, but since the temperature is lower than a supercharger, you don't need as much fuel to make the same amount of horsepower."

Radical nitrous systems might mandate additional plumbing as well. "When you get into nitrous and you start running a separate system, where you are trying to branch off and run something to a fuel solenoid, etc., you've got to take into consideration that instant spike, when the pressure is going to drop on your main fuel source going to either the injectors or the carburetor. You've got to make sure that you have a pump and a fuel system that are designed to not

have that problem," Kelly emphasized. "It seems to me so many people just want to stick a T in the line and pray. It doesn't work."

Because the nitrous can't really boost fuel pressure that much, you can either switch to larger injectors on a dry system or come up with a separate pump and line for the nitrous system. "If it's anything larger than a 125 shot, I suggest they put a dedicated fuel system on simply for the nitrous. You don't have to put on anything killer, but just something to support the nitrous," he added. "It's not that expensive and it's a whole lot cheaper and a whole lot easier than a blown head gasket."

Pump Voltage
Voltage has a big impact on an electric fuel pump's output. In fact, Jim Bell said every volt is worth about 10 percent in fuel flow. He discovered that running around at night with the headlights on and the radio blaring reduced the voltage received by the pump and, as a result, leaned out the car's air/fuel ratio. This revelation brought about Kenne Bell's marketing the Boost-a-Pump. This unit is essentially a step-up transformer that not only increases voltage to the pump, but maintains that voltage with as little as 8 volts from the battery.

According to Bell, the Boost-a-Pump can increase pump flow by as much as 50 percent without affecting its longevity. Best of all, the Boost-a-Pump can be activated in response to boost, so you don't have to up the voltage all the time.

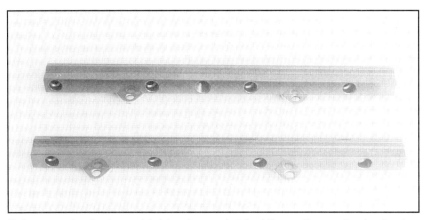

If they are plumbed up with big aftermarket fuel lines—Downs Ford sells nice adapters to easily achieve this—the stock fuel rails will support up to 600 horsepower. This is plenty of power for the street, but if you are running a street/strip or race 5.0, a move to aftermarket rails, like these from Paxton, will ensure that you have plenty of fuel volume and even distribution at the fuel injectors. *Paxton Automotive*

While Bell likes to add voltage to street pumps to make more power, J.R. Granatelli, formerly of Paxton Automotive, perpetuates an inverse theory—reducing the voltage on racy pumps to run them on the street. "You are better off taking a pump that's designed to run at 90 gallons an hour at 12 volts and then take it down to 80 gallons an hour, then you are trying to take a pump that's at 80 gallons and try to hyperactivate it up to 90," Granatelli said.

Paxton's answer for such duty is called the Brain. This little step-down box cuts pump voltage, thus flow, in half to preserve a big pump running continuously on the street. It can be activated via a switch for manual engagement at the track or by a wide-open-throttle switch.

Whether or not either of these products meets your needs, it's safe to say fuel pump voltage is yet another statistic to factor into your fuel system thought process.

Lines and Rails

There is more to a fuel system than the pump, however. The fuel has to make it from the pump to the injectors. "The stock fuel line was marginal at 190, so when you go to 255 it's really a total waste of time.

You are not benefiting from it. You can maintain more pressure, but you can't get the flow," Granatelli said. "Flow, just like in supercharging, is really what makes the power."

The consensus is that the stock fuel rails should get most of you by, unless you are going racing. "By the time the fuel gets to the rail," Granatelli added, "the rail has enough capacity to make up for it, unlike the scenario in which you might run a small line from the back of the car. Then the whole line becomes a restriction. So, yeah, the stock fuel rail is a restriction, but historically, the pump can keep up, so that means the pump can feed the rails faster than the rail can evacuate the fuel. The stock rail will, in fact, support 600 horsepower."

"Trying to get the volume to the rails will help," said Kelly, "but the bottom line is that you want to address restrictions in the order that they come. So you can narrow that down to the stock in-tank pump to the stock lines to the stock rails. It works that way, from the rear of the car to the front of the car."

Getting that volume there means investing in some serious footage of braided stainless-steel

line. With the Cartech, Paxton, and SX pumps, you should start out with -8 (1/2-inch) pressure line and -6 (3/8-inch) return line. It would be wise to step up line size when moving to the monster racing pumps. Central Florida Motorsports offers a prebent stainless-steel line arrangement that should cut the cost of a total fuel system and ease its installation.

Despite working with what some would call a compromised fuel system, people make lots of power by adding bigger pumps and bigger injectors. This is because bigger injectors require less pressure, so you can squeeze more flow out of the existing lines and rails. "We've had great success with a 190 in the tank, a new line, a T-Rex, a stock fuel filter, but in good shape, stock lines, and 36-pound injectors," Iacobelli said. "We've had plenty of cars that have 351s in them survive with that, but the boost cannot be any higher than like 10 pounds."

Still, if you can afford it, upgrading the entire fuel path is the way to go for ultimate power and safety.

Regulators and FMUs

Fuel-injected 5.0s rely on fuel pressure to ensure proper fuel delivery through the injectors. The computer and mass air meter are assuming the fuel injectors are getting 38 pounds of pressure, so increasing or decreasing the pressure is a mechanical way of changing the air/fuel ratio.

The most prominent fuel pressure controller is the fuel management unit (FMU) delivered as part of most supercharger kits. The FMU mechanically raises fuel pressure in response to boost pressure, essentially making smaller injectors act big under boost. FMUs are particularly useful at wide-open throttle, when the EEC-IV simply relies on a default program and doesn't know to add enough fuel for the increased airflow.

An FMU is essentially a secondary fuel pressure regulator. The fuel pressure regulator on the fuel rail controls fuel pressure at idle and increases or decreases that pressure, based on boost or vacuum signals. An FMU instantly overrides the on-rail regulator by pinching off the return line in response to boost.

Typically, FMUs are available in 12:1, 10:1, 8:1, 6:1, and 4:1 calibrations to accommodate 19-, 24-, 30-, 36/38-, and 42-pound/hour injectors. The first number refers to the number of psi the fuel pressure will increase in response to 1 pound of boost. Fuel pressure multiplication is achieved by a diaphragm. Increasing the dia-phragm size increases the multiplication and reducing it reduces the multiplication. This is because a larger diaphragm exerts more force in response to the same amount of boost than a smaller one.

Supercharger manufacturers offer upgrade kits for FMUs to alter the diaphragm size to accommodate an injector change. There are also a few adjustable FMUs on the market that allow you to set base fuel pressure, adjust the slope of the fuel pressure curve, and adjust the amount of pressure placed on the diaphragm. These are useful on heavily boosted cars, particularly those with aftermarket pumps, lines, and rails.

"They always ramp up to the same pressure every time we do it, so we've always been comfortable with them," Anderson said of FMUs. "I think a lot of times they're blaming the FMU for a fuel problem—not enough pump and not enough volume."

The general problem with FMUs is that people rely on them too much, asking them to crank excessive fuel pressure through fuel injectors that are too small. Another knock on FMUs is a historical lack of repeatability. This, it seems, can be traced to the use of air bleeds to adjust when the FMU kicks in.

"An FMU is good up to about 450 horsepower. After that they

just don't repeat," Granatelli said. "I am not a fan of any FMU where a guy installs a controlled air bleed. To me, controlled air bleeds are a waste of time. As the pressure increases, the dynamics of the air change. As the boost increases, the valve cannot move the same amount of air, so it's naturally gonna spike the fuel pressure sooner or later."

Temperature and barometric pressure are other air bleed consistency culprits, according to Granatelli. "So if a guy was doing a steady state 8 pounds of boost or 12 pounds of boost, or if he was going up a hill towing, the fuel pressure would actually decrease as the guy got to the top of the hill, because the air temperature increased and it would take pressure off that controlled air bleed, which is not good."

The other piece of the fuel pressure puzzle is the fuel pressure

regulator. It is used to adjust the base fuel pressure, which can be useful for minor richening or leaning. However, most tuners recommend that you stick with stock base pressure so as not to confuse the computer.

Other than resetting the base pressure to stock when adding mega fuel pumps, a boost-sensitive fuel pressure regulator can work with properly sized fuel injectors to alleviate the need for a high-pressure FMU. As Granatelli observed, "Basically, what the regulator does is it allows you to articulate the fuel as the boost increases. A lot of regulators didn't have the surface area, so they could not maintain the flow to go with the pressure. As the pressure would increase, the flow would decrease, because the diaphragm was never large enough. Paxton regulators are so large because the footprint of the diaphragm needs the leverage on

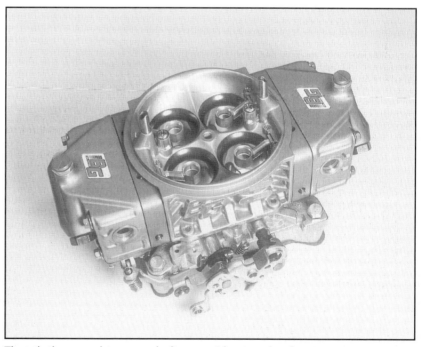

Though they are cheaper and often provide an easier shot at more power, carburetors are not intuitive. It's possible to jet them for good all-around street performance for your application, but for racing you have to keep a close watch on weather conditions and adjust the carburetor accordingly. In general you don't want to go with too large a carburetor, but you can go as large as 750 cfm (with a tuned-up carb like this Barry Grant Demon) if you don't mind steep rear gears and less torque. *Barry Grant Fuels*

Paxton and Barry Grant both market step-down transformers that allow you to run larger, racing-style fuel pumps on the street. Even with a good bypass regulator, too large a fuel pump will cause the fuel pressure to rise at idle and affect emissions and drivability. Paxton's Brain allows you to step down the voltage on the street and step it up at the track via a switch. In addition to the drivability issues, reducing pump voltage should extend the life span of a racy pump run on the street. *Paxton Automotive*

the rail. Having a large diaphragm allows moving a lot more fuel and making more finite adjustments."

Secondary Injectors

The downside of an FMU is that you really can't control it precisely, even the adjustables, so it becomes an on/off fuel pressure switch, which usually leaves the mixture rich when it engages. This can be cured with electronics and with larger injectors, but there is a streetable limit to injector sizing.

"Nobody's got a 302 anymore," said Rick Anderson. "I think the 347s are gonna be 351s, 414s, and 450s before we know it. And, the guys are gonna still want to drive them on the street. A lot of guys just want their Mustang to be big cubic inches, they don't want a PMS, they don't want a laptop, they don't want to mess with all that. So they want to put 36s or 38s in and go with it. Well, if you do that you're not going to have enough injector. So with the S.I.D., those injectors don't come on until you want them to and you correlate all rpm and boost. And then you can adjust the rate of gain to how hard you want the injectors to run."

S.I.D. stands for Secondary Injector Driver, which is built by EFI Systems but is primarily marketed by Anderson Ford Motorsport. It is a small control box, wiring harness, and MAP sensor that work in concert to allow you to engage a second set of fuel injectors, based on rpm and boost. You can also adjust the secondary injectors' pulse width from 1 to 15 milliseconds.

Adding the extra fuel to the upper intake has a positive side effect. "Another thing that we've seen with it is it cools down the intake charge about another 10 to 15 degrees," Anderson added. "I could run 1 or 2 degrees more timing without any detonation because I was running the 16 injectors."

You can either run 16 additional injectors in a Vortech Shootout intake or have your existing upper intake modified by Anderson to accommodate the extra injectors. Additionally, their new Power Plate puts three injectors just behind the throttle body for easy installation on any 1986–93 5.0. The only caveat with the secondary injector arrangement is it requires boost to keep the fuel mixed with the air.

Though many critics say it affects fuel pump life, stepping up the voltage of small in-tank pumps is Kenne Bell's preferred method of increasing fuel pump volume. This is achieved with their Boost-a-Pump, which is nothing more than an adjustable step-up transformer. It allows you to increase the flow of your pump by up to 50 percent. Besides easy installation and improved fuel pump flow, the Boost-a-Pump (pictured here with Kenne Bell's Boost-a-Pump and Optimizer) offers two unique benefits. It stabilizes pump voltage, so it doesn't drop when the stereo, headlights, and A/C steal voltage away. Plus it can be activated under boost, so it will work like an electric FMU, increasing fuel flow in response to boost. *Kenne Bell*

Injectors

Where large fuel injectors used to be the bane of 5.0 tuners, they are ubiquitous, thanks to the proliferation of inexpensive mass air metering. The big-power modern

5.0s need the bigger injectors anyway, and they aren't really a drivability problem until you get over a certain flow rate. And, with electronics, tuners can make even enormous injectors idle and cold-start right there with the small ones.

"When you start the car up, the car looks at the throttle angle and the water temp," Anderson said. "Then it looks at the program that's already there that's for 19-pound injectors. So the 38s are just to that point, that you don't have a problem with cold start-up." He does caution that 38s will make warm start-up a bit tougher, so 38 pound/hour injectors remain his upper limit on street cars.

This seems to be the thinking of choice today. Why not just step up to a large injector on a mildly modified car? Then, as you add more power you don't suddenly run out of injector. Bell said, "To anybody who's thinking about going to a bigger injector on a Mustang, I say, 'Always go 36.' Why not? There's no reason not to."

An interesting thing to note on supercharged cars is that the fuel injector flow rates are factored at atmospheric pressure. Supercharging increases manifold pressure well beyond atmospheric pressure, so you have manifold pressure leveraging against fuel pressure, which is why a boost-sensitive fuel pressure regulator is a must when swapping an FMU for big injectors.

"You've got to remember that when you're rating the injector at 45 pounds of fuel pressure, say 30 pounds per hour at 45 pounds, and you've got 10 pounds of boost, you do not have a 30-pound injector at 45 pounds. You have what used to be a 30-pound injector, only at 35 pounds, because you've got manifold pressure," Bell explained.

Supercharging isn't the only arena where bigger fuel injectors come in handy. "When you are talking about guys that are running nitrous, for example," Granatelli observes, "they don't have the benefit of the blower to spike the fuel pressure. So even though they can bleed a little bit of pressure off the nitrous through a makeshift regulator, the guys that try to make big power don't do that. They are forced to run a wet system. Well, they could actually run it dry if they just went to a 24- or 30-pound injector. Because then with a 30-pound injector, they could support 340 horsepower at 45 psi."

High-rpm engines present a challenge to selecting the proper injector size. "Something else everybody likes to forget is rpm," Anderson explained. "They go by all these little formulas that everybody publishes. A 7,500-rpm motor—that changes the whole story on injectors, because one thing people forget is the higher the rpm, the shorter the time you need. It's as simple as this: You need bigger injectors to get the same amount of fuel in there."

Electronics

The mass air meter calibration is the most important electronic consideration of properly fueling your EFI 5.0. It has the biggest impact on drivability. All the common air meters work fine with naturally aspirated and centrifugally supercharged cars, but they can become a problem with low-rpm boost.

"Well, it's the load tables, when they change the voltage to compensate for the injector at wide-open throttle. What happens when you floor it at 2,000 rpm, the computer says .04 of a volt instead of .06 of a volt. Lean it out and give this guy mileage and advance the timing," Bell explained. As a result, he started converting to larger injectors using a computer chip, which is similar to the factory's method of calibrating at the processor.

The voltage-shifting meters work fine on centrifugal and naturally aspirated applications, because there isn't boost present at low rpm to mingle with the advanced timing and lean air/fuel ratio to cause detonation. The shifted load tables do eventually become a limitation, when running 72 pound/hour and larger injectors, because the meter voltage becomes so low at wide-open throttle that the EEC-IV starts looking at load tables other than those meant for WOT. Of course, most cars running injectors this large have already switched over to aftermarket programmable speed-density injection.

The dark side of larger injectors and recalibrated mass air meters is that these items are not technically emissions legal. Most of the people I chatted with said you can smog a car with up to 36 pound/hour injectors, but making it through a tailpipe test isn't quite an IM-240 dyno emissions test either. Electronics can go a long way to getting injectors to work under emission constraints, but eventually the gargantuan fuel injectors can't pulse quickly enough to keep excess fuel out at idle.

You can get pretty far in a street/strip 5.0 Mustang with a big in-tank pump and an inline booster pump or voltage enhancer feeding a set of 36 or 38 pound/hour injectors and a good fuel pressure regulator. This setup will take care of the lion's share of naturally aspirated, 150-shot-nitrous and 10-pounds-of-boost 5.0s roaming around the street. Even at that point, but especially with anything more serious, you need a big external pump, large lines, and larger injectors. The truth of the matter is, you really can't have too much fuel system capacity so long as you have appropriately sized lines and a way to step down voltage on the really big fuel pumps. Remember, fuel is like insurance, so start shopping for a better policy.

Cooling System

9

The cooling system isn't the first thing that comes to mind when thinking about high-performance modifications, but it should. Why? Because making more horsepower creates more heat. Think about it. As more air and fuel enter the combustion chamber, more power is created. A byproduct of this equation is the increased heat. Think of the cylinder as a campfire. Throw more wood on the fire and it creates more heat.

While it's not difficult to figure out the relationship between horsepower and heat, the cooling system is often overlooked and overwhelmed by a barrage of horsepower bolt-ons. Not that the stock system is bad—it will often handle a lot more horsepower than specifications indicate. But depending on the climate, it can be overrun, especially when the pile of horsepower bolt-ons is accentuated by underdrive pulleys, which slow the water pump.

Thermostats

In the early days of fuel-injected 5.0s, switching to a much cooler 160-degree thermostat was a way to get a cooler, denser mixture and get the EEC-IV to richen the mixture. As tuners became adept at manipulating the 5.0, these crude methods were no longer recommended. In general, most 5.0s will cool better with a 180-degree thermostat. In hot climates, 5.0 owners can stick with the 180 year-round. In cold climates, 5.0 owners can go with the 180 during the warmer months, then switch to a stock 192-degree unit during the winter.

While there are certainly modern ways of enriching the air/fuel mixture, why is running too-cool a thermostat bad? It is bad for three reasons. It artificially enriches the fuel mixture, which can hurt drivability. The rich condition can increase engine wear by fueling-down the cylinder walls, which keeps the oil from properly lubricating them. Additionally, a too-cool thermostat can actually make a car run hot, as it is open all the time and the coolant doesn't stay in the radiator long enough to dissipate the proper heat. A thermostat really needs to cycle open and closed to maintain proper operating temperature.

Coolant

The lifeblood of most cooling systems is antifreeze and water. Most coolant and auto manufacturers recommend a 50/50 mix of water and coolant. This provides maximum corrosion protection, effectively raises the water's boiling point, and, naturally, prevents the coolant mixture from freezing. Unfortunately for those in hot climates, antifreeze doesn't cool as well as water. So, you can increase the system's efficiency by running more water and less coolant—80/20 is a practical limit.

To go even further, you can use pure water (preferably mineral-free distilled) doped with Redline's Water Wetter and topped with a high-pressure radiator cap. Water Wetter is said to improve water's cooling properties while adding corrosion protection, and an 18-psi

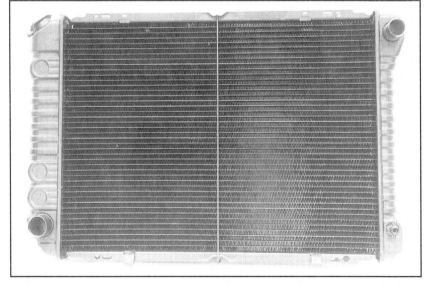

Adding a thicker radiator can increase cooling capacity. The economical choice is a copper-brass radiator like this three-core unit. While they are inexpensive, they are heavier and less efficient than aluminum radiators. This is because copper-brass radiators are soldered together, which insulates the inherent heat-transfer abilities of the copper-brass arrangement. These radiators also must use narrower internal tubes, so less coolant has direct contact with the tubing wall, which means less heat transfer. No matter what, a thicker radiator mandates increased airflow from the fan. *Ford Racing Performance Parts*

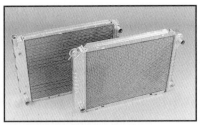

Aluminum radiators are the more expensive and more efficient cooling choice. They allow wider coolant tubes without adding too much weight and their welded construction doesn't impede heat transfer. Whether you choose aluminum or copper-brass, it's worth noting the 1979–93 and 1994–95 radiators are different. Griffin offers aluminum radiators for all 5.0 Mustangs.

The factory fan clutch does a nice job of engaging and releasing the fan in response to engine temperature. However, it eventually wears and slips, which can lead to overheating problems. If you plan to stick with the factory belt-driven fan, you might consider a Special Service fan clutch as sold by Performance Parts, Inc. The Special Service clutch, which was standard equipment on police-package 5.0s, features revised lock-up and release points said to improve cooling and free up horsepower.

cap will increase the water's boiling point over 250 degrees. A high-pressure cap mandates a healthy cooling system with good hoses and clamps. Whether you run water or a water/coolant mixture, a healthy radiator cap will reduce the chances for overheating.

Radiators

Likely the first item selected for replacement is the radiator. While a larger radiator certainly can't hurt the cooling cause, it may or may not be necessary. If your 5.0 runs cool on the open highway, but heats up idling in traffic, the radiator is not the culprit. If the coolant temperature is at or below the thermostat's rating, the radiator is doing its job.

If the cooling system has some age and miles on it, as most 5.0s do by now, it wouldn't be a bad idea to replace it. Then it becomes a matter of choosing which material you want: copper-brass or aluminum. Copper is an excellent heat conductor, but it has two main disadvantages as a radiator medium. Its foremost disadvantage is that the coolant-carrying tubes must be soldered to the cooling fins and end tanks. The solder acts as an insulator, which limits the tubes' heat-transfer abilities. Additionally, it's accepted among radiator builders that larger tube width provides more heat transfer because it allows more coolant to come directly in contact with the tube wall. Unfortunately, making copper-brass tubes wider requires making them prohibitively thick and heavy. Thick copper-brass radiators also add weight to the front of the car. The upside of copper-brass radiators is that they are relatively cheap.

The more expensive, but max-performance option is an aluminum radiator. Because aluminum is so much lighter, it allows manufacturers to construct much wider tubes, without adding too much bulk and weight to the radi-

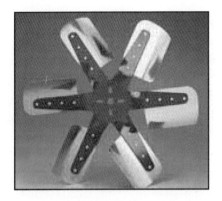

Flex fans like this unit from Flex-a-lite feature flexible aluminum blades, which are steeply pitched to improve airflow at low engine rpm. At higher engine rpm, the blades flex and flatten out, letting the down-the-road airflow take over, while reducing drag. These lightweight fans are usually good to 10,000 rpm and beyond and can be a good choice for 5.0s with thick radiators, cracked fan blades, and slipping fan clutches. *Flex-a-lite Consolidated*

ator. Not only does aluminum allow more coolant-to-tube contact for improved cooling, but aluminum is a fine conductor of heat and is welded, not soldered, so its efficiency is not limited. As such, a two-row aluminum radiator will out-cool a four-row copper-brass heat exchanger. The two are dimensionally similar, but the aluminum is more efficient and lighter.

Let your budget be your guide here. A naturally aspirated street 5.0 will probably do just fine with a copper-brass radiator, while a supercharged open-track 5.0 can use all the cooling and weight reduction of an aluminum radiator. And, a radiator is only one facet of the cooling system, so make sure the basics are in order before you start spending money on a high-zoot radiator.

Fans

Ford did a great job with the stock cooling fan. So long as the stock shroud is in place and the fan clutch is in good shape, it will cool all but the gnarliest 5.0s. The key is maintaining the stock parts. The plastic fan will eventually wear and crack at the junction where the blades meet the hub. Not only will this hurt cooling efficiency, but eventually one of those blades could break off when you are powershifting at 6,000 rpm. As for the clutch, which is supposed to spin faster when heated, it will eventually wear and slip.

Typical overheating problems occur at idle. Most 5.0 engines producing more horsepower are

Electric fans are generally a better choice for race cars or as a secondary cooling device. However, Flex-a-lite offers a direct-fit electric fan for 5.0 Mustangs (shown here mounted to a polished Be Cool radiator). It moves 2,400 cfm and features an adjustable thermostat and automatic air conditioning relay. Unfortunately, this fan will not fit 5.0s equipped with superchargers, as its motor will interfere with the blower belt.

A popular retrofit for 1979–93 5.0s is the factory electric fan from 1994 and later Mustangs. This fan survived Ford's rigorous testing procedures on newer Mustangs and is a great solution for hot-running Fox-body 5.0s. Most people wire these fans up to a relay that engages the fan with key power so it runs all the time. This works fine, but it's not a bad idea to have a switch wired in as well, since the spinning fan can be an airflow restriction at highway speeds. These fans also need a heavy-duty relay, like those used on golf carts, to survive the sustained current these fans draw.

outfitted with underdrive pulleys, so the fan is turning more slowly and less air is moving over the radiator. If the fan clutch is slipping too, these factors can add up quickly. Even with a healthy fan clutch and standard pulleys, idle is a critical cooling time, and a common way to move more air over the radiator is replacing the stock fan with a flex fan.

Flex fans are so named because they are constructed with flexible metal blades that are sharply pitched at low rpm and flatten out at high rpm. As such, these fans move lots of air during critical low-rpm duty, and they are lighter, thus more durable at high rpm, than the stocker. While these fans can help, they can be a clearance issue when coupled with superchargers requiring additional serpentine belts in front of the stock accessory belt; the stock fan shroud may also interfere with such belts when mounted on a thicker-than-stock radiator.

The last resort for moving more air over the radiator is an electric fan. These fans deliver practically the same airflow, when provided with consistent current, at all rpm. Only a properly sized electric fan can be used for primary cooling on a daily-driven 5.0. In some cases multiple electric fans may be necessary, though going with a stock electric fan from a 1994–95 Mustang is the best choice. An upgraded charging system is a given with any electric fan, and likewise a 1994–95 alternator is a perfect upgrade for earlier 5.0 Mustangs.

With regard to the electric fan-equipped SN95 5.0s, the stock fan is great, but activating it earlier than the stock settings promotes better cooling. This can be achieved with a computer chip or Best Products' stand-alone controller.

Water Pumps

The stock water pump is probably the last thing replaced on a 5.0 cooling system. Provided the rest of the system is functioning properly, it will do a fine job. If it finally

starts weeping, or you just think its time is about up, it's worth considering an aftermarket replacement. Performance aftermarket water pumps cost considerably more than those found at the corner auto parts store, but they offer improvement for that money. Most aftermarket pumps increase coolant flow, and some focus on balancing that flow evenly throughout the engine.

This is another place to let your budget and climate be your guide. In cooler climes, you can probably get by with a stock replacement pump. In hot climates, an aftermarket pump, particularly one that increases flow at low rpm, would be the final piece in a performance cooling system.

Oil Coolers

While the coolant naturally gets lots of cooling attention, the engine oil doesn't get much respect. After all, the oil is the engine's lifeblood. It's expected to lubricate and cool the crankshaft, rods, pistons, cam, valves, valve springs, and rocker arms without the benefit of a proper heat exchanger. The standard cooling

A choice replacement water pump for hot-running 5.0s is the FlowKooler pump. These pumps are specifically designed for hopped up street machines that need to remain cool in traffic. Brassworks designed the FlowKooler impeller to double coolant flow at idle and continue pumping increases up to 3,500 rpm. It's also said to increase coolant pressure by 22 percent. These pumps are also available for standard- and reverse-rotation accessory drives.

A low-cost, easy-to-install horsepower boost is available from underdrive pulleys. These accessory drive pulleys slow down the engine accessories, which reduces engine drag. While most manufacturers say they do not cause overheating, they are generally referring to bolt-on 5.0s. Once you significantly increase horsepower, a slower-turning fan and water pump can be a detriment. In these cases, you have to carefully balance horsepower and drivability. The best solution is to swap out the large underdrive water pump pulley with a pulley from the 1993 Cobra. This will allow you to retain the underdrive crank and alternator pulleys and their horsepower, while increasing cooling.

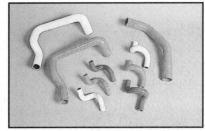

Special Service hoses are a popular 5.0 cooling system addition because their silicone construction offers increased durability over rubber. Unfortunately, those hoses soil quickly. These silicone hoses—manufactured by Samco Sport and marketed by Incon Systems—offer durability and grime resistance. They are also available in a variety of eye-catching colors, such as red, yellow, black, blue, and purple.

system principally benefits the cylinder heads and upper engine block. The crank and rods are left simmering in a boiling vat of oil.

You never want the engine oil too cool because it won't burn off contaminants, and cool, thick oil eats up some horsepower and gas mileage. Even so, the oil is being

stressed by heat, even if the engine is running within its specified range. As such, an engine oil cooler is a good idea for most any engine, particularly max-power street cars and high-endurance road racers.

There are two types of engine oil coolers: those that dissipate heat via the existing cooling system, known as oil-to-water coolers, and those that exchange heat oil-to-air via a dedicated heat exchanger. Oil-to-water coolers, as used on highway patrol 5.0 Mustangs, place extra strain on the engine cooling system, so it must be up to the task. Oil-to-air coolers bring their own cooling capacity, but they require mounting a heat exchanger somewhere in the vehicle's front-end air path. Not only is this area crowded, but obstructing the air path in front of the radiator can hurt overall engine cooling.

If you choose to add an oil cooler to your engine, you should make sure to use quality hoses and fittings to minimize the chances for a leak. It's also worth considering some type of thermostatic bypass, which only circulates oil through the cooler when the engine has reached operating temperature; this is only necessary with oil-to-air coolers.

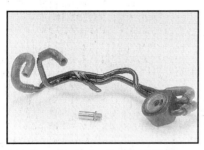

An oil cooler is worth considering, as the standard cooling system really only cools the upper block and heads, leaving the crankcase oil to fend for itself. Oil coolers come in two versions: air-to-oil, like the PermaCool unit (right), and oil-to-water, like those found on Special Service and Cobra R Mustangs (left).

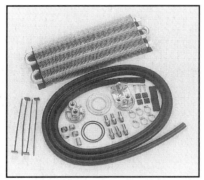

Oil-to-air coolers are tougher to mount, while oil-to-water coolers place more strain on the standard cooling system. Both can aid engine durability in heavy-duty applications.

Electronics

10

If you own a carbureted 5.0, you might as well turn to the next chapter. Owners of fuel-injected 5.0s should keep reading, though, as there are numerous horsepower and drivability benefits available via electronic tuning. It's not that the factory Electronic Engine Control-IV is a bad system, but it works under emissions, fuel economy, and drivability constraints that don't necessarily maximize performance.

Even among stock systems all EEC-IVs are not created equally. Calibrations change from year to year and even within the same model year. The biggest difference among EEC-IVs is those set up for speed density, as found in 1986–88 5.0 Mustangs, and those set up for mass airflow, as found in 1988 California 5.0s and all 1989–95 5.0s. In short, speed-density 5.0s are less accepting of performance modifications than mass-air 5.0s.

Speed Density

Speed-density systems infer airflow by consulting the oxygen sensors, manifold absolute pressure sensor, and throttle position sensor. With this inferred data, the EEC-IV assumes airflow, engine load, and so forth and uses them as guidelines to consult the internal programming, or look-up tables, to determine fuel and spark settings. This, however, is an imprecise way of factoring air/fuel ratio, which influences emissions and reduces its acceptance of increased airflow, as it doesn't have the programming to deal with it.

Mass Airflow

As emissions and fuel economy became more of a factor, Ford switched to mass airflow EEC-IV.

Mass airflow places a sensor between the air filter and the throttle body in the intake stream to directly measure the mass of air coming into the engine. The mass-air sensor achieves this measurement by placing a hot wire in the air stream. The computer attempts to keep the wire at 200 degrees above ambient temperature by applying voltage to the wire. The more voltage, the more flow. A second wire in the sensor measures air temperature.

Because the computer is now informed precisely how much air is coming into the engine, it can more accurately add fuel to match.

Ford's fourth Electronic Engine Control, or EEC-IV, really is a powerful system, especially when programmed for mass airflow. Ford proved the EEC-IV in the highly competitive Indy car racing ranks. Naturally, Ford harnessed its processing power for emissions, drivability, and fuel economy in all its production car lines. Still, in the early days of 5.0s, gearheads got exceptional performance by simply advancing the initial timing at the distributor. It was eventually replaced by the more-powerful, and restrictive, EEC-V, which includes sophisticated on-board diagnostics designed to ensure emissions compliance versus tampering and age.

This real-time method allows the EEC-IV to respond to improvements in engine airflow. Where an aftermarket camshaft will cause erratic idling in a speed-density 5.0, the mass-air system will compensate and idle.

The later-model 1994–95 Mustangs are even more reliant on the mass-air meter at all times, even checking it at wide-open throttle to determine spark advance. The EEC-IVs found in 1986–93 5.0s simply default to programmed timing data at WOT. The new strategy, a result of stringent emissions requirements, makes SN95 Mustangs less accepting of modi-

This is what started it all. When Ford introduced mass airflow to the Mustang in 1989 (1988 in California) and Ford Racing Performance Parts followed it up with a conversion kit for the 1986–88 5.0s, the 5.0 aftermarket exploded. All those who ripped off EFI manifolds and installed carburetors were proven wrong by the performance and drivability offered by mass-air 5.0s tweaked with common hot rodding techniques like ported cylinder heads and performance camshafts. Mass-air EEC-IVs actually measure incoming airflow via a hot-wire sensor, rather than inferring it from the MAP and oxygen sensors. *Ford Racing Performance Parts*

fication. In this case, the computer's information-gathering power allows the computer to tweak out performance at WOT.

In short, if you own a speed-density 5.0, you should place converting to mass air at the top of your list of modifications. Ford Racing Performance Parts, Best Products, and Interactive Systems and Technologies all offer mass air conversion kits.

Air/Fuel Strategy

Regardless of your EEC-IV's setup, it operates in two modes important to your tuning: closed loop and open loop. In low and medium load and rpm situations, the computer constantly checks the oxygen sensor voltage to determine

Ford Racing Performance Parts also offers a mass-air upgrade kit for existing mass-air cars. This 70-millimeter Mass Air Induction Kit, or Cobra mass-air kit as it is known on the street, includes the same parts found on the 1993 Mustang Cobra: a 70-millimeter throttle body, eight 24 pound/hour fuel injectors, and the Cobra-spec EEC-IV. This kit is a good value for those wanting to step up to 24-pound injectors with a factory calibration. However, the Cobra mass-air meter is bisected by a backflow inhibitor that reduces its flow to little more than the stock 55-millimeter meter. Also the Cobra EEC features some performance-killing features. Its programming contains a spark timing retard that occurs at over 93 miles per hour and between 3,800 and 4,200 rpm. Owners of 1993 Cobras can eliminate these issues with a chip or Best Products' Cobra Finisher box.

how much oxygen is in the exhaust gas. More voltage means more oxygen and a lean mixture, while less voltage conveys less oxygen and a rich mixture. The computer tries to achieve a stoichiometric or ideal air/fuel mixture, which, for a gas engine, happens to be 14.7 parts of air to 1 part of fuel. The engine will run at richer (up to 10:1) or leaner (near to 17:1) mixtures, but 14.7:1 provides the most efficient and emissions-friendly results.

Since achieving this ratio is fleeting because of all the atmospheric and combustion variables, the computer removes or adds fuel in response to oxygen sensor voltage to keep the ratio bouncing back and forth right around that ideal ratio. This is important, as the computer will do all it can to circumvent some tuning changes, like increasing base fuel pressure with a regulator or injector pulse width with a piggyback system. Of course,

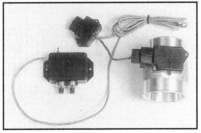

Best Products calibrates mass air meters by sandblasting the electronics till the voltage output is reduced by enough to fool the mass-air meter into pulsing larger injectors quickly enough to make the car idle, while pulsing slowly enough in the upper rpm ranges to perform. Most customers send their meters back for recalibration to a different injector flow rate, but Best also offers its Mass Air Calibrator, which allows you to alter the voltage output of the meter, thus allowing you to adjust the meter yourself. The device is provided with a complete instruction manual, including a chart of voltage outputs as they correspond to injector sizes. Interactive Systems and Technologies offers a similar product called the Air Adjuster, but it lacks comprehensive documentation.

it is limited by how quickly it can open and close the fuel injectors, so at some point excessive base fuel pressure will out-muscle the EEC-IV—and trigger an error code and check-engine light.

By comparing the mass airflow to the engine rpm and oxygen sensor data, the EEC determines how much fuel it is supplying, compared to the amount of air entering the cylinder. If things don't add up, the computer will store away the troubled areas in its Keep Alive Memory so it can apply the compensation in the future. This is known as the EEC's adaptive control, which is designed to compensate for aging sensors and fuel delivery hardware. The Keep Alive Memory can be cleared by disconnecting the battery. Then the learning process starts all over again.

Like all chips for EEC-IV 5.0s, the chips from Mike Wesley's Autologic invade the stock programming via a factory test port. The Autologic chips are only available for Fords—mostly Mustangs and F-150s. These chips are also unique because the Chipmaster software and hardware used to create them are licensed to individual shops. These shops use dynos and data-acquisition hardware to tune them for individual combinations. Autologic also licenses a special version of this chip to Kenne Bell. Dubbed the Switch Chip, the Kenne Bell version allows them to download two programs to the chip. Then the end-user flips a simple rocker switch to toggle between the two programs. This can be useful for changing from a program for 93-octane pump gas to a program for 100-octane race gas.

Kenne Bell's Optimizer tuning tool, which had not been released before this book's deadline, is a piggyback processor similar to those covered elsewhere in this chapter. It differs because rather than intercepting the stock computer's signals before they go back to the engine, it allows tweaking the sensor signals going into the EEC-IV to enhance the vehicle's performance. It does so by making the EEC react to the altered sensor inputs. *Kenne Bell*

Superchips offers its chips one of two ways. It can create a program for you based on a comprehensive questionnaire, or you can buy one from one of its Modem Dealers. These dealers are shops, usually with chassis dynos, that tell Superchips what tuning the vehicle needs, then download several program variations from the Superchips bulletin board system, and dyno the car with each version to determine the best program.

Conversely in open loop, which usually takes hold above 2,500 rpm below 10 inches of vacuum, the computer does not actively attempt to adjust the air/fuel ratio after consulting sensors. Instead, it relies on

preprogrammed look-up tables to determine the fuel and spark settings; SN95 computers consult and react to the sensors at all rpm. The stock computer sends the air/fuel ratio rich in these modes to protect

the engine from damage, so you can lean out the mixture for more naturally aspirated power or richen it for more forced-induction power without fear of being counteracted by the computer. This is why supercharger FMUs don't cause the computer any grief, as they usually spike fuel pressure in open loop.

Chips

An attractive electronic tuning solution for the average enthusiast, computer chips offer an easy way to add increased performance. Since Ford solders its read-only-memory chips into the EEC-IV, they cannot be removed and replaced as is possible with some Brand X cars. The computer's programming is stored on these chips, but chip programmers work around the fixed ROM chips by accessing the programming via the EEC-IV's test port. This port is designed for dealership technicians to reprogram the computer's ROM to improve an emissions or drivability problem.

Aftermarket chip makers use this factory back door to plug in a piggyback EEPROM chip, which alters the factory programming for performance. A number of companies use this method, and Autologic and Superchips are the premier chip programmers for 5.0 Mustangs, as they both offer individually tuned chips, where most other manufacturers sell one-size-fits-all chips.

All the chip makers actually break into the stock hexadecimal code and reprogram it. As such, they can effect change in just about any facet of a 5.0's performance. Chip tuners can adjust important features such as idle speed, timing, fuel injector pulse width, rev limiters, speed limiters, and automatic transmission shift points and shift firmness. Naturally, this power is contingent on the programmer's knowledge of the factory software and what adjustments optimize performance. A rare combination of computer and automotive

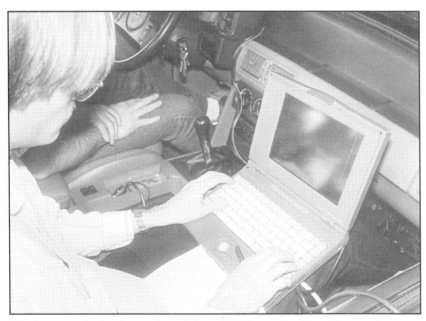

Also from Autologic, the much-anticipated Calibrator is said to allow end-users to tune their cars via an IBM-compatible computer. The Calibrator is essentially a more-powerful rewriteable chip that allows switching between two programs without a computer connected. Two versions of the Calibrator should become available—the DL (Download), which allows tuning after shutting the car off, and RT (Real Time), which allows tuning while the car runs. The RT version also incorporates a 16-channel data logger.

EFI Systems' Programmable Management System is the most user-friendly tuning tool available for 5.0 Mustangs. It allows making tuning changes with a small handheld controller, thus allowing the driver to make tuning changes while driving. The PMS is also expandable with software that allows it to rival many stand-alone EFI systems. This software allows for more powerful tuning changes, plus the ability to record comprehensive data logs. Rick Anderson of Anderson Ford Motorsport is the foremost PMS advocate and offers tech support to buyers.

knowledge can yield impressive performance results.

While many chip makers offer chips via speed shops and catalog vendors, Autologic and Superchips offer two distinct chip services. Autologic licenses its Chipmaster software to performance shops, most of them equipped with chassis dynamometers. These shops use their tuning experience, rear-wheel dynos, air/fuel ratio monitors, and other data logging to burn custom chips for each individual vehicle. Chipmaster offers a user-friendly front-end, so the shops needn't be fluent in hex.

Superchips, on the other hand, offers a double service. It will sell you a mail-order chip based on an extensive tech sheet. Their tuners have a good grasp on tuning, so this is a good way to get a chip if you aren't near one of their modem dealers. Modem dealers, on the other hand, tune cars much like Autologic licensees, except Superchips, rather than the shop, still programs the chips. The Modem Dealer tells Superchips what parameters need changing, then downloads a variety of programs from the Superchips com-

puter bulletin board system—they usually get five programs for the price of one chip. Then they test each program to find the best version before saving the program to a chip, known in the trade as burning a chip.

Chips are a powerful tuning aid, but they do have a downside—chips are a static tune. In other words, once you significantly alter your combination, the chip formerly tuned for your specific application is no longer as effective. This means going to the time and, more importantly, the expense of having a new chip burned. While this likely should be cheaper the second time around, it's still an added cost.

Chips also suffer from being tied to the stock electronics. They don't have the opportunity to be informed by outside sensors, like some aftermarket EFI systems. In other words, a chip can be tuned for maximum supercharged performance, but if the belt breaks at WOT, the retarded timing set up for boosted performance will reduce naturally aspirated performance.

Despite their fixed tune, chips offer a cost-effective, low-maintenance, easy-to-install option for owners who are maximizing a completed combination.

Piggyback Systems

As evidence of the power of the 5.0 phenomenon, computer chips are not the only tuning tool available. A few highly intelligent gearheads spent considerable time and money developing a number of piggyback systems designed to maximize the performance of the 5.0 Mustang by working in concert with the stock EEC-IV computer. By doing so, these systems capitalize on the stock computer's penchant for good drivability manners, while improving performance. This differentiates the piggyback systems from the stand-alone systems I'll cover a bit later in this chapter.

Interceptor
The grandpappy of all EEC-IV piggyback systems is the Crane

Interceptor. Created by hardware genius Doug Wallis, who also created the first computer chip for EEC-IV Mustangs, and programmed by Paul Pisarchuk, the Interceptor technology was quickly scooped up by Crane Cams' then-new electronics division. Unlike chips using the EEC-IV's service port, Interceptors simply plug in between the factory wiring harness and the EEC-IV computer and allow most factory signals to pass through, while substituting performance commands in key performance areas like fuel and timing.

Wallis, who previously sold his chip technology to a mass-market chip maker, worked with Crane while it marketed the Interceptor and the improved Interceptor II. Eventually, Crane gave up marketing the Interceptor, which was really ahead of its time, and Wallis revised the unit and began selling it himself as the Programmable Management System.

While Interceptors are no longer sold, they are still available on the used market and likely a good performance bargain. Interceptors allow the user to adjust fuel and timing tables at low load (through 2,200 rpm), medium load (through 4,000), high load (through 5,800), and wide-open throttle. Users program adjustments at those points via a handheld keypad, and the computer averages the difference between the settings. Interceptors also offered a way to circumvent the factory 6,250-rpm rev limiter and switch on two powered devices like nitrous solenoids, shift lights, and transbrakes.

Interceptor II added the ability to respond to boost from a supercharger (via a GM MAP sensor) or the engagement of nitrous oxide. Thereby, forced-induction 5.0 owners could enrich the fuel mixture and retard the timing for maximum performance without using cruder mechanical methods; in the boost table you set fuel enrichment and timing retard numbers for 1 pound and maximum boost, and the Interceptor II averages between those numbers for the intermediate boost numbers. Both systems allow you to monitor basic engine functions, such as rpm, fuel injector duty cycle, fuel injector pulse width, mass airflow, oxygen sensor voltage, engine load, and total timing.

PMS

After Crane ceased marketing the Interceptor, Wallis decided to improve it and bring it out under his own EFI Systems banner. Since Crane was bent on selling the Interceptor as a street-legal unit, Wallis was restricted as to how much power he could give it. His Programmable Management System is sold as an off-road piece, so he was able to throw out all the stops. The only real difference is more tunability.

The PMS (an appropriate name given the grumpy nature of some performance cars) is packed into a more compact, anodized purple case and outfitted with a handheld display that is easier to

read, thanks to backlighting. The PMS also picked up processor speed and an open architecture designed to interface with a laptop for data-logging via a program called *InterACQ*. PMS computers are available for other cars, but most of those sold to Mustang owners come from Anderson Ford Motorsport's Rick Anderson. He has a lot of experience with the unit and provides great tech support to those who buy it.

In addition to the low-load, medium-load, high-load, and WOT adjustments, the PMS stand-alone mode takes over at 4,000 rpm, rather than only with the extended rev limiter with the interceptor. PMS units will also support up to 9,200 rpm if your engine can. Later versions can support up to 30 pounds of boost versus the 15-pound limit on early PMS and Interceptor computers. PMS units also incorporate a number a drivability options. Users can adjust start-up fuel (great for taming large fuel injectors), idle fuel, idle timing, idle rpm, and the sensitivity of the idle-air bypass valve. These

capabilities are great for corralling a grumpy camshaft.

Though it all sounds complicated, the PMS is actually quite easy to master. The PMS compact handheld controller makes it easy to make one-handed changes while driving, which is great for tuning drivability. While the standard PMS is powerful—Anderson has tuned a supercharged Mustang to 8-second quarter-miles with the hand-held unit—it does have limitations in resolution, or the number of rpm points you can tune. Also, some of the low-load changes are subject to be overridden by the EEC-IV's adaptive, closed-loop air/fuel strategy.

To remedy those limitations, Wallis again called on Pisarchuk to program more software for the PMS; Pisarchuk already had penned the aforementioned DOS-based data-logging program. This time he coded a Windows-based tuning interface, dubbed *InterACQ for Windows*. This powerful software allows tuners to build complete fuel and timing maps for pinpoint tuning. The maps can be built from scratch or learned from the existing setup and tweaked from there. Like the handheld PMS adjustments, all the *InterACQ for Windows* tables allow for interpolation, so you can fill in two cells and have the software fill in all the blanks between those points. Once downloaded to the PMS, these tables run in the background, so you can still tweak them with the hand-held controller. More importantly, the new tables run standalone without meddling from the EEC-IV.

Besides the obvious fuel and timing tuning, *InterACQ for Windows* incorporates all of the standard PMS functions. It allows you to substitute revised fuel and spark tables in response to boost, nitrous, air temperature, water temperature, and acceleration. Just like the keypad, the software allows tweaking idle, part-throttle, and wide-open throttle performance as well. The new

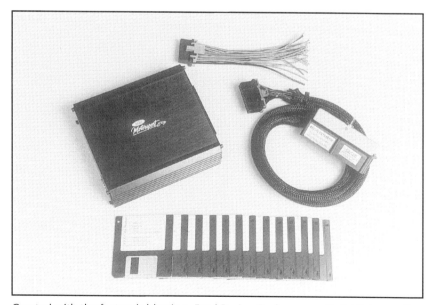

Created with the factory's blessing, Ford Racing Performance Parts' Extreme Performance Engine Control is likely the most powerful piggyback processor available for 5.0 Mustangs. It offers so much tunability it can even be wired up as a stand-alone system. It also offers sophisticated data logging capabilities tracking up to 16 different signals, 4 of which can be sensors outside the EEC wiring harness. Jim LaRocca of LaRocca's Performance is EPEC's biggest proponent.

features allow for the PMS to control a turbo wastegate, be tuned for an aftermarket mass air meter, and compensate for larger injectors. Perhaps its most intuitive function is the ability to tell it what injectors you are running and what pressure you are running and have it figure out, for example, that 19 pound/hour injectors at 45 psi act like 22 pound/hour injectors—way cool!

InterACQ for Windows also incorporates all the data-logging features of its DOS cousin, plus it adds trick reports like volumetric efficiency and estimated horsepower. In all, *InterACQ for Windows* turns the piggyback PMS into a hybrid piggyback/stand-alone EFI computer, offering the ease of use of the former and ultimate power of the latter.

Extender

After the Interceptor and before the PMS, Sam Guido of General Systems Research built the Extender for Ford Racing Performance Parts. This piggyback processor offered powerful control over the rev limiter and air/fuel ratio. For just over $500, racers could twist their 5.0s to 13,000 rpm, engine willing, and set their air/fuel ratio anywhere from a superfat 9.5:1 to 14:1 in 25 percent increments.

Like most piggyback systems, the Extender uses a wiring harness and stock-style connectors to splice in between the EEC-IV and the factory wiring harness; these complicated wiring harnesses are really what drive the pricing. Once plugged in, an Extender allows the user to manipulate the aforementioned rpm and air/fuel settings. These adjustments are achieved by turning two mini dials with a small screwdriver.

While the Extender is simple, it does the job for a number of applications, particularly high-rpm naturally aspirated 5.0s. This two-function, manual dial arrangement does have limitations. You can't stow the Extender box in a cramped out-of-the-way place, because you need free access

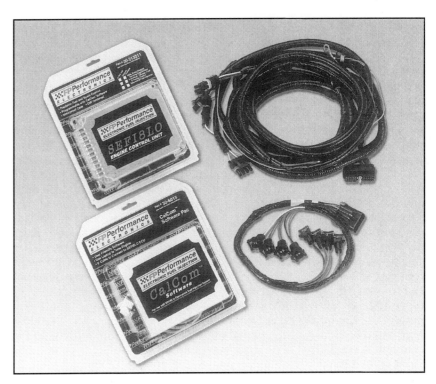

The most popular stand-alone EFI system used on race 5.0s is SEFI8LO speed-density system from FP Performance. It offers a user-friendly Windows interface and allows the user to set up a program with only four initial inputs. Knowledgeable users can use the system's powerful data logging feature to further tune the program for maximum power. It also uses a wide-band oxygen sensor to correct to the user-programmed air/fuel ratios during closed-loop operation. *FP Performance*

to the dials. Plus the settings controlled by those dials are dependent on your hardware. To spin a 5.0 past the rev limiter, it best be equipped with some heavy-duty reciprocating parts, and setting the air/fuel ratio is dependent on your car having a fuel system to pace the engine airflow.

This is important to note because you still have to add larger injectors using an aftermarket-calibrated mass-air meter because the Extender is limited to tuning two functions. As you've likely figured out, that also means you'd still need a timing retard of some kind for forced-induction 5.0s, and you'd still have to trick the computer into advancing the timing quicker by twisting the distributor.

The Extender is powerful yet limited. Its adjustability is a plus, but its limited functionality is outpaced by most other forms of

electronic tuning. If you only have need for its two functions, it's a relative bargain.

EPEC

In response to racer requests and competitive products, Guido's General Systems Research built what is likely the most powerful piggyback EFI system on the market—the Extreme Performance Engine Control, originally codenamed the Super Extender. Most folks just refer to it by its acronym EPEC, pronounced "epic." Whatever you call it, the EPEC represents a staggering collaboration between GSR and Ford. Essentially, EPEC is an EEC processor that can be programmed via a Windows interface. It can run in conjunction with EEC-IV or override it completely. It can even be wired as a stand-alone system, so it's really a hybrid system.

EPEC's Windows interface allows for tuning, switching, and data logging, all in a $1,300 package, which is downright affordable when compared with buying an EFI setup, a data logging arrangement, plus any number of analog switch gear for shift lights, nitrous solenoids, and the like.

Naturally, tuning is EPEC's prime directive. It takes the basic idea of tweaking the timing curve and air/fuel ratio to a new level. Of course, it allows you to tune basic fuel parameters at idle, at part throttle, at wide-open throttle. It also allows you to adjust fuel in response to air-charge temperature, engine coolant temperature, throttle position, manifold pressure (boost), acceleration, voltage (as it influences injector opening time), external analog sensors, and when one or more of the output signals (switches) is triggered.

Spark adjustments are available in response to most of the same parameters as the fuel adjustments, with a few exceptions. EPEC allows you to add or subtract spark, based on barometric pressure and subtract spark in response to boost or nitrous (two stages).

As staggering as all this sounds, EPEC allows you to use as little or as much of it as you need. You can rely on the EEC-IV for the basics and just tweak for power, or reprogram the whole strategy. It's a fully customizable system.

Tuning isn't all you get, though. Data logging is an EPEC strong suit as well. It isn't as comprehensive as some dedicated systems in the $5,000 range, but it does a superb job for 95 percent of enthusiasts. EPEC will log up to 16 different channels, or sensors, including analog inputs. It will sample up to 100 times per second, but the number of samples must be balanced with the length of recording.

Calibrator
Autologic isn't just in the chip business. The man behind Autologic has long been promising to release

the power behind his Chipmaster software as a piggyback EEC-IV tuning device. The man behind Autologic and its hard parts counterpart is Mike Wesley, another one of those electromechanical geniuses who combine computer virtuosity with automotive tuning acumen. Wesley also runs a hardware company dubbed C&M Racing, which stands for computers and Mustangs.

Tantamount to letting the cat out of the bag, Wesley's long-promised Calibrator package promises a user-programmable front-end to the EEC. Naturally, it requires an IBM-compatible computer, preferably a laptop. In other words, it requires little more hardware than a chip, but allows most of the tuning capabilities of a traditional piggyback processor.

Essentially, the Calibrator will be available in a DL (for Download) version, which requires you to turn the car off before tuning, and an RT (for Real Time) version, which allows real-time tuning and accepts 16 channels of data-logging input, four of which can come from sensors beyond the usual EEC-IV wiring harness. As such, the DL version, said to be about the size of a pack of cigarettes, should offer powerful tuning in the affordable range of $500. The RT version, reportedly as big as a paperback book, is targeted at professional tuners and costs considerably more. A stand-alone data logger could also be offered to bring those capabilities to Calibrator DL owners.

Both versions will offer control over fuel injector pulse width and spark timing (in response to air temperature, coolant temperature, rpm, and load), rpm limits, speed limits, idle speed, and injector size. SN95 Mustangs with electronically controlled transmissions can also benefit from the Calibrator's ability to tweak shift rpm, firmness, and torque converter lock-up. Additionally, the Calibrator allows you to download two performance programs and manually switch between them without hooking up

the laptop—great for a stealthy performance increase.

Though demo versions of the Calibrator software (which is essentially the same as the Chipmaster interface) have been around for years, the hardware end has been a long time coming. So far, the Calibrator has been the vaporware, but should it actually appear, powerful tuning should be in the hands of the 5.0 proletariat.

With prices ranging from $500 to $1,300, piggyback computers are definitely more expensive than chips, but they do allow you to make infinite tuning changes without burning a new chip each time. Additionally, the systems that incorporate data-logging features provide vital information to help you constantly refine your combination. Unfortunately, to maximize these systems, you usually must supply an IBM-compatible laptop computer running a fairly recent version of Microsoft Windows—adding even more to the cost.

The bottom line on piggyback systems is how much do you need and how much can you use? Some 5.0s can work wonders with a basic Extender, while others could use the increased functionality of the PMS or Calibrator, and yet another group of cars could use the omnipotent EPEC. Of course, as the system's power increases, its ease of use diminishes. These systems require a good handle on computers and electronics plus an absolute aptitude for knowing what a combustion engine wants.

Tuners like Rick Anderson at Anderson Ford Motorsport and Jim LaRocca at LaRocca's Performance overflow with wisdom about the PMS and EPEC respectively, while many Chipmaster shops will be able to aid Calibrator owners. These tuners can send you a box, give you a ballpark program, and have you up and running in no time. Of course, there is no substitute for time on a tuner's dyno, but the increasing popularity of the Internet means you could e-mail your data log run to a tuner and they could e-mail you back the proper adjustments to maximize your combo. By taking UPS and FedEx out of this loop, the cost for such services is sure to be minimal. There is also the possibility of program trading via the Internet, but be sure to check out new programs for viruses and malicious tuning before damaging your setup.

Also keep in mind that all these systems retain mass airflow, which is definitely more accurate and easier to live with, due to its inherent adaptability, than speed-density systems—even programmable speed density.

Stand-Alone EFI

While chips and piggyback systems are designed for street cars or street/track hybrids, aftermarket EFI systems are for race cars. Granted, some daredevils run these setups on the street, but they are really designed for racers who want to constantly tweak every last drop of power out of their combinations. There are a variety of aftermarket EFI systems, including those from Electromotive and Motec, but these high-end systems aren't quite as popular with 5.0 racers as ACCEL's Digital Fuel Injection, known as DFI, and FP Performance's Sequential Electronic Fuel Injector 8 Low Impedance Injector Drivers, or SEFI8LO. All are programmable speed-density arrangements and all are more expensive than chips or piggyback systems.

Essentially, these systems allow you to build a complete speed-density program tuned to your engine's needs. Unlike the factory speed density, which also can be tuned for performance with a chip, these systems allow for minuscule fuel and timing adjustments that maximize performance and drivability. This is because the parameters you set are based on your combination and can be changed as the combination changes.

Any programmable EFI system is only as powerful as its user's knowledge. A professional tuner can set up your programming with an all-around setup. This can even be done on a dyno of some kind, but speed-density systems will always need to be tweaked in response to weather changes, as they are not able to actually measure the air mass entering the engine. As such, racers will need to know how to operate the software and what to change to make the car work in different situations.

This is especially true of early aftermarket systems, but FP's SEFI8LO raised the bar for aftermarket EFI systems by adding power and increasing usability, while quickly becoming the choice for 5.0 racers. The FP system added a user-friendly Windows-based interface named CalCom. The FP SEFI8LO software and hardware was created by John Meaney, who also created DFI and sold it to ACCEL. Apparently, DFI was not upgraded to his liking, so he created the SEFI8LO system and sold it to Fel-Pro's FP Performance division.

This system allows adjusting all the usual parameters: cranking and starting fuel, air/fuel ratio, spark timing, idle speed, rev limit, plus nice touches like fuel pump priming time and cooling fan switching. Additionally, this system includes a wide-band oxygen sensor which allows it to actively correct the air/fuel ratio.

While this isn't quite as self-contained as a mass airflow system, the FP software and hardware make it much easier on new users. You need only provide the CalCom software with four parameters, and it will build you a base program that will allow you to get the car started. Then you can use its powerful data acquisition feature to fine-tune the combination.

You can set the FP system up to run in closed loop and have the

software correct the air/fuel ratio in response to readings from the system's seven-wire NGK oxygen sensor. Where closed loop can be a bad thing with the factory computer, the FP closed-loop function works to maintain the air/fuel ratios you set for performance, not those set by a factory engineer for emissions and economy. Different closed-loop parameters can be set for low rpm, high rpm, and WOT. The FP system also features a powerful nitrous calibration capability and the ability to tune each cylinder individually to compensate for variances in air and fuel flow.

No doubt the nuances offered by FP will drive further improvements in competitive products, but no matter which aftermarket EFI system you choose, be sure you need it. These systems can be tuned to a safe level to run well all the time for street duty, but their real advantage is constant tuning. It is also advantageous that there are a number of racers using these systems, and several of these racers run shops that offer tuning support for these systems. If you aren't computer and tuning savvy, you will be best served to find a tuner for installation and tech support.

As with any performance component, selecting an electronics package requires an honest analysis of your goals. If you just want to tweak out your combination and forget about it, a chip is the way to go. If you think you might go racing, or you just know your combination is going to evolve, a piggyback system is a good choice. If you are building a race car, you can either go with a high-end piggyback system and retain mass airflow or ditch all the factory stuff and head for programmable speed-density management. Fortunately for 5.0 power fiends, your knowledge and finances are the only limitations.

Transmissions

11

It's easy to see, just by flipping through the pages of this book, the 5.0 Mustang is a fertile performer from the factory. Add just a few bolt-ons and these cars, particularly the 1987–93 variety, will embarrass those big, bad musclecars of yore. While bolting a bunch of parts under the hood, it's easy to overlook the transmission that is trying to handle more power than it was designed to accept.

Durability and performance are the two limitations of the stock transmissions. Naturally, Ford only wanted to build transmissions that were strong enough to work with the stock horsepower rating. Too much more durability is unnecessary, from its vantage point, and certainly unprofitable. Meanwhile, the characteristics exuded by a performance transmission often contradict those exhibited by a transmission maximized for drivability.

The durability and drivability lines can pretty well be divided between the manual and automatic transmissions. The stock T-5 is upgradeable to improve its durability, but these changes have little effect on a 5.0s drivability, as when and how hard the shifts come are still determined by the driver. Conversely, modifying an automatic transmission for performance and durability often affects the car's drivability, based on when and how hard the shifts occur.

Both the T-5 five-speed manual transmission and the Automatic OverDrive have reputations for being susceptible to breakage. Drivers usually mangle the T-5's third-gear synchronizers, while full-throttle upshifts into third wreak havoc on the AOD's two-piece input shaft. Despite these weaknesses, both transmissions can be upgraded to supply durable, drivable shifting for most any street or street/strip 5.0s. The SROD four-speed manual and Cruise-O-Matic three-speed manuals in early 5.0s aren't worth considering for any performance applications. Race 5.0s, on the other hand, need race transmissions.

Manual Upgrades

Despite its questionable reputation, the T-5 transmission found in most 5.0 Mustangs is a durable, smooth-shifting performer. Of course, this is most true of the later, more-refined T-5s. As the 5.0-liter gained more power from the factory, Ford gradually had Borg-Warner upgrade the T-5 right along with it. (These days Tremec builds T-5s.) The early T-5s found in the 1983–84 5.0 Mustangs are only good for 265 lb-ft of torque. Of course, the stock 5.0 was only kicking out 245 lb-ft of torque.

In 1985 Borg-Warner stepped

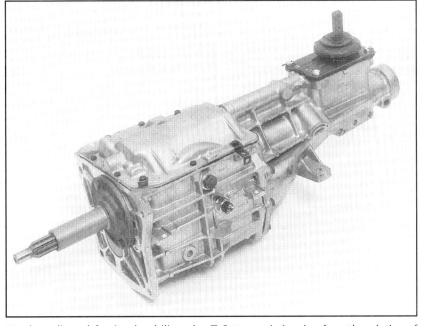

Much maligned for its durability, the T-5 transmission is often the victim of improper driving and shifting techniques. While stock T-5s may outlive their usefulness behind a high-horsepower 5.0, aftermarket T-5s like this Ford Racing Performance Parts version can support up to 330 lb-ft of torque. This transmission should be quite durable in a street car that doesn't see a drag strip regularly. High-powered 5.0s regularly launching on slicks will likely be biding time between rebuilds, but driving technique and some give in the clutch can extend an otherwise outmatched T-5's life span. It's possible to upgrade a stock T-5 to 330 lb-ft capacity. Two shops, D&D Performance and Hanlon Motorsport, specialize in rebuilding and upgrading all 5.0 manual transmissions. *Ford Racing Performance Parts*

One of the more popular shifters for the T-5 is Pro-5.0's Power Tower. It offers billet construction for durability, adjustable stops to prevent overextending shifts, and a short handle for quicker shifts. What differentiates it from other shifters is its unique Offset Shift Mechanism designed to ease the two-three shift where most 5.0 powershifters try to use muscle rather than finesse. Pro-5.0's shifter is the most expensive of the 5.0 shifters, likely because it's manufactured by a small company, but it does offer nice shifting feel. While its shorter handle does hasten shifts, it can make you stretch for fifth gear. Power Towers are also available for all Tremecs and T-56s. All 5.0 shifters are easy-to-install, gratifying bolt-ons.

the T-5's capability to 265 lb-ft and it stayed that way until 1989, despite the 5.0's stock torque peak swelling from 260 to 300 lb-ft over that same period. In 1990 the T-5 capacity matched the engine's output at 300 lb-ft, where it would stay till the end of 5.0 Mustang production in 1995. All that differentiates the T-5s found in Fox Mustangs and SN95 Mustangs is that the later T-5s have longer input shafts—a failed attempt by Ford to allow installing the engine and transmission as one. Naturally, these transmissions are not interchangeable.

One other factory T-5 did exceed the 300 lb-ft. Birthed in 1993, the Mustang Cobra received tapered roller pocket bearings and picked up an additional 10 lb-ft of torque capacity. Of course, all 5.0 Cobras through 1995 received this upgraded T-5.

Though the Cobra T-5 represents the ultimate factory 5.0 five-speed, it is possible to get more

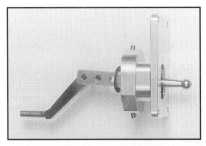

Steeda Autosports took the best parts of existing shifters and added several goodies to its Tri-Ax shifter. Naturally it features a billet base, adjustable shifter stops, and a shorter handle. The Tri-Ax shifter differs from other T-5 shifters by its handle, designed to gently bend toward the driver so the shorter throws don't require stretching for fifth gear. (The handle is available separately.) The base also allows two shifter heights to further tune it to the driver. Tri-Ax shifters also come with a Boot Saver. This thin washer slides over the base of the handle and prevents the factory rubber weather boot from being pinched between the handle and the positive stops.

torque capacity in the aftermarket. There are two main manual transmission resources in the aftermarket: D&D Performance in Wixom, Michigan, and Hanlon Motorsports in St. Peters, Pennsylvania. Both outfits are quite knowledgeable and offer everything from basic rebuild kits to upgrade kits taking the T-5 up to a maximum torque capacity of 330 lb-ft, thanks to a less steep 2.95:1 first gear ratio and numerous detail improvements.

Shifters
A popular addition to any stock or aftermarket T-5 is an aftermarket short-throw shifter. In general the stock Ford shifter offers a long, sloppy shifting motion, due to its long handle and rubber isolator bushings. The long handle lengthens the time it takes to actuate the shifts, while the rubber isolator bushings deliver imprecise feel.

Of course, not all stock shifters are exactly alike. During the late 1980s, Ford switched to a shorter-

throw, higher-effort shifter designated by its gold base. The standard-throw shifters are designated by a black base.

For those on a budget, it's easy enough to replace the rubber isolators with solid bushings and install a shorter handle to speed up shifts. However, this budget plan doesn't provide the biggest benefit of aftermarket shifters—adjustable shift-lever stops. These bolts prevent aggressive drivers from overextending the shift lever and damaging the transmission. The shifters from B&M, Hurst, Pro-5.0, and Steeda are all constructed of stronger materials than stock to withstand abusive driving—some drivers have actually ripped the stock handle off its base.

Clutches
Coupling the engine to the manual transmission is the clutch. Obviously, like all stock parts, the stock clutch is not designed to handle greater-than-stock horsepower. So, eventually increasing horsepower will eventually mandate a clutch

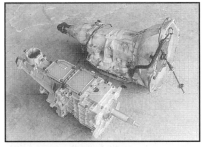

Here is the popular Tremec five-speed compared with the unfairly maligned AOD. Standard Tremecs can support 450 lb-ft of torque, while the TKO version pictured here can handle up to 490 lb-ft. TKOs require special clutches and U-joints for installation. These transmissions do sacrifice some shift feel for their durability. Despite its enhanced strength, the Tremec is lighter and more compact than an AOD. As such, it's popular to swap out an AOD for a Tremec in a high-powered 5.0. Don't discount the AOD, however. A performance-built AOD can carry a 5.0 Mustang to 9-second quarter-miles.

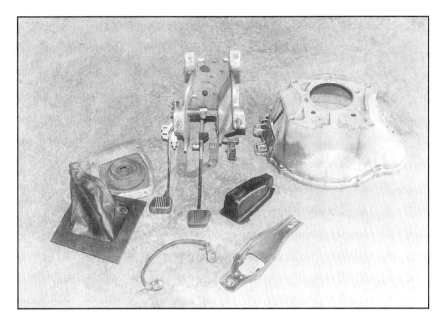

AOD-to-Tremec conversions are so popular Mustang Parts Specialties offers complete swap kits. Some of the major items needed are pictured here: an SROD bellhousing, a pedal assembly, weather seal, shift boot, clutch fork, and a neutral safety switch harness. You'll also need a starter index plate, flywheel, clutch, throwout bearing, shift knob, clutch cable, clutch quadrant, pivot ball, speedometer gear, backup light harness, and a cross-member.

A lesser-known transmission option for high-powered 5.0 Mustangs is the Richmond six-speed. Richmond four-speeds are popular in the rigors of NASCAR racing, and the six-speed contains the same hardened, CNC-cut gears and durable brass synchronizers. Richmond allows choosing custom gear ratios. Anything from a 4.42:1 first gear to a .49:1 sixth gear is available. However, fifth gear is fixed at 1:1, which can make second through fifth tightly spaced. The six-speed's installation requirements are on par with those of a Tremec TKO, but the price is more than most other aftermarket transmissions.

improvement. Most aftermarket performance clutches provide increased clamping force via increased diaphragm pressure and high-tech friction surfaces. The trick is determining how much clutch you need.

Here's a comparison of the stock cast-aluminum T-5 bellhousing (right) and Lakewood's steel version (left). The stock bellhousing is fine for a pure street 5.0. However, when you start adding horsepower and rpm a steel bellhousing is a good idea. It will protect you and your vehicle from an unforeseen driveline failure, which can send the flywheel cutting through everything in its wake. An SROD bellhousing is a cheaper alternative for Tremec swaps, but steel bellhousings selling around $200 are cheap insurance.

Like choosing any other performance part, it's easy to get carried away and put the most aggressive clutch in your street or street/strip car. However, a racing clutch can be really out of place in a street vehicle, as it can dramatically increase clutch pedal effort while chattering at low rpm. These are undesirables in a street vehicle, but the clutch's grip must

cope with engine output. That's the trick.

It is worth a reminder that the clutch is a wear item, and too aggressive a clutch will turn the transmission into a wear item. So, even if your engine makes a ton of power, it would be smart to use a slightly overpowered clutch as a buffer for your transmission. It's much easier and cheaper to replace a clutch than a transmission. This is especially true of the T-5 transmission, but those upgrading to stronger aftermarket transmissions may opt for equally aggressive aftermarket clutches.

Flywheels
When the clutch pedal is released, the pressure plate levers the clutch disc against the flywheel, kind of like a brake pad on a rotor. Just as different brake rotor designs can affect braking, flywheel materials can influence an engine's personality. The cast stock flywheel is fine for moderate-horsepower street cars living under the factory rev limiter. Start spinning the engine in a drag or road race environment and more durability is a safety requirement.

Billet steel and aluminum are the two popular replacement flywheel materials. Steel flywheels

Electronic Shifting

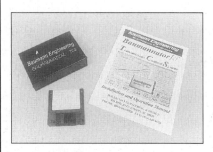

Electronic controls supplement the hydraulic controls inside AODE transmissions in 1994–95 Mustangs. While these transmissions can certainly benefit from all the usual mechanical upgrades, performance can be further enhanced with electronic tuning. Like engine electronics, transmission electronics come in chip, piggyback, and stand-alone varieties. As is the case with the fuel-injected 5.0 Mustang, the electronic transmission brings some limitations while simultaneously expanding the performance potential.

Naturally the most common form of electronic transmission tuning comes alongside engine tuning in a computer chip. Most any computer chip offers some form of transmission tuning for AODs, but custom chips can raise shift points and firm up shifts to accommodate a modified engine. The downside with all chip tuning is its fixed nature. You must pick shift points and firmness and live with them at all times.

Piggyback transmission tuning tools don't offer any engine tuning, but they do offer flexibility a chip doesn't. Two notable piggyback units are the ShiftPlus from B&M and the ATG Interceptor from AutoTrans Group. Simply splicing the ShiftPlus wiring into an AODE-equipped 5.0's wiring allows switching between firm shifts, stock shifts, and very firm shifts. Also offering two adjustments, ATG's Interceptor plugs in line with the factory wiring harness and allows adjusting line pressure and torque converter clutch timing while improving shift quality.

The aforementioned tuning tools offer nice features and easy installation for a moderate cost. Chips and piggyback adjusters are nice additions for street 5.0s already equipped with an electronically controlled transmission. To gain ultimate control and the ability to swap an electronically controlled transmission into an early 5.0 means turning to a stand-alone processor like Baumann Engineering's Baumannator Transmission Control System (pictured) or AutoTrans Group's E-Place.

Longtime Ford transmission tuner and electronics wizard Karl Baumann has developed a number of valve body improvement kits for AOD, AODE, E4OD, and 4R7OW transmissions. He also developed the Baumannator TCS. It is designed to wire up to the stock AODE harness and allows adjusting shift points, line pressure, and torque converter clutch operation. All these settings are tuned via Windows-compatible software, which can store two programs. The second program may be activated on the fly with a switch; great for street and race settings. Its ManuTronic option is perhaps the coolest feature of the Baumannator. This feature allows for manual shifting via the stock cruise control buttons on the steering wheel.

While the Baumannator requires a computer to tune its functions, AutoTrans Group's E-Place provides similar functionality with dial adjustments. The E-Place differs from the Bauman-nator in its intent. Where the Baumann piece is a Ford-specific part designed to work in vehicles with and without stock electronic transmissions, E-Place is specifically meant for swapping electronic transmissions into earlier vehicles and street rods. It also, however, offers adjustable shift points, torque converter clutch control, and manual shifting. Its hardware based adjustability makes it more expensive than the Baumannator, which requires a personal computer.

In addition to increased tunability, the Baumannator and E-Place both offer 1994-95 5.0 Mustang owners the option of adding Best Products Performance Improvement conversion (see Chapter 10) or aftermarket EFI while retaining an electronic transmission.

On the subject of AODEs, it's worth mentioning Level 10 Performance in Hamburg, New Jersey. Level 10 Performance specializes in matching mechanical improvements with electronic tuning. It reprograms EEC-IV computers to enhance shift points, shift firmness, torque converter engagement, and line pressure. Level 10 can also correct the computer for gear ratios greater than 3.73:1, as well as larger-than-stock tire diameters. Otherwise, the computer is confused by the quicker drive-shaft rotation.

With so many choices for electronic transmission tuning, the choices are surprisingly easy. It's a matter of how much you can spend. Chips and piggyback controller are relatively inexpensive and offer nice upgrades for a street 5.0. Stand-alone controllers are costly, but offer numerous tuning advantages for serious street/strip and race 5.0s. There's more to an AODE than a valve body kit.

---

store more inertial energy, thus providing more torque off the line. This is desirable in heavy drag cars and most any street car. Conversely, rev-happy drag or road race vehicles benefit from the snappy throttle response provided by an aluminum flywheel. Both flywheel constructions offer increased high-rpm durability, but aluminum fly-wheels are obviously not as durable in a daily driver.

Bellhousings
Serving as the hard mounting point between the transmission and the engine block, the bellhousing serves to shield the clutch and flywheel from the elements and vice versa. Each transmission uses a unique bellhousing bolt pattern, so the bellhousing used on the early 5.0s with SROD four-speeds will not accommodate the later T-5 five-speed. Conversely, many of the heavy-duty aftermarket transmissions, like the Tremec five-speed and Richmond six-speed, utilize the earlier SROD bellhousing, which Ford originally

It is certainly cheaper to resurface the stock flywheel when installing a performance clutch. Those planning on racing in a sanctioned class will need to step up to a billet steel unit, like this one from Centerforce. It is SFI approved for racing and offers vastly improved high-rpm durability. An aluminum flywheel is another alternative for high-rpm durability. Aluminum flywheels let 5.0s rev more freely at the expense of some low-end torque. *Midway Industries/ Centerforce*

One of the most popular high-performance clutches for 5.0 liter Mustangs is the Dual-Friction clutch from Centerforce. It offers a reported 90-percent increase in clamping force, yet retains stock pedal feel. Naturally, Dual-Friction clutches have more aggressive friction materials than Centerforce's I and II clutches, offering 30 and 60 percent more grip than stock, but all Centerforce clutches actually grip harder as rpm rises. These clutches achieve grip without heavy springs. Instead, they harness centrifugal force by strategically weighting the clutch fingers. Ford Racing Performance Parts, McLeod, and Ram are also popular 5.0 clutch vendors.

used to fit Toploader four-speeds to 289s and 302s.

The cast construction of both factory bellhousings is fine for a street car seeing street rpm. However, as the engine is revved higher in a street or race environment, these bellhousings become a safety liability. Think of the heavy flywheel and clutch spinning inside the bellhousing. Should an unforeseeable failure occur, these pieces, particularly the flywheel, can cut through the bellhousing like a saw. This deadly projectile will also cut through the floor pan and anything else in its way, like your legs. This is why steel safety bellhousings are required by race-sanctioning bodies. These bellhousing are designed to contain such dangerous failures.

Both Lakewood and McLeod offer blowproof steel bellhousings. They are available with SROD, T-5, or both transmission bolt patterns. The T-5 dual-pattern housings are a good choice, as they allow for adding safety to the stock transmission, while leaving the door open for a stronger aftermarket

trans as the vehicle's horsepower and torque are increased.

Automatic Upgrades

In stock form, 5.0 Mustangs equipped with manual transmissions are quicker than those fitted with the gentle Automatic Over-Drive transmissions. The reason for this reduced performance is twofold. Foremost is the gentle shift calibrations programmed by Ford. They aren't much different from the overlapping shifts Grandpa so enjoys in his Crown Vic. Secondly, automatic transmissions siphon off more frictional losses than their manual cousins.

A quick overview of how an automatic works shows why these transmissions eat up more power, while ultimately offering more durability. Rather than directly transferring engine torque through a frictional union, known as a clutch, automatic transmissions convert the engine's energy into hydraulic energy. This viscous coupling eats up more power, but since there are no direct physical links

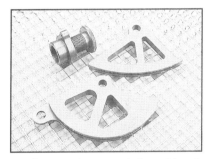

Another popular transmission add-on is an adjustable clutch quadrant. When the pedal engages the clutch, it controls tension on the clutch cable. While the factory unit is self-adjusting to compensate for clutch wear, power shifting can jar the stock plastic quadrant out of its proper setting. There are many aftermarket aluminum quadrants, which allow tailoring pedal engagement to a driver's taste. The most popular versions, like this one from Unlimited Performance, adjust at the firewall under the hood, rather than at the clutch fork under the car. This unit also allows retaining a stock clutch cable, while most others mandate a special cable.

Installing a high-performance torque converter with a higher stall speed is a good way to get an AOD to work with the elevated powerband of a modified 5.0. Of course, it's important to buy a converter that will work with your engine's powerband and your differential's gearing. It's just as important to buy a well-built converter. Most often you get what you pay for with torque converters, and good ones usually cost around $600. This 9.5-inch Stallion converter from Precision Industries is shown being installed by 5.0 Racer Dennis Ramsey of Ramsey's Performance. It features a one-piece, billet steel front cover, which provides more durable mounting ears than those with ears welded to their covers.

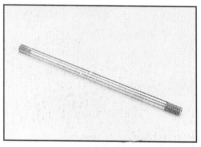

Another torque converter decision is choosing lockup for fuel economy or nonlockup and a one-piece input shaft for maximum durability. For street and even street/strip AOD cars, lockup is the way to go. This hardened billet steel piece from Precision Industries allows a substantial durability over the breakage-prone stock shaft, yet retains lockup for good fuel economy.

between engine and transmission, these transmissions are more durable, especially in high-performance form.

Torque Converters

The aforementioned viscous coupling is achieved via the AOD's

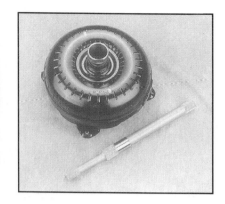

torque converter. A torque converter is made up of an impeller, a turbine, and a stator. Bolted to the flywheel, the impeller converts the engine's torque into hydraulic energy. This energy is transferred to the turbine by way of the automatic transmission fluid. Finally, the stator returns the fluid back to the inlet side of the impeller.

A converter's diameter is the most common spec described as determining its stall speed. This is because smaller converters generate less centrifugal force than those with larger diameters. As such, smaller torque converters stall later than larger units. Spacing between the fins on the impeller and turbine is another factor determining the torque converter's stall speed. Wider spacing raises the stall, allowing a modified 5.0 to work in its elevated powerband. Such wider spacing does sacrifice low-end efficiency delivered by converters with tighter fins. While converter diameter and fin spacing are a good indicator of stall speed, other factors, such as the shape and number of fins, also contribute to a torque converter's stall speed.

Above all, different engine combinations will react differently to the same torque converter. So, as with most parts, don't expect the converter that works so well in your friend's car to act the same way in your 5.0. It is wise to order a torque converter for your specific application. Powerband, induction, cam specs, rear-end gears, driving style, and other transmission modifications should be consid-

Where Precision Industries' billet input shaft will work with stock and stock-style aftermarket torque converters, Art Carr's nonlockup converter and one-piece input shaft must work as a pair. The heavy-duty shaft greatly reduces the chances of input shaft breakage, but adds a few hundred cruising rpm. How much horsepower the transmission must handle and how much fuel mileage is desired must be balanced when choosing a one-piece shaft. Generally, they are best suited to serious street/strip and race 5.0s.

ered when purchasing a torque converter. It's not a bad idea, even if you are going to do the work yourself, to work with one transmission shop or vendor in order to execute a well-thought-out transmission build.

A final consideration for choosing a torque converter is whether to lock up or not to lock up. AODs and AODEs feature two-piece input shafts. While the vehicle is cruising at highway speeds, AODs lock the third gear and overdrive clutches to reduce slippage and improve efficiency. While this aids fuel mileage, it cuts down on torque multiplication and opens the door to breakage, especially when a high-horsepower 5.0 with a firm-shifting AOD slams into third gear. Switching to a nonlockup converter and one-piece input shaft is a good choice for ultimate durability in a drag car, but swapping in a stronger two-piece shaft is better for gas mileage in street cars. One-piece and two-piece input shafts for AODs are available from Art Carr and Precision Industries respectively. Art Carr's one-piece shaft requires a unique torque converter.

Valve Bodies

Automatic transmission fluid not only transfers engine torque, it also controls the transmission's shifting. It travels through a series of passages and works to actuate clutches in response to shift lever position and throttle position. In the later AODE transmissions found in 1994–95 5.0s, shift rpm, shift firmness, and converter lockup are controlled via the EEC-IV computer and carried out by the hydraulic mechanisms. As such, either model can benefit from a valve-body improvement kit. Numerous transmission vendors sell the kits, which allow the shifts to be customized to a driver's needs by drilling new orifices, plugging existing holes, adding stiffer springs, and so forth. AODEs can benefit from mechanical and electronic shift tuning.

Transbrakes

A variation on the valve-body reprogramming theme is a transbrake. A transbrake allows a drag racer with an automatic transmission to, in effect, rev up the engine and dump the clutch. Pioneered for the AOD by Performance Automatic, a transbrake offers a great improvement in performance. The PA transbrake locks up reverse and first gears, allowing the driver to rev up the engine while the gear selector is in first and a momentary switch (controlling a solenoid in the valve body) is depressed. When the tree goes green and the driver releases the switch, the car launches with authority. The PA brake also converts an AOD to manual shifting. First, second, and third gears are selected via the shifter, while overdrive must be engaged with a remote switch when the shifter is engaged in third gear. These fully manual characteristics are likely only attractive on full-time race 5.0s or serious street/strip 5.0s.

Wide-Ratio Conversion

As you can see in the "Transmission Gear Ratios By Year" sidebar, 5.0 Mustang manual transmissions have a distinct gearing advantage versus comparable automatic transmissions. This contributes to the AOD's sluggish performance and forces owners of AOD Mustangs to run more rear-end gear ratio than owners of manual-transmission 5/0s to obtain similar straight-line performance. Fortunately, Ford Racing

Performance Parts released a product to give AODs more favorable low-end gearing with little effect on overdrive rpm. It's known as the AOD Wide Ratio Upgrade Kit, and is really made up of many of the internals from the modern 4R7OW transmission (an AODE with the Wide Ratio kit).

Ford Racing Performance Parts' conversion kit features new first and second gears, low-inertia high clutches, a heavy-duty overdrive band, a 6,000-rpm one-way clutch, heavy-duty intermediate clutch, and needle-bearing thrust washers. If these parts don't mean much to you, it should at least be apparent that the Wide Ratio kit replaces many of the AOD's internals, which explains why its price exceeds $650. What it does, though, is improve low-end performance without subtracting fuel mileage like a steep rear-end gear ratio. It converts first gear from 2.40:1 to 2.84:1, second gear from 1.47:1 to 1.55:1, third gear is

The best way to hasten and firm shifts in an AOD or AODE is a valve-body improvement kit. Although garages commonly call this a "Shift Kit," TransGo owns the trademark to the term and has long offered its parts to professional rebuilders. TransGo's consumer Shift Kits come with full documentation and even an installation how-to video. TransGo offers AOD, AODE, and even a manual AODE conversion kit. In the case of TransGo's AODE kit, it also improves transmission durability by lessening rpm between downshifts and providing a relief valve to protect against an Electronic Pressure Control failure. *TransGo*

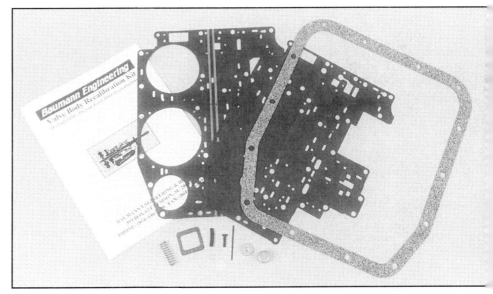

While TransGo has been in the Shift Kit business for a long time, Baumann Engineering was first on the block with an AOD valve-body improvement kit. Dubbed ReCal Pro Valve Body Recalibration Kits, they are available for most every Ford transmission. Karl Baumann, proprietor of Baumann Engineering, saw the need for an AOD kit and filled it. He has since developed a full line of Ford automatic transmission tweaks, including an electronically controlled conversion for standard AODs, a stand-alone electronic controller for AODEs, and a number of detail improvements for both transmissions. Baumann's ReCal Pro kits are popular and, like most valve-body kits, allow tailoring firmness and rpm to a driver's needs.

Besides the standard torque converter and valve-body improvements, there are a number of internal durability tweaks for AOD transmissions. This A servo, sourced from the Thunderbird Super Coupe's transmission, provides 16 percent more clamping force on the overdrive band than the standard AOD's B servo. This piece reduces slippage during the transition from third gear to overdrive. This part is integral to any performance AOD buildup.

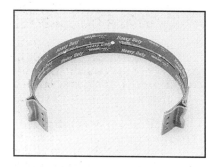

unchanged, and overdrive is stepped up slightly from .67:1 to .70:1.

The downside of the Wide Ratio kit is that it doesn't address shifts, stall speed, or durability, so it should be considered a good basis for a complete street performance rebuild. Race 5.0 owners can simply install steep rear gears and forget the fuel mileage penalty.

Coolers

Since automatic transmission fluid is the AOD's workhorse, it's obvious that heat is its enemy. It is the enemy of any automatic transmission, but one bolted to a performance engine has to deal with even more heat. The stock transmission cooler tube is woefully inadequate, so the first thing you should do for your AOD, even if it's stock, is install a tranny cooler. Simply splice into the factory tubing and plumb in the best cooler

Stepping up to the A servo suggests improving the overdrive band as well. This is a 1 3/4-inch-wide band from Precision Industries. It is lined with Kevlar to further enhance clamping force and reduce slippage. The stock AOD overdrive band measures a paltry 1 1/2 inches wide, while the band in the AODE is 2 inches wide. Baumann Engineering offers a retrofit kit to install the 2-inch band in an earlier AOD.

you can fit on the front of your 5.0. It will increase the life of your transmission by slowing down the heat breakdown of the fluid. Weakened fluid can cause premature wear in just about every area of the AOD. Replacing mineral-based automatic transmission fluid with synthetic ATF will also add longevity.

Replacements

Eventually the lust for horsepower and the durability of stock transmissions reach a crossroads. It's easy enough to run 9-second quarter-mile elapsed times with a built

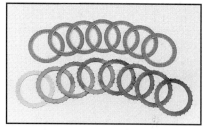

Another weakness of the AOD transmission is the stock clutch pack. Stock AODs have only five or six clutches, and increasing the number of clutches improves grip for improved third gear performance and reduced heat. These Kolene steel plates are a popular upgrade, as are Raybestos Blue Plate Special and Alto clutches.

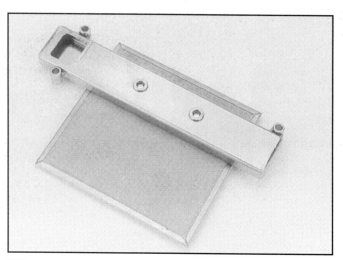

A commonly overlooked AOD modification is the transmission's internal filter. The stock Dacron fiber filter can become a flow restriction and cause leakage between the valve body separator plates. This is a replacement racing filter from Precision Industries. It is constructed of high-flow wire mesh to eliminate restrictions. *Chuck James*

AOD, but try it with a built T-5 and you'll be sweeping gear, synchronizer, and input shaft bits off the starting line. While manual transmissioned 5.0s are easily the best performing cars in stock form, eventually pushing the performance envelope in a straight line means an automatic transmission is in order. This is not to say there aren't other options in the aftermarket.

Tremec

For those wanting to shift their own gears without breaking them, there are a number of alternative manual transmissions. The most popular T-5 substitute is the Tremec five-speed, essentially a five-speed cousin of the rugged Toploader four-speed. Tremecs weigh some 23 pounds more than T-5s, due to larger gears and shafts. Standard Tremec 3550s are good for 425 lb-ft of torque, while the upgraded Tremec TKO can withstand up to 490 lb-ft. This increased durability is thanks largely to a stronger 31-spline output shaft and stronger 26-spline input shaft. These changes mandate a TKO-specific clutch and drive shaft U-joint. Tremecs are durable, but they do trade the relative smooth shifting of a T-5 for a more industrial feel.

T-56

At the other end of the smooth-shifting spectrum is the T-56 six-speed. This is the older and better brother of the butter-smooth T-45 found in modern 4.6 liter Mustangs. While the T-45 has shown its glass jaw in modified cars, the T-56 doesn't give up any strength in exchange for its smooth shifting. It is the factory manual trans choice for Corvettes and Vipers, so it has to be smooth and durable. Standard T-56s can support 440 lb-ft of torque, while the race-prepped T-56 from the R-model Viper can withstand a whopping 550 lb-ft. With the small-block Ford-specific bellhousing (there is no steel bellhousing available for the T-56), this cream-of-the-crop manual can be

Transmission Gear Ratios By Year					
	1st	2nd	3rd	4th	5th
1979–83					
SROD	3.07	1.72	1.00	.700	n/a
Cruise-O-Matic	2.46	1.46	1.00	n/a	n/a
1984					
T-5	2.95	1.94	1.34	1.00	.625 ('83 1/2: .725)
AOD	2.40	1.47	1.00	.667	n/a
1985–89					
T-5	3.35	1.93	1.29	1.00	.675
AOD	2.40	1.47	1.00	.667	n/a
1990–93					
T-5	3.35	1.99	1.33	1.00	.675
AOD	2.40	1.47	1.00	.667	n/a
1994–95					
T-5	3.35	1.99	1.33	1.00	.675
AODE	2.40	1.47	1.00	.667	n/a

Automatic transmissions rely on automatic transmission fluid to transfer engine horsepower to the differential, as the impetus for gear changes, and, naturally, for internal lubrication. Internal friction stresses the ATF with heat, which can reduce its lubrication capabilities. Substituting synthetic ATF, which is more resistant to heat, is a good place to start, but a transmission cooler is an absolute requirement for a performance-minded AOD. B&M's aluminum SuperCooler features a stacked-plate design, which is said to promote efficiency while reducing fluid pressure drop. *B&M Racing and Performance*

The Hammer is the only direct-fit shifter for AOD- and AODE-equipped 5.0 Mustangs. For the most part, automatic shifters are an aesthetic improvement, but the Hammer incorporates a reverse lockout, making it legal for use in National Hot Rod Association-sanctioned drag racing. It also features B&M's ergonomically designed shift handle, which is available individually. A direct-fit Hammer shifter is also available for 5.0 Mustangs with C-4 conversions. *B&M Racing and Performance*

installed in 5.0 Mustangs using swap kits from D&D Performance and Kenny Brown Performance. It's a little heavy at 115 pounds, but it offers up nice gear ratios: a 2.97:1 first, a 2.07:1 second, a 1.43:1 third, a 1.00:1 fourth, a .80:1 fifth, and a .62:1 sixth. The two overdrives mean you can run steep rear-end gear ratios and still see manageable cruising rpm. It is the manual choice for any ultra-horsepower 5.0

street or race car. It does, naturally, command a higher price than a replacement T-5. Standard T-56s sell in the mid $2,000 range, while the race version commands nearly $3,000.

Richmond

A final, less-popular manual transmission choice for high-powered 5.0s is from Richmond Gear. It offers four-, five-, and six-speed transmissions that can withstand up to 450 lb-ft of torque. The four- and five-speed transmissions are geared toward

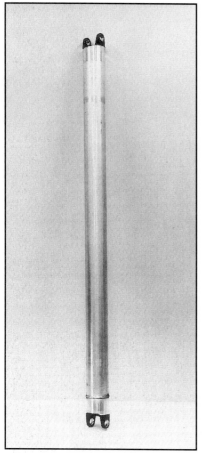

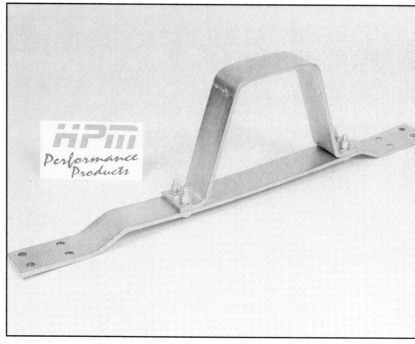

Those racing 5.0-liter Mustangs will want to invest in a drive-shaft safety loop. In the event of a U-joint or drive-shaft failure, the safety loop will help prevent the drive shaft from pole-vaulting up through the floor pan and wreaking havoc. Lakewood's loop provides plenty of clearance for the stock drive shaft, while this larger version from HP Motorsports offers ample room to clear the larger-diameter aluminum drive shaft from Ford Racing Performance Parts. *Chuck James*

Often, increasing rear-end gear ratios can lead to driveline vibrations. A good solution is this aluminum drive shaft from Ford Racing Performance Parts. It features more precise balancing than the stock shaft and comes complete, U-joints and all. Naturally, the aluminum drive shaft reduces reciprocating mass, which can free up a smidgen of power as well.

racing, as they lack overdrives. However, Richmond's six-speed is completely streetable and offers customizable gear ratios for all but fifth gear, which is always 1:1. This fixed fifth gear means third, fourth, and fifth end up tightly spaced, but sixth can really drop cruising rpm all the way down to 0.49:1. Richmonds require SROD-style bellhousings, special drive shaft U-joints, and a custom cross-member, which is available

from Richmond. Its downside is the external rod shifter, which is tricky to set up in the tight confines of the transmission tunnel and offers notchy shifts. Additionally, its steep price tag of nearly $3,000 makes other manual choices more attractive.

C4/C6/E4OD
When straight-line performance is the ultimate goal of a 5.0 Mustang, it's time to look to the Mustang's past for a performance automatic transmission. Many racers have the AOD's father, the C4, upgraded for strip performance. When built for performance duty, these lightweight three-speeds can withstand nine-second ETs in a light 5.0 Mustang, but heavier cars and quicker ETs often mandate stepping up to the heavier and sturdier C6 three-

speed. Racers often complain the C6 saps much more power than the lighter C4. As a result, many change to light durable Brand-C Powerglide two-speeds if their class rulebooks allow doing so.

A modern alternative to the vintage three-speed automatics, particularly for big-power street/strip 5.0s, is the E4OD. This modern transmission is found in trucks, like the 5.8-liter Lightning pickup. It is essentially a C6 with overdrive and electronic controls. To install one in a 5.0, especially a pre-1994 car, it will be necessary to employ an aftermarket electronic controller from Baumann Engineering or AutoTrans Group (see the "Electronic Shifting" sidebar). When built for performance duty, these transmissions offer durability without giving up overdrive or electronic tuning.

Rear End

12

For the next to last stop on the horsepower and torque delivery line, the rear end is often the first item modified on a 5.0 Mustang. This is because a change in rear-end gear ratio yields more torque multiplication and a quicker Mustang. Often 5.0 owners on a budget simply change gears and leave everything else stock. While this is fine for a bolt-on street car, the rear end often must be revisited as horsepower reaches critical mass.

Before getting into the teeth of rear-end modifications, it's important to determine what rear end is under your vehicle. Stock 1979 and 1982–85 Mustangs were fitted with 7.5-inch rears. This rear end is fine for a mildly modified Mustang, but becomes a liability when coupled with more power and a drag strip. In 1986 Ford stepped up the stock rear end to the rugged 8.8-inch unit, said to be 35 percent stronger than the 7.5. While not as durable as the legendary 9-inch found in many 1957 to 1987 Fords, the 8.8 is lighter and more efficient.

Of course, there aren't many stock 5.0-liter Mustangs on the road these days, so it would be best

This is the 8.8-inch axle found under 1986–95 5.0-liter Mustangs. It is exceptionally durable and remarkably adaptable to all manner of performance endeavors. It is recognizable by its nearly square cover. This version, from an 1989 5.0 but found in all 1986–93 5.0s, features four-lug, 28-spline axles and drum brakes. With the exception of the 1993 Mustang Cobra, 5.0s first received five-lug axles and disc brakes in 1994. As shown here, it's often easier to remove the rear end to take it in for a performance makeover. The toughest part of the job is freeing the stubborn drive-shaft bolts.

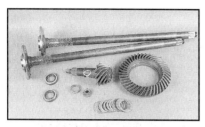

Swapping in a numerically higher rear axle ratio is a cost-effective way to hasten a 5.0 Mustang's acceleration. The Ford Racing Performance Parts is by far the most popular vendor of gears for 5.0 Mustangs. Their gears are said to be the quietest on the market. The 3.73:1 ring (the round gear) and pinion (the shaft with the gear on the end) pictured here is thought to be the maximum ratio for streetable five-speed 5.0s and the minimum ratio for streetable automatic 5.0s. It is pictured with Motorsport's heavy-duty 31-spline axles. These axles are a great upgrade for street and street/strip Mustangs around 400 horsepower. Beyond that level it's time for forged aftermarket axles. The grooves in the splined end of the axle are where the C-clips (the weak link of stock-style axles) slide around the axles to retain them.

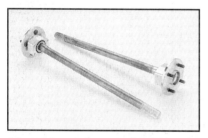

A huge step up from stock axles on the durability ladder are these forged racing axles from Moser Engineering. They are forged from a stout steel alloy and hardened to withstand abuse. These 31-spline axles are larger in diameter than the Motorsport axles for even more strength. Notice that the splined ends have no provision for C-clips. Moser does offer forged C-clip axles, but these are equipped with C-clip eliminators.

to jack the car up to see which rear is under it. Obviously, the 7.5-inch rear is smaller than the 8.8, but it can most easily be distinguished by looking at its cover. The top and bottom of the cover are flat and

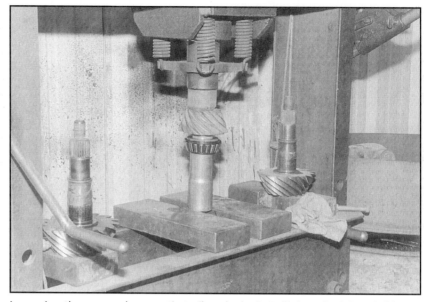

Increasing the rear-end gear ratio trails only the installation of a K&N air filter as the most popular first modification for 5.0 Mustangs. It is a job best left to professional mechanics versed in rear-end work, since it requires a number of special tools, like the press used to install the bearing on the pinion gear. It also necessitates setting a number of clearances. If they are right, the gears will be quiet and durable. If they are wrong, the gears will certainly be noisy and may well fail.

the sides rounded on a 7.5. On the other hand, 8.8 covers are flat on all four sides, but the corners are rounded. If you are lucky, you might even find a 9-inch under your 5.0. These rears do not feature removable covers, and their gear housings are nearly round.

While you are unlikely to find a 9-inch under your 5.0 Mustang, 7.5- and 8.8-inch axles are nice, durable rears straight from Ford. They feature 28-spline axles, Traction-Lok differentials, and 2.73:1, 3.08:1, or 3.27:1 gearing. Some non-5.0 differentials are open, but any 7.5 or 8.8 with an L on its tag has a Traction-Lok. Other pertinent rear-end tag codes are E for 3.27 gears, Z for 3.08 gears, and M for 2.73 gears. Typically 3.27 and 3.08 gears are found in automatic 5.0s, while 2.73s are found in manual 5.0s.

Gears

As already mentioned, a rear-end gear swap is an affordable way to hasten a 5.0s acceleration. Such a swap has its downsides, however.

Most importantly, the swap usually is not a do-it-yourself proposition. Unless you are mechanically experienced and have all the proper tools, it is a job best suited for a professional mechanic. Make sure to select a shop that frequently installs gears and has the proper tools, otherwise you may get a noisy, short-lived rear because of improper setup. While you're having the gears swapped, it's also a good idea, even though some parts may be reused, to go ahead and install all new bearings and other hardware. Richmond and Zoom offer complete installation kits with new bearings and hardware. Zoom also offers adjustable carrier shims and adjustable bearing spacers, which ease installation and enhance durability.

The gear swap requires a number of tools usually lacking in the home garage. A press is needed to install the bearing on the pinion gear. Pinion depth must be checked using Ford's Differential Service Tool, and if it is not within spec, it must be shimmed to the

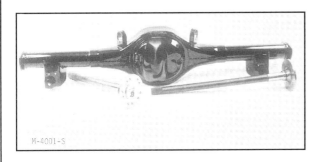

M-4001-S

The 9-inch Option

Ford's 9-inch rear end is so durable it's a wonder Ford stopped making it. Its strength was borne of heavy-duty construction which made it heavy. Heavy parts cost fuel economy, and quite simply they don't build them like they used to. Not all 9-inch rears were created equal, with the N housing being the most rare, durable, and desirable. It's distinguished by a cast N above the pinion retainer and is cast of nodular iron. While this is the one to seek if you are fishing for bargains at the boneyard, you really can't go wrong with any 9-inch. Plus, many aftermarket vendors, such as Currie Enterprises, Moser Engineering, and Strange Engineering, offer bolt-in 9-inch rears for Fox-body Fords, including 5.0 Mustangs.

Naturally, these durable rear ends were designed to bolt into early Fords, including big-block musclecars. Today's aftermarket rear-end specialists outfit 9-inch rear-end cores with the proper bracketry and all manner of durability improvements to fit in and survive in most any performance environment. Besides the great leap in durability offered by the 9-inch, it doesn't use C-clips for axle retention, so it's legal for racing in most any sanction. Additionally, the 9-inch's removable carrier makes swapping gears for different tracks an at-the-track proposition. All the rear-end setup is done to the carriers, which can be bolted in and out of the housing with one setup. While it's not cheap, this allows having a selection of different gear ratios available for easy change.

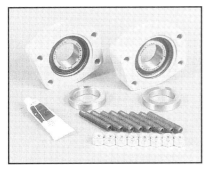

C-clip-retained axles are not allowed for cars running 11-second and quicker ETs at NHRA-sanctioned drag races. This is because the C-clip could easily come loose when walloped with a big power hit. The axle would then be free to slide out of the housing, and if it did so dow- track, the results could be catastrophic. For this reason, C-clip eliminators were created to externally retain the axles. These eliminators from Moser Engineering feature a bearing surrounded by an aluminum housing. The bearing must be pressed on the axle. C-clip eliminators are great safety upgrades for drag-only 5.0s, but will not hold up to cornering on street and road race 5.0s. The all-around solution is to install 9-inch bearing retainers on the 8.8 axle tubes.

proper depth. When finally installing the pinion, a torque wrench is required to set pinion preload. Additionally, clearance between the pinion and ring gear

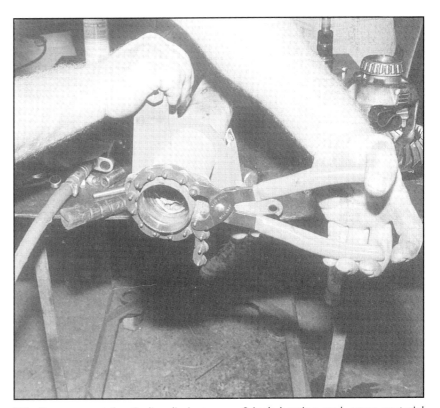

Whether you opt for C-clip eliminators or 9-inch bearing end, some material must be trimmed from the stock axle tubes to allow grafting on the new retainers. In the case of C-clip eliminators, a half-inch of material, including the stock axle bearing, must be cut from the axle tube. Then the eliminators bolt to the stock axle flange. Here Dennis Ramsey of Ramsey's Performance does the trimming with a chain tubing cutter. Be sure to deburr the trimmed axle tube before installing the eliminator-equipped axles. Doing so will reduce the chance for gear oil leaks at the eliminator. Converting to 9-inch bearing ends requires cutting the ends off the 8.8 axle tubes and welding on 9-inch housing ends.

Rather than a large spring and clutch packs, AuburnGear's Auburn differential uses short, stiff springs for preload, and cone-shaped clutches to engage the rear axles. Auburn and Auburn Pro differentials are popular in street, road racing, and drag racing. Their internal torque bias ensures most of the torque always goes to the wheel with the most traction. Everything about the Auburn is more durable than the stock Traction-Lok, but because it uses frictional material to overcome the rear end's natural tendency to send power to the unloaded wheel, it can still wear out over time. However, it is affordable, streetable, and available for 28- or 31-spline axles. Auburns are even available for 7.5-inch rears. *AuburnGear*

teeth, known as backlash, must be checked using a dial indicator and, if it isn't within specifications, must be adjusted with shims; looser backlash usually results in quieter gears. Those are just some of the specialized aspects of the job; a gear swap is not for the inexperienced.

While installing the gears is not for most people, choosing the proper ratio is just as important as a proper installation. Many aftermarket gear vendors including Ford Racing Performance Parts, Precision Gear, Richmond Gear, and Zoom offer a wide variety of gear ratios. For instance, Ford Racing offers 3.08, 3.27, 3.55, 3.73, 4.10, 4.30, 4.56, 4.88, and 5.13:1, which will suit anything from a mild grocery-getter to a 9,000-rpm drag

racer. The trick is deciding which gears your combination needs.

For street cars there are oft-repeated rules of thumb that apply pretty well. The recommendations printed over and over in magazines say five-speed cars get 3.55s and AODs get 3.73s. These numbers actually ring pretty true for pure street cars whose owners are more concerned with fuel mileage and overall drivability. Aggressive street/strip cars will actually perform both duties well with a bit more gear, 3.73s for five-speeds and 4.10s for AODs. The aforementioned rules of thumb are geared toward straight-line acceleration, so if road racing or top-speed racing are your thing, the more rear axle gear you run (higher numerically), the lower its top speed.

There are other considerations to choosing a rear-end gear ratio. Before slapping in the same gear as your buddy's car runs, there are several factors to consider. Are highway cruising rpm and fuel

The stock Traction-Lok differential is immediately identifiable by the S-shaped spring in its midsection. This spring preloads the internal gears inside the differential. When torque is applied to the Traction-Lok, it pushes its side gears apart and engages them via stacks of clutch packs to turn the axles. This arrangement provides smooth, quiet differentiation, but its clutches can wear out over time or from trying to cope with increased horsepower and traction. The Traction-Lok is the ideal diff for bolt-on street 5.0s. *Ford Racing Performance Parts*

mileage or ultimate quarter-mile performance the overriding concerns? Often the previously mentioned recommendations will help you walk this tightrope. It is, however, possible to determine the ultimate gear for your intended purpose by plugging a few numbers into a formula. This requires knowing at what rpm an engine reaches its torque peak, meaning a trip to a chassis dyno. It's also possible to ballpark what a gear change can do for your 5.0's quarter-mile performance by plugging your car's specs into Mr. Gasket's *Desktop Drag Strip* software. It allows you to change engine and drivetrain specs and view their influence on a virtual drag strip pass. While it can't perfectly match up to your 5.0, it does give an indication of the worth of a gear-ratio change.

The bottom line on gear ratios is that a 5.0 with any performance intentions needs more rear-end gear. How much more is up to your driving habits and drivability

Where the racy GoldTrak will not accept C-clips, the smooth, streetable Torsen differential will. Like the aforementioned diff, it uses helical gears for quiet, smooth differentiation. It also sends torque to the wheel with the most traction. Torsens are available for 8.8-inch rear ends in 28- and 31-spline versions from Ford Racing Performance Parts and Saleen Performance. *Ford Racing Performance Parts*

requirements. Changing rear-end gear also means recalibrating the speedometer via the driven gears in the transmission. These gears are sold at Ford dealers, but determining the necessary gears requires more math (see sidebar). Most shops familiar with gear swaps will likely know which gears to use.

Should you radically increase the rear-end ratio, it is necessary to change the drive gear inside the transmission. On a T-5 the drive gear is accessible by removing the transmission's tailshaft. AODs, on the other hand, have drive gears machined as part of the output shaft, meaning the transmission must be removed and disassembled to change the drive gear. Interactive Systems and Technologies offers a Speed Sensor Adapter that allows the factory speed sensor to be attached to a gear-reduction box from a speedometer shop. This is a cost-effective and durable way of calibrating a speedometer, as Ford speedometers with 21 or more teeth have short lifespans of about 20,000 miles.

Differentials

While a change in rear-end gear ratio is a good first change to even a stock 5.0-liter Mustang, the swap entails disassembling the rear end, which includes removing the factory Traction-Lok differential. This diff is good for pure street 5.0s, as it offers adequate traction coupled with smooth differentiation between the rear axles. As with many driveline parts, Traction-Loks become a liability in racing arenas, particularly drag racing. In that function they provide unequal torque to the rear wheels, and as power increases they are likely to fail. So, changing the differential at the same time as a gear swap is a good idea, as it will save you money on labor. Again there are several differential designs, and each performs more favorably in a specific driving environment.

Limited Slips

Ford's Traction-Lok differential,

The most unusual, versatile, and expensive differential solution for street/strip 5.0 Mustangs is the ARB Air Locker. Originally designed for dual-purpose street/off-road vehicles, the Air Locker can switch from being an open differential for carefree, fuel-efficient highway use, to a fully locked spool, for maximum traction, at the push of a button. Because the locking actuation of the Air Locker comes from compressed air, hence the name, its installation is more complex than a standard aftermarket differential. The compressor must be mounted in the car, it must be wired for power and the on/off switch, and the compressed-air lines must be routed to the rear end. Additionally, the differential housing must be drilled and tapped for the compressed-air line. On the plus side, ARB offers an optional kit that allows using the compressor to add air to tires, a nice feature on the roadside or at the racetrack.

found in 5.0 Mustangs, is a limited-slip design. Unlike open differentials, which send equal torque to each wheel all the time, limited slips use internal friction to direct most of the torque to the wheel with traction, thus reducing wheel spin. Open differentials have no way to control wheel spin, so they are obviously not well suited for a torquey 5.0 Mustang. Limited slips still allow smooth cornering, by shuttling some torque to the outside wheel. Limited slips are the first choice for street and road racing 5.0 Mustangs because of their favorable cornering traction.

The two main limited slips available to 5.0 Mustang owners are the stock Traction-Lok and those offered by AuburnGear. Ford's Traction-Lok is a clutch-based differential. It utilizes stacks

Locking differentials, such as Tractech's Detroit Locker and EZ Locker, and Powertrax's LockRight, lock both wheels together when the vehicle is traveling straight. In a turn, these lockers disengage and send all the torque to the wheel with the most traction. When they disengage, their internal gears ratchet and lock into place when the car returns to the straight and narrow. This racheting is audible and can become downright clunky in slow, sharp turns. The solution to this is shifting into neutral and coasting through these turns, but drivability purists likely won't enjoy the sound or feel. As the photo shows, the LockRight offers an easy bolt-in replacement for the factory Traction-Lok that doesn't require removing the carrier (as does Tractech's similarly designed EZ Locker). This is beneficial for those who have already installed steeper gears and want a more durable differential without more labor charges. The full-on Detroit Locker is part of a new carrier, but is reportedly more durable than the drop-in lockers.

of spacers and clutches attached to the side gears. An S-shaped spring between the two side gears preloads the differential. As torque is applied to the differential, the side gears are pressed outward to engage the clutches, which causes the axles to rotate simultaneously. When torque dissipates, the axles are allowed to rotate independent of one another. These diffs are generally smooth and quiet, though some people try to increase their effectiveness by adding more clutch plates. A byproduct of this arrangement is increased rear-end noise.

Auburn differentials use cone clutches, rather than stacks of clutch plates, to engage the rear

Here is the original TA rear-end girdle for the 8.8-inch axle. The increased structural rigidity of the cast-aluminum cover is readily apparent. While the structure gives the overall 8.8 housing more strength, the big benefit of the TA cover, and all rear-end girdles, is the adjustable load bolts designed to preload the differential's bearing caps. Unsupported, the bearing caps are known to break when wedged between big horsepower and drag-slick traction. These bolts help the caps resist breakage. Also pictured here is TA's optional bearing cap stud kit. Like all other studs, these make full use of all available threads to further enhance the caps' rigidity. While early TA covers (like this one) didn't have drain or fill plugs, the latest models have both. Since the factory fill plug is difficult to access and the stock cover lacks a drain plug, these are great additions to any 8.8.

axles in response to pressure from stiff springs. This arrangement delivers what Auburn deems a High-Bias differential, or one that automatically sends most of the torque to the wheel with more traction. Auburn differentials feature thicker housings and more durable materials than the stock diff, plus they offer an even stronger Auburn Pro differential for really high-powered vehicles. Naturally both versions are more expensive than a replacement Traction-Lok. Auburn is also one of the few outfits offering a streetable performance differential for 7.5-inch rear ends.

Though Auburns are certainly more durable, both designs will eventually need maintenance. An Auburn's cone clutches will eventually need replacement, to ensure optimum performance, as the springs lose some tension over

time. Obviously the stock clutch plates will also need replacement as well. Both differential styles require gear oil augmented with friction modifier to operate properly.

Lockers

Where limited-slip differentials distribute engine rotations to the axles in response to torque, locking differentials make decisions solely based on wheel speed. When traveling straight, both wheels are locked together and turn simultaneously. When entering a turn, it automatically sends torque to the slower turning wheel, which is the inside wheel. The outside wheel is allowed to freewheel. This is unlike a limited slip, which sends some torque to the outside wheel. Lockers are a good street/strip differential, as they supply equal torque to the rear wheels when traveling in a straight line, but to the wheel with most traction in a turn.

Locking differentials for 8.8-inch rear ends are available from ARB Air Locker, Dan Press Industries, Powertrax, Tractech, and Zexel Torsen. These represent three types of locking differentials. The ARB Air Locker operates as an open differential, but may be locked at the touch of the button. LockRight lockers from Powertrax and Detroit Lockers from Tractech are constructed with rugged toothed cogs that remain locked while the vehicle travels in a straight line, but differentiate by ratcheting. At low speeds the clicking is audible, and they are not very agreeable to sharp, low-speed turns, as they can communicate clunking through the drivetrain. Also, particularly in manual transmission cars, they can lock back together slightly out of alignment and noisily, randomly pop back into place.

While the aforementioned ratcheting lockers exude their durable nature, the more expensive GoldTrak, TrueTrak, and Torsen locking differentials, from Dan Press Industries, Tractech, and Zexel Torsen respectively, offer more elegant durability via helical

gears. If you read Chapter 6, you know helically geared superchargers are quieter than those with straight-cut gears. This is much the same difference between the helical- and straight-geared lockers. These diffs use groups of straight and helical gears to distribute torque and provide differentiation in a turn. Because of their smooth delivery and enhanced durability, these differentials are the choice of those wanting much improved durability without deducting drivability or adding noise. GoldTraks are even available in loose, medium, and tight versions to further accommodate specific horsepower ranges and vehicle weights.

Since they are designed to accommodate high horsepower while retaining street drivability, lockers are among the most expensive differentials for 5.0 Mustangs. ARB Air Lockers are the most expensive due to their air compressor actuation. Helical-geared diffs are next up on the price ladder due to their complicated, expensive-to-machine internals. Straight-toothed lockers are the cheapest locking choices, particularly those, such as Powertrax's LockRight and Tractech's EZ Locker designed to fit inside the stock Traction-Lok case. Full-fledged straight-toothed differentials, like the Detroit Locker, are more durable than the replacement lockers, and thus more expensive.

Spools

There are no springs, spacers, cones, or clutch plates in a spool. It is as simple as an automotive part gets. Where limited slip and locking differentials try to serve straight-line and cornering traction, spools are made to go straight ahead. A spool is simply a solid piece of steel that joins the rear axles as one unit. As such, both wheels receive equal torque at all times, which is great for a drag 5.0, but not so great for a street 5.0, which will understeer a great deal in corners. If used in a street car, a spool will quickly wear tires and

Like shifters and subframe connectors, rear-end covers and girdles are driven to innovation by rabid market demand. LPW's cast-aluminum 8.8 cover features the requisite drain plug and adjustable bearing cap load bolts, but adds a unique feature. It uses the cover as an attachment point for adjustable tie rods, shown being installed by Mitch Masten at the now-defunct Crawford Performance. With tabs welded to the ends of the axle tubes, these rods are adjusted to preload the axle tubes to prevent them from bending under load—a trick welded onto many drag 9-inch rears as well. You can also see this passenger-side axle tube was welded to the 8.8 housing. From the factory, the tubes are only press-fit, so they can rotate out of position. Even welded tubes can twist, so some shops go so far as to replace the stock axle tubes with much thicker tubing to ensure reliability. Obviously this level of modification is for extremely quick drag 5.0s.

rear-end hardware. Currie Enterprises, Mark Williams, Reider Racing, and Strange Engineering all offer spools for the 8.8-inch axle.

Axles

With moderate gearing, a stock differential, and bolt-on horsepower, the stock 28-spline axles are just fine, especially for a pure street 5.0. The stock axles become a liability when coupled with big horsepower, good traction, and a drag strip. Not only are the stock 28-spline axles not sturdy enough to be wedged between a sticky track and 400 lb-ft, but Ford's method of retaining the axles via C-clips is not built to withstand the sudden application of power much beyond that of a stock engine. C-clips are not allowed on cars running quicker than 11.99-second quarter-mile ETs at National Hot Rod Association-sanctioned drag races.

The first way to shore up axles is to replace the stock axles with 31-spline axles from Ford Racing Performance Parts. These are sturdier axles from Ford's 8.8-equipped trucks and allow the use of the stock C-clips for axle retention. These axles are a nice upgrade for any modified 5.0, but they still offer limited durability because of the C-clips. The ultimate step-up in durability comes from forged axles sold by Currie Enterprises, Moser Engineering, and Strange Engineering. These rear-end specialists offer forged steel axles with just about any spline configuration,

and even their 31-splines are larger in diameter and feature stronger hardened alloys than the off-the-shelf Ford Racing Performance Parts 31-spline axles.

Though some of these race-quality axles are available with grooves for C-clip retainers, that really defeats the purpose of installing these sturdy axles. There are two choices for durable axle retention. The most common method is the C-clip eliminator. These pieces retain the axles via a bearing captured in an aluminum housing. The bearing is pressed onto the axle, and then the housing bolts to the stock flange on the end of the housing. They do require removing a half-inch of material, including the stock bearing, off each axle tube end. C-clip eliminators are great for drag cars, but their bearings are not stout enough to handle the side loading of cornering, so they are not suited for street or road racing duty. When subjected to a lot of cornering, they will leak.

The most uncommon, but best, way to retain heavy-duty axles in an 8.8-inch housing is to convert it to 9-inch bearing ends. These ends incorporate heavy-duty bearings retained by pressed-on locking collars and steel plates. These ends can handle side loads, allow numerous brake choices, and, most importantly, eliminate the C-clips. These are the ultimate all-purpose bearings and axle retainers for 8.8s. Currie Enterprises

and Moser Engineering both offer conversion kits for 8.8 rear ends.

Covers

In the old days the only kind of rear-end cover that mattered was chrome, so everyone could see it at cruise night. Because 5.0-liter Mustangs were producing so much more power than Ford had intended and trying to funnel it all through the factory rear end, this created a subaftermarket for 8.8 durability parts. TA Performance developed the often-imitated rear-end girdle for 8.8s. There are even a few girdles available for 7.5-inch rears as well.

Not only does this cast-aluminum cover increase the rigidity of the housing by adding structure, it features adjustable load bolts designed to support the 8.8's bearing caps. These load bolts help the caps resist the gear's natural impetus to spin right out the back of the rear end. TA also offers a stud kit for the bearing caps to further bolster the bearing caps.

Accufab and Ground Pounder offer variations on the 8.8 girdle theme and TA private-label girdles for a number of aftermarket vendors. Whatever the source, these covers/girdles allow an 8.8 to approach the durability of the much heavier 9-inch. All of the aftermarket girdles not only aid durability but make servicing easier thanks to built-in drain plugs. Servicing gear oil usually means removing the factory cover.

Chassis

13

A chassis is a car's skeleton, and like our own skeletons, it must provide a rigid framework for the rest of the entity to function. With a stiff chassis, the suspension is predictable and easy to tune, which ultimately makes the car much easier to drive. This holds true on the street, at the drag strip, or on a road course. When it comes to chassis, stiffer is definitely better.

To look at it another way, a flexible chassis acts like a huge, poorly controlled spring in the suspension. By deflecting a little here and twisting there, a flexi-flyer chassis makes front-end alignment a hit-or-miss affair. A flexible chassis can cause unpredictable, twisted launches at the drag strip, make

steering a series of back and forth corrections in midcorner, and require overly hard springs and sway bars, which ruin the ride. A stiff chassis also lasts longer, especially under the brutal assault of drag strip launches with a high-torque engine.

While it would be nice to say 5.0 Mustangs are blessed with great chassis, just the opposite is true. The 1993 and earlier cars are one of the limpest chassis around. This is especially true of the open-topped convertibles, with the T-tops not too far behind. Even the common hatchbacks suffer from the huge rear hatch opening, and while the coupes are the stiffest of the lot, that's not saying much. The Fox

chassis of the 5.0 Mustang was built in an era of gasoline crunches, when reduced cost and light weight were the goals. The result is a somewhat flimsy construction that responds well to nearly any form of chassis stiffening.

If you are working with a 1994–95 5.0, then half the work has been done for you. Ford realized the Mustang desperately needed a beefed-up chassis, so it greatly improved the rigidity of the sleek 1994–95 body. In fact, the demise of the practical and handy hatchback body style is a direct result of this desire to stiffen the platform. The hatchback's opening was deemed simply too large to obtain the desired rigidity, and was thus retired in favor of the trunk body style. As for the convertible, a certain amount of flexibility must be accepted, as the rockers and floor pan are the only section joining the two halves of the car, but

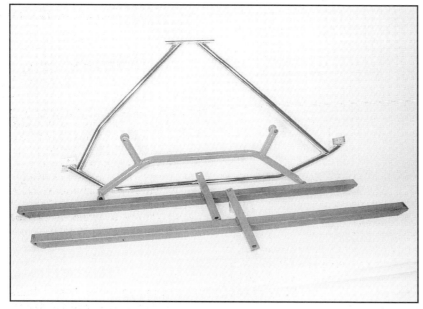

Package kits are typically money savers, such as this dose of much needed medicine for pre-1993 Mustangs. It is Kenny Brown's Chassis Support Kit, made up of the strut tower brace in the back, a four-point lower chassis brace in the middle, and a pair of subframe connectors lying down in front. Brown's strut tower brace clears both GT-40 intakes and Vortech blowers, allowing them to fit the vast majority of modified 5.0s. *Kenny Brown Performance*

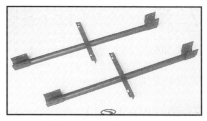

Steeda's Double-Cross pieces are good examples of a typical 5.0 Mustang subframe connector. The channel-like tabs at each end of the connectors fit over the Ford frame rails, while the crosspieces at midspan bolt to the seat attachment hardware. Such crossbraces considerably stiffen the connector against bending, but even a plain subconnector without them is a huge improvement. Steeda offers these in cost-effective mild steel and durable, but pricey chrome moly. *Steeda Autosports*

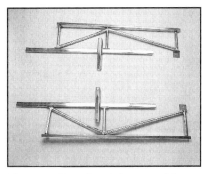

Like any other chassis brace, subframe connectors work best with extra bracing. These Kenny Brown Extreme Subframe Connectors are veritable trusses, but by spreading loads to both the rocker panels and "frame rails" the chassis is that much stiffer. This is a three-part kit, consisting of subframe connectors, matrix bracing, and jacking rails. The connectors do a familiar job and the jacking rails allow jacking up the car from all along its side. Meanwhile the matrix braces tie the aforementioned pieces together for ultimate rigidity. These are a bit much for the casual air-filter-and-wheels car, but a help as tire size and horsepower grow.
Kenny Brown Performance

Subframe connectors must be welded to the parent chassis to be effective. You'll find bolt holes in the flanges of some subconnectors, but at best they're for holding the connector in place while welding. Bolts allow too much flex from the heavy loads these pieces carry, so get out the smoke wrench. Here Brandon Switzer of Racers Edge is welding in his popular torque-box-replacement subframe connectors, which shore up two weak areas of the chassis.

the 1994–95 cars are hundreds of percent stiffer in torsional rigidity than their predecessors. Thus they don't need the same amount of chassis stiffening from you as their older brothers to provide the same level of ride and handling.

Aside from chassis stiffening, the other 5.0 Mustang chassis characteristic that requires attention is the tendency for certain high-stress areas to pull apart when subjected to hard use. The torque boxes where the rear upper control arms attach to the unibody are the best example of such an area.

Furthermore, the K-member may require replacement for simple header clearance, to reduce weight, or you may want to change it for a modified version that features modified suspension pick-up points.

The final chassis consideration covered here is a roll bar or cage. Naturally, these devices are fitted to protect the occupants in case of a rollover mishap, but they can also

provide much needed chassis stiffening along the way.

Subframe Connectors

Subframe connectors run parallel to the drive shaft, joining the two separate built-up sheet-metal "frame rails" found under the Mustang chassis. When welded to the existing frame rails, the subframe connectors form full-length frame sections and make the chassis much more rigid in both bending and twisting. While some subframe connectors are sold with bolt holes in their mounting flanges, and are labeled "bolt-in" parts, they must be welded in place to do any good. Consider them a weld-in part.

Because subframe connectors address one of the weakest spots on the Fox chassis, they should be the first chassis stiffener added to your car. On the 1993 and earlier Mustangs, they should be one of *the* first additions.

If your Mustang is older, and never had subframe connectors, then its chassis has loosened up. This is all the more reason to add subframe connectors, as they'll

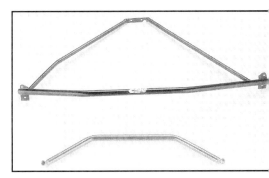

Eibach's upper strut tower brace is a great example of a basic strut tower brace. Light and effective, it will help a bolt-on type car greatly. More aggressive cars would likely want more mounting area along the cowl flange. At the bottom is Eibach's lower chassis brace. A simple two-point design, it too is well suited for the loads imposed by performance street driving.

noticeably tighten a chassis that's gotten a case of the creaks with age.

When shopping for subframe connectors, you'll come across everything from simple flat bars to trapeze-like constructions. The simpler units are good for basic

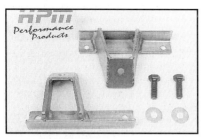

Because of the lower center of gravity that results, dedicated race cars and all-out street cars benefit from lowering the engine in the chassis. This is done with shorter engine mounts, such as these from HP Motorsports. There are multiple side effects from this, such as exhaust system fit, so leave this modification for highly specialized machines. Engine lowering can also be done through the mounts on a tubular K-member. *HP Motorsports*

street-driven cars, and are the best bang for the buck, assuming they are built of sufficiently thick tubing to be of structural value. The more complex designs are often part of a total chassis stiffening system, which is great. If any sort of track use is planned, hook up with a chassis supplier you like and stick to his stuff. This will pay off, as other parts attach to or near the subframe connectors. The best example of this is a torque arm. The torque arm's cross-member welds to the subframe connector, and if the two don't match well, you'll be down at a chassis or muffler shop looking for some blacksmith work; Griggs Racing offers torque arm mounts to accommodate square- and round-tube connectors.

Griggs Racing, Kenny Brown Performance, and Racers Edge all offer popular subframe connector variations addressing specific concerns, but just about any Mustang tuner worth its salt has subframe connectors.

Through-Floor Subframe Connectors

When getting serious about handling, either for extremely high-performance street use, road racing, or drag-strip duty, under-

car subframe connectors are not used in favor of through-floor connectors.

These are really just boxed sections run through the floor pan to connect the front and rear frame sections from Ford. They are a lot of work to install, as the floor is cut open, thick-wall tubing is laid in the floor, and the whole thing zippered shut with a welder. Also, these pieces surface through the rear floor pan as they rise to meet the rear lower control arm mounting points, thus costing footroom for rear seat passengers.

The benefit is a strong floor pan/chassis, which is a must for track-dedicated cars. Plus, while the rest of the world doesn't seem to bother with convertibles as track machines, 5.0 Mustangers seem enamored of them; they benefit most of all from these connectors.

G-Load Braces

Not quite as fundamental as subframe connectors, but still important to improving steering precision and front-end alignment is a brace joining the two frame rails in the bellhousing area. These are known by a variety of trade names. Saleen popularized such braces under the G-load brace moniker, but they are also known as lower cross-braces, or similar names. Mainly they seem to be known simply as a "chassis brace."

No matter the name, these are typically small tubular braces that do their job via triangulation, not simply through massive material strength like a subframe connector. They reduce the frame rails' inward deflections caused by large tires and hard cornering, or from spreading loadings during big downward movements of the car's front end.

Such braces are available as either simple cross-car tubes that attach using two bolts, or slightly more involved braces with sweptback arms to pick the chassis up in four spots; the latter are more effective.

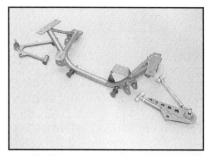

This tubular K-member, which gives much improved front suspension geometry with more Ackerman, a more favorable scrub radius, and double the stock caster. All this means better front-end grip and more precise steering. It's also considerably lighter than the stock stamped steel K-member, and its vastly more compact dimensions allow much greater freedom when fitting long-tube headers on race cars.

Strut Tower Brace

Granddaddy of all 5.0 braces is the strut tower brace. This is the familiar little jungle gym of tubes that joins the two front shock towers and the firewall together. For years various tuners and even the factory have argued the merits of this brace, but the bottom line is that it works, especially on the 1993 and earlier machines. Ironically, the later SN-95 cars, which need this brace the least, came with this link as stock for a while. That ended when the Mustang Cobra could no longer get the brace around its larger engine, and the accountants killed it across the board as a cost measure.

What you really need to know is, if you ever drive around a corner, and can fit a strut tower brace in your Mustang's engine compartment, then do it. You'll certainly have your choice of braces. Look for a brace with a generously sized mating area along the firewall. This attachment point should use more than a pair of bolts, too. The more area it is firmly bonded to along the firewall, the better. Also, the ends that attach to the shock towers should distribute the loads through a couple of fasteners, not just a single point.

Upper strut tower braces are a pain to work around when doing engine maintenance, and are often deleted on drag cars where frequent valvetrain work is required. Also, the towering intake systems on many drag engines make it impossible to fit a strut tower brace. In such cases, it's easier to look at a strut tower brace as more extra front-end weight than anything else, and given the straight-line nature of the sport, this is more true than not.

Jamex, Maier Racing, Steeda Autosport, and Saleen Performance Parts are among those offering strut tower braces. Again, just about any Mustang specialist offers a version of this triangular support.

Rear Strut Tower Braces

If the front strut tower braces need reinforcement, why not the rears? Well, the rear strut towers are more heavily reinforced by the body structure than the fronts, so an add-on brace is not as necessary. Furthermore, by the time such stiffening is needed, either in a big-power drag car or a serious road racing or slalom machine, such reinforcement is taken care of by the roll cage. JBA was the only

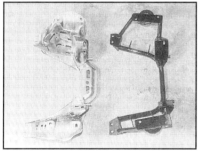

Racer's Chassis specializes in drag racing suspension and chassis parts. It offers two K-members for the 5.0. The Light Weight is for bolt-in applications with stock engine, lower control arm, and spring perch mounts. The Ultra Light Weight is for use with a motor plate in dedicated race cars, which accounts for the lack of spring perches and engine mounts in the example shown. Both use slightly relocated mounting holes for improved front-end geometry.

aftermarket 5.0 supplier to market a rear shock tower brace.

Torque Boxes

Mustangs subjected to hard drag strip launches can eventually tear the rear upper control arm attachment points out of the chassis. These are commonly called the torque boxes, and torque box replacement is a familiar job to owners of high-powered cars with minimal chassis preparation. The more torque the engine has and the stickier the tires (slicks), plus any rear traction aids such as slapper bars, the faster these upper control arm attachment points tear out.

For the common street 5.0 that sees the occasional burnout, there's nothing to worry about here. However, older cars driven very hard and drag strip warriors are definite candidates for inspection and possible reinforcement or repair in this area. Such work is normally done by a chassis shop, but there are torque box reinforcement kits available, should you have a welder at home.

Two outfits offer torque box enhancements. Racers Edge markets a subframe connector that not only joins the subframes, but welds in place of the stock torque box. These pieces are quite popular on drag-race-only 5.0s. Those looking for a bolt-in piece can turn to Wild Rides. They sell torque box supports designed to bolt into the stock torque box.

Floor Pan

Yet another area where the Fox chassis gives up is the floor pan, where the front seats bolt through. This is especially true of the driver's seat. Look for cracks from underneath the car. These too can be repaired with the smoke wrench, but it's easier to reinforce this area with special subframe connectors that feature side extensions that pick up the seat studs before this area rips out. Performance Parts, Inc. also offers a steel panel designed as a weld-in or bolt-

The Name Game

When the all-new 1979 Mustang was developed, Ford was using code names for its platforms. The term "Fox" was chosen for the Ford Fairmont/Mercury Zephyr chassis, from which the Mustang was eventually built. That's how the 1979–93 Mustangs came to be known as Fox-chassis cars.

In 1994, when the fully redesigned Mustang debuted, it used all new bodywork, but retained a modified version of the Fox chassis. Ford insiders sometimes call this platform the "Fox-4," but it's a name that hasn't really stuck. Instead, the new car is best known by its "SN-95" designation, which follows the new alphanumeric platform code Ford adopted after using names.

in support. It can brace pans against breakage or be employed to repair damaged pans.

One caution with these seat studs; you don't want to attach anything to them that is in contact with the driveline. If you do, you can end up transmitting all sorts of road and mechanical noise into the passenger compartment via the floorboards. The most common way of making this mistake is to attach a torque arm cross-member to the seat studs. Attach such a cross-member to the subframe connectors instead.

Ground Clearance

This brings up the idea of planning your underchassis real estate. While normally space can be found for just about anything you want to weld, bolt, or clamp to the bottom of a 5.0, if you can plan out your undercar plans at all, it's best. Also, ground clearance is occasionally an issue. The most vulnerable area is equidistant between the axles, where the chassis is most prone to high centering over speed bumps and steep driveway approaches. Bulky subframe connectors on heavily lowered cars are the typical culprit, as are mufflers. The answer here is to use floor-hugging subframe

5.0 Chassis Construction

While the later cars are certainly more rigid, both the pre-1994 and the later SN-95 chassis share the same basic construction. Both are unibodies, meaning the body and frame (load carrying structure) are joined in the same sheet-metal assembly.

Ford starts with the floor pan, which is pretty much the transmission tunnel and the flat floor sections on either side of it. On each side of this are welded the rockers, which form the lower, outer perimeter of the body. The rockers run from the front to the rear tires, which is apparent when you study the outside of the car and notice the body gaps and how the rockers run uninterrupted below the doors.

To the floor pan and rockers, Ford welds on the cowl, which is the firewall (Ford's lawyers prefer the less inflammatory "engine bulkhead" description) and outer sheet-metal structure where the windshield wipers mount. The front inner fenders and radiator support are then welded onto the front of the inner fenders and atop the front frame rails. These are a pair of built-up, heavy-gauge sheet-metal sections extending forward from the floor pan. They are easily visible from under the car, and there are similar built-up sheet-metal sections in back, the rear frame rails, but the two box sections are not joined. (This is where subframe connectors finish Ford's job of building a stout chassis.)

In the area under the engine, the K-member is bolted to the chassis. The K-member is a cross-member—Ford engineer's refer to it as the "No. 2 cross-member"—and is what the lower part of the front suspension bolts to. It gets its name because when viewed from the top, it is shaped like a K. An important part, the K-member serves as the attachment point for the front suspension and the steering rack, and also provides the engine mounts. By fiddling with any of these mounting points, or where the K-member itself bolts to the chassis, a tremendous number of variables can be changed, from the car's wheelbase to the front suspension geometry, and even how the engine sits in the car.

In back, another pair of sheet-metal "frame rails" sprout from the floor pan. These, and reinforced sections of the sheet metal humping up and over to clear the rear axle, are where the rear suspension bolts to the chassis. Aft of the rear axle there isn't much more than enough to provide the rear hatch or truck floor.

Most rigid of the three Fox body styles is the coupe, because it has a full roof and relatively small openings in the rear body structure. The hatchback is wonderfully convenient the way it opens up hugely to swallow drag slicks and floor jacks, but that large opening noticeably detracts from chassis rigidity. T-top cars are probably just as bad, and the convertibles are simply hopeless in stock trim. They need subframe connectors right off the showroom floor.

The chief defect of the basic Fox design is generally lightweight material everywhere, plus the fact that the front and rear "frame" sections are not joined together.

---

connectors. The flat, rectangular tubing models seem to work just as well, yet offer more ground clearance than the massive round tubes.

Back Halving

When drag racing, there comes a point in the low-10-second bracket where the stock chassis, even with a fair amount of reinforcement, is simply overwhelmed. This is a squirrelly, dangerous situation, and many an excellent driver has slapped the wall when such a 5.0 has gotten away from him as he tried to drive into the nines.

The answer is to back-half the chassis. That is, the entire rear of the car is cut away except the outer fender skins. This leaves quite a hole, as the rear floor, gas tank, spare tire well, and inner fenders are all torched out. This allows fitting either a three-link or typically a four-link drag racing rear sus-

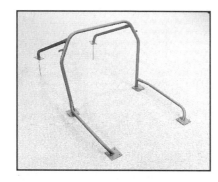

pension, all attached to the roll cage. Thus a tube chassis is effectively built inside the 5.0 body. Finally, aluminum inner panels and wheel tubs are fitted to help seal the interior.

While a few radical street machines have been back halved, the drag racing suspension can barely make it around a street corner, so back halving is a pure-racing operation.

Several outfits make dedicated 5.0 roll bars and cages, so getting one of these life-saving and chassis-stiffening tools in a Mustang is no big deal. Roll bar specialist Autopower is one popular cage builder, as are Dugan Racing and Kenny Brown. This Kenny Brown Super Street Cage for 1994 and later chassis uses low-mounted front braces to allow easier entry and exit for the driver and passengers. That's a prime consideration on the street, where higher mounted front braces can really make life a pain, although such braces are required by many racing sanctions. Always use roll bar padding to protect against impact injuries, especially around your head! Otherwise, your Mustang is more dangerous with a cage than without. *Kenny Brown Performance*

Suspension

14

One of the 5.0 Mustang's greatest charms is its low cost. Naturally, one of the downsides of this low cost is that the saving comes from somewhere. One of those areas is the suspension, which, along with the basic platform, was derived from the economy car Fairmont. This is in keeping with long-standing Mustang tradition; the first Mustang, after all, was a spin-off of the lowly Falcon.

Thus, 5.0 Mustangs get along with a MacPherson strut front end and a simple, live-axle rear suspension. Before maligning the 5.0's suspension any further, let's pause to reflect on two of its great strengths. First, it was inexpensive to produce, so we all could afford

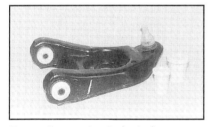

Energy Suspension is the industry specialist in urethane bushings, and can outfit a Mustang bumper-to-bumper with them. Note the inner steel sleeve in the A-arm bushings, which provides a wear surface for the pass-through bolt. The stiff-but-not-solid urethane surrounding the steel bushing is much less resilient than the rubber used by Ford, but without being unyielding like all-steel racing joints. This slight give allows a precision bushing that withstands constant street-car use with easily acceptable ride harshness and noise limits. Global West is another noted source for bushings, plus Steeda, Saleen, Griggs Racing, HP Motorsport, and others offer bushing kits. Many are repackaged Energy Suspension parts.

it, and secondly, the simple, strong live-axle rear end is well suited to drag racing, a pastime popular with many 5.0 enthusiasts.

Now, what are the practical disadvantages of the Mustang suspension? For starters, the ride is pretty rough, and the rougher the road, the rougher the ride gets. This is especially true of the rear axle, which seems to magnify bumps and potholes.

Additionally, the handling leaves something to be desired. The strut front end gives up pretty easily, promoting understeer. Understeer means the front tires must steer more than the car turns. It is the opposite of oversteer, where the rear end comes around and the driver has to "steer into the skid," as all those driver's training manuals put it. In the 5.0, understeer sets in early, limiting the cornering power and causing the outer edge of the front tires to wear quickly. If you slalom or open-track your 5.0, we don't have to tell you front tire wear is a huge factor.

Besides too much understeer, the 5.0's handling is fairly unpredictable near the limit. In other words, driven hard, a 5.0 begins to lose steering precision and can step out into oversteer in a real hurry when upset by a bump or when bouncing off the suspension stops. This is apparent on loose surfaces, such as snow, and even rain. Then the 5.0 is often left in the garage, and rightly so. You could say the 5.0 is a "white-knuckle car" when driven fast.

Even at the strip, the 5.0 isn't all polite manners. When launching hard, the rear tires often seem to bite right away, then break loose and spin uncontrollably.

Another 5.0 characteristic is

For a casual street driver with only a few bolt-on suspension modifications, progressive-rate springs are best because of their easy ride when just driving around. More sophisticated handling cars, especially those with torque arms or improved front-end geometry, should stick with linear-rate springs for more predictable handling. The center spring is progressive rate, as indicated by its unevenly spaced coils; the others are linear rate. These happen to be Neuspeed units. Thanks to aggressive marketing, Eibach is the best known and most widely used brand; Steeda Autosports windings are also popular. *Neuspeed*

excessive brake dive. Clamp on the binders and the 5.0 drags its nose like a bloodhound on the trail. This limits braking power because the rear tires are barely on the ground, thus requiring that the fronts do all the braking work. Furthermore, with the front suspension heavily compressed, the Mustang doesn't steer very well, and the transition into a corner or onto the gas is more dramatic than it needs to be.

Balance
To be perfectly fair, some of the 5.0's handling dramatics are not all the fault of the suspension. Being derived from a sedan and not designed from the ground up as a sports car, Mustangs have a conventional powertrain layout,

Good shocks are a must and worth the money. Koni is an excellent brand with a long history of building a superior product; Bilstein and Tokico are also first-rung makers. For general street use, a non- or single-adjustable shock is fine, while the extra cost of a double-adjustable shock pays off best when tuning for widely varying conditions.

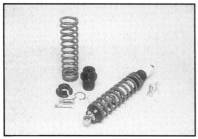

Coil-over shocks and struts are relatively new to high-performance street cars, although they've been the racer's choice for many decades. Griggs Racing is the primary proponent of these excellent spring/shock assemblies, mainly because its chassis preparation and suspension system is sophisticated enough to use coil-overs profitably. Advantages of coil-over units are that the shocks are superb, with excellent valving and low sticktion, ride height and corner weights are adjustable, spring choice is nearly unlimited, and weight is reduced. As usual, cost is the disadvantage. Griggs Racing offers its conversion kit, shown here, with either rubber or metal mounts and in four packages for drag, road race, and street machines. Coil-overs are worth the cost once you've moved to a full torque arm or other seriously upgraded suspension design.

Fox-body Mustangs have limited camber and no caster adjustment from the factory, so adding camber plates is necessary. With its urethane upper bushing, this replacement plate is a good choice for a street car, in which noise and vibration need suppression. Expect to enlarge and elongate the holes in the inner fender to allow the camber plate a full range of motion. The large studs are loosened for camber adjustment; the small Allen-headed hardware controls caster.

with the engine sitting nearly atop the front axle. The resulting 57-percent-front, 43-percent-rear weight distribution means the 5.0 Mustang is inherently front-heavy, and, given the powerful torque of its 302 engine pouring through the rear tires, can be easily provoked into oversteer at the limit or on loose surfaces. Short of moving heavy items rearward in the car, there isn't much to be done about this.

Sometimes, heavy objects can be moved rearward. On race cars, where major chassis modifications are the norm, the driver's seat is often moved rearward and the steering column extended. Furthermore, the engine is often set back in the chassis.

On the street the only real practical advice when it comes to balance is to move the battery to the trunk or rear hatch area. Relocating the battery over the right rear tire helps load that tire against axle wind-up and to offset the driver's weight laterally. It's a change sufficiently large that a sensitive driver can feel it when cornering.

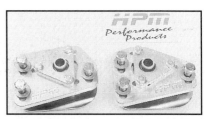

HP Motorsport offers a camber plate with dual adjustment and a spherical rod-end bearing for the upper strut mount. Such bearings offer more precision than a urethane bushing, so they are good on race cars. Metal bearings do tend to wear out faster than urethane but are normally easily replaced, and race cars don't see much mileage compared to a street car anyway. Metal bearings' worst feature on a street car is that they introduce road noise into the body structure. *HP Motorsports*

This is the same corner of the car where a nitrous bottle should go, for the same reason.

The opposite effect should also be kept in mind. The tendency is to add weight up front, in the engine compartment. Superchargers, turbos, and shopping cart loads of electronic boxes all contribute to front-end weight. Naturally, the power increase from these overrides their degradation in handling, but it is something to keep in mind. Whenever possible, move weight rearward.

What's the Problem?

OK, we've documented the 5.0 as not the happiest-handling car, either on the road or the strip. Why? Most of the trouble lies with the rear suspension. The 8.8-inch axle is located by four trailing arms. Two of these arms attach to the lower outboard axle; these double as the attachment points for the rear coil springs. The upper arms are shorter, angled heavily outward, and attach to the differential housing near the center of the axle.

Obviously, as the rear suspension compresses and extends, all of these arms move through arcs. What isn't visible is that the arcs of the lower arms are different from the uppers. In the middle of the

Baer Racing's bumpsteer correction kit is basically a pair of taller tie-rod ends. They replace the stock tie-rod ends, thus lowering the tie rods, thereby reducing bumpsteer on lowered cars. Don't let the metal rod end bearings scare you; little vibration gets through the isolator-filled steering system to the steering wheel, but precision is enhanced. Use these to get the tie-rod ends parallel to the ground when the car is at its static ride height. The result will be calmer, more precise steering that doesn't wander through bumps or need many small corrections in mid-corner. *Baer Racing*

suspension travel this isn't much of a concern, but toward the end of its travel the upper and lower arms bind each other because the arc of the upper arms wants to pull the axle one way while the lower arms arc differently and want to swing the axle another way. This binding is definitely not good, and causes much of the oversteering and unpredictability from the rear end. The harder you compress the suspension, either through bumps or launching at the drag strip, the worse the binding gets.

Ford tip-toes around this suspension arm misalignment by fitting fairly soft bushings to the upper arms, especially at their chassis end. This allows the upper arms to give way at the extremes of their travel, but obviously it is not the most satisfactory solution.

The front suspension is also not quite textbook. The main problem there is inadequate negative-camber gain during suspension compression. Such camber gain is what keeps the outside tire flat against the ground while cornering. Of course, little negative camber can be dialed in on the

alignment rack before tire wear becomes excessive (with street cars), so the need for increased caster shows up. Without getting into the details of front-end suspension geometry, more caster helps gain negative camber during suspension compression, which keeps the outside tire flatter to the pavement.

Mustang front ends do not have enough Ackerman built into them, either. Ackerman allows the inside front tire to steer more into a corner than the outside tire, necessary because the inside tire describes a tighter radius. Ackerman is built into front suspension geometries by the factory, and Ford didn't put enough in the 5.0's steering.

What's to Be Done?
Broadly speaking, there are two philosophies when upgrading 5.0 Mustang suspension. The first is to make detail improvements to the existing suspension using harder bushings and stiffer suspension arms and replacing a few key parts with modified versions. The second school of thought is to start over by removing much of the stock suspension and either substituting a different suspension system altogether or using radically different parts. This is especially true of the rear suspension.

As you'd suspect, the detail improvement plan can make a noticeable difference and is cost effective. This is the route taken by most owners, because it is easier on the pocketbook, as the parts are bought one by one and the total cost can be fairly low. Replacing

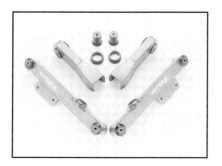

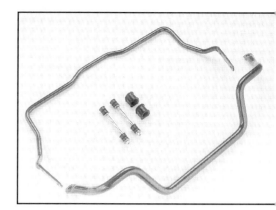

Changing sway bars on late-model Mustangs is not often necessary. The stock sway bars are huge, and the higher rate springs and shocks commonly installed by tuners only increase roll stiffness, so larger bars are rarely needed. However, the stock bars are solid, like these, and thus heavy. A hollow aftermarket bar, like Steeda's, can therefore shed several pounds, although mounted this low in the chassis, such a weight saving is not the sort of thing you'll feel. Aftermarket bars may also be needed on highly modified cars where so many changes are in place that the roll couple is out of whack. Steeda offers an additional rear sway bar that can help under such conditions. It goes on with the stock bar, but behind the rear axle.

the suspension with a complete aftermarket suspension system is considerably more expensive, but returns huge benefits because most of the fundamental flaws of the Fox chassis can be cured.

Often an owner starts off trying a bolt-on part for his suspension and it seems to help, so he tries another. Pretty soon he's added springs, shocks, urethane bushings here and there, maybe a

Replacement rear control arms are the same dimensions as stock Ford arms, but are thicker, heavier, and use well-thought-out urethane bushings with grease fittings. Their advantage is a bit less flex from the heavier arms and considerably less flex from the bushings. This set uses nonadjustable upper arms; the replacement also has an adjustable upper arm.

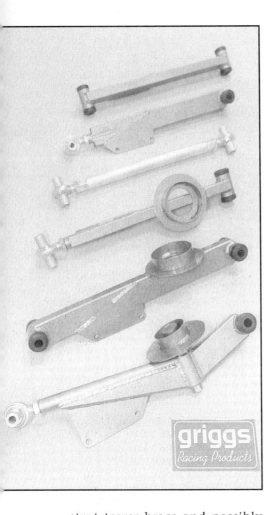

Griggs Racing offers no less than six rear lower control arms to accommodate both stock springs or coil-overs, low budgets, or higher dollar efforts. From the bottom up, they are:

- Adjustable length, adjustable spring (ride height) for street, road race, drag. An excellent all-around piece that is the most adaptable, most expensive Griggs Racing option. It's super rigid, lighter than stock. Uses stock springs.
- Fixed length, fixed spring perch. This is good for increased rear roll resistance and lower expenditures. Typically installed in drag cars or those already wearing Eibach air bags, or drag springs. It's very light and has some roll bind due to the bushing design. Uses stock springs.
- Here the roll bind is removed and the arm is adjustable in length. Uses stock springs.
- This straight tube design is for full race, road, or drag racing coil-over application.
- Adjustable length, no roll-bind with stock sway bar. Coil-over application.
- An inexpensive, street drag piece. The quietest arm, it has more compliance in the bushings and is for coil-over applications.

These Kenny Brown adjustable rear upper control arms combine the racy feature of adjustability with rubber bushings at the chassis end for dead-quiet street operation. Stock bushings are used in the axle end to provide adequate compliance while cornering. Kenny Brown also offers this arm with spherical rod bearings for racers. *Kenny Brown Performance*

For extra hit on the rear tires at the drag strip, Southside Machine Lift Bars are the ticket. The bracket fixed to the axle end of the lower arms gives them the geometry of an aggressive slapper bar, and they definitely shock the tire. This arrangement is biased heavily toward drag racing, especially with a small or not-grippy tire, but it does work on the street, too.

strut tower brace and possibly camber plates, not to mention wheels and tires. The car responds with better handling, and often this better handling is plenty and our owner is happy.

But it's also not uncommon for the owner to have discovered that he really likes going around corners, and after a while he realizes that stripping off much of his stock suspension and nearly all of his aftermarket parts so he could add a reengineered aftermarket suspension system would give even better handling. He's right, but has to go through the financial torture of discarding plenty of hard-earned hardware to get to the fancy suspension.

The point is, if you have any inclination toward sharp handling, you are money ahead going for the reengineered suspension from the get-go.

Detail Improvements

Common 5.0 suspension detail improvements are a wide and varied lot. Hard bushings, replacement suspension arms, stiffer springs and better shocks, adjustable caster/camber plates, and relocated steering rack bushings are all examples. Others are replacement rear control arms, both upper and lower, and these can be either adjustable or nonadjustable.

Polyurethane Bushings

A great starting point is hard polyurethane bushings; they're available from many sources, and basically, the more used, the greater the benefit. There is one exception to this rule: the forward bushings in the rear upper control arms. These should remain stock to allow sufficient compliance in the rear suspension. This is doubly important when installing hard bushings, as compliance in the rest of the suspension is being reduced.

One of the best places for a hard bushing is the upper front strut. This is often replaced by a metal Heim joint (rod end) bearing as part of a camber plate installation, but if a simple hard bushing replacement is desired, this is a good place to reduce unwanted suspension movement. Hard bushings in the remainder of the front suspension will reduce

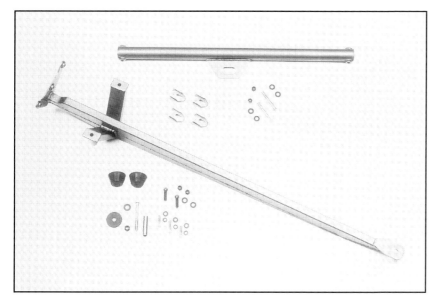

Think of a torque arm as a giant traction bar that works—really works!—not only under acceleration but braking, too. Griggs Racing has popularized torque arms for Mustangs, but they are offered by Maximum Motorsport, Roush Performance Parts, and others as well. Don't mix and match vendors on torque arm and associated parts, as each has its own idea of how long the arm should be. All mount, like this standard Griggs Racing example, to the differential cover bolts in the rear and at a single point in front to a new cross-member. The cross-member itself attaches to subframe connectors.

slop in the handling and steering in trade for an increase in road noise. Now that the 5.0 fleet has aged and the stock bushings are beginning to rot away, hard bushing replacement makes a lot of sense for those wanting a simple, low-cost improvement of the basic 5.0 chassis. Hard bushings are also important in delivering the benefits from upgraded suspension arms and locating links.

One drawback of polyurethane bushings can be squeaks and groans. Lubrication is the key to eliminating these, and grease fittings are the key to getting the lube to the bushings. Of course, you may not end up with zerk fittings, so slather on the white lithium or silicone lube supplied with the bushings during installation. Sometimes problem-child bushings may require occasional disassembly and relubing, not an appealing proposition.

Energy Suspension is the primary vendor of urethane bushings.

Springs

A 5.0's four coil springs support the weight of the car on the suspension and provide the flexibility in the suspension to soften the impacts from irregularities in the road. The stiffer the spring, the less the body and suspension will move relative to each other for a given input. Said another way, with stiffer springs, the more energy it takes to move the suspension. Springs are measured by their rate, or the amount of energy it takes to move them a given distance. In the United States, spring rate is listed in pounds per inch or how many pounds of force it takes to compress the spring 1 inch.

The general rule is, you want to use the lightest spring rate that still gives you responsive handling. That way the suspension is still free to comply with the road so the tires stay on the pavement where they can do some good. If the spring rate is too high, your Mustang will feel darty, go-karty quick on dead

Suspension Modifications Made Easy

Deciding on what to do with the suspension is difficult. Unlike powertrain modifications where the object (more power) is easy to define and quantify, suspension improvements are less clear-cut. One enthusiast wants to drag race, another to slalom, and everyone wants a nice street driver. Furthermore, there are different ways of getting to the same goal with the suspension, and like engine modifications, mixing and matching parts from different suppliers can build a real disaster.

With all that in mind, here's a collection of unvarnished facts and coarse guideline to follow when improving your 5.0's suspension:

• Decide what you want from your suspension, find a supplier that follows your philosophy, and stick with him.

• Avoid mixing parts from different manufacturers.

• If you drive on the street, use parts labeled for street use. Metal-to-metal joints and flimsy drag racing tubular arms may look neat, but are noisy, wear out fast, and may not be strong enough for bumping against curbs or slamming through potholes and across manhole covers.

• Always build more suspension than horsepower.

smooth roads, but even small bumps will upset the suspension, chattering the tires across the pavement and losing traction. The ride is terrible, too, and pretty soon you get tired of it.

Softer springs can make a Mustang feel a bit floaty, but they do allow the tires to follow the road better than rock hard springs, especially at street driving speeds.

Good examples of the two philosophies are found in the 5.0 line-up. The late 1980s GTs and LXs are firmly sprung, while the 1993–97 Mustang Cobras are lightly sprung. Those Cobras are often criticized for being too soft, but no one will deny they are at

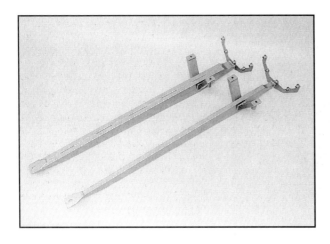

For up to 400 lb-ft of torque, the standard Griggs Racing torque arm, at the bottom, is sufficient. The upper example is the double arm, which simply has a second bar sistered alongside for increased torque capacity. It's good up to 600 lb-ft, and is also best for slalom racers who are constantly on and off the gas in low gears. Griggs Racing's double arm is normally available only to fit TA rear axle covers.

least as good in the corners as a GT. The message is, rock hard springs feel go-kart quick in the steering and help keep the nose up when cornering and braking, but fall apart on real-world roads—the ones with bumps in them. Keep in mind that road racing cars use high spring rates, but they also spend all their time at high speed, where bumps are magnified. At average street speeds a road racer rides like an ox cart.

In practice, the basic idea behind 90 percent of 5.0 Mustang spring sales is lowering, however. A shorter spring instantly lowers a Mustang, giving it a low-slung look that's undeniably cool. Furthermore, up to 1 1/2 inches of lowering is, overall, a beneficial thing on the 1993 and earlier cars. Any more and what is gained by lowering the car's center of gravity is easily offset by the many bad things going on in the suspension geometry.

Let's also not forget a lowering spring means the suspension is closer to full compression by the amount the spring is lower. A 1-inch lowering spring means the suspension is effectively compressed 1-inch. That's 1-inch closer to bottoming out, where the locating arms hit the limits. Bottoming is bad. It upsets the handling tremendously, and places extreme loads on the suspension arms. So, to keep the suspension from crashing, lowering springs use a higher rate. Naturally, this ruins the ride.

To compromise, variable-rate springs are common. Unlike the stock springs, which are linear rate (sometimes called specific rate), variable-rate springs are wound with some of the coils closer together than others. Where the coils are closer together, the spring is softer. That allows that part of the spring to move fairly easily in response to most of the jiggles and bumps in the real world, while the rest of the spring is much firmer to withstand big impacts and hard driving.

The trouble with variable-rate springs is the energy absorbed and released by the spring varies with suspension travel, and this leads to a bit of unpredictability in the handling. Road racers insist on linear-rate springs for precise car control, and a touch of this comes across on street cars when driven very hard. But for the vast majority of street-driven 5.0s, the softer ride is really what's needed to keep the car livable.

So, if you want the last word in precision, if you're a handling sort of person, use a linear-rate spring. Otherwise, a variable rate is a better real-word street spring. Eibach, H&R, Neuspeed, and Steeda are popular outlets for performance replacement coil springs.

Struts and Shocks

Shock absorbers are misnamed. The English more properly call them dampeners because that's what they do, dampen spring movement. Without dampeners, a

Panhard rods, like this TracKit Plus street kit, locate the chassis side-to-side over the suspension. They also locate the rear roll center, and by moving it lower, reduce the Mustang's roll and understeer. Panhard bars must be big and beefy to hold up to the stress, but you also have to get an exhaust system around them. Kenny Brown offers panhard bars designed to clear 2 1/2-inch exhaust systems, plus a choice of rod-end or urethane bushings. Griggs Racing, Maximum Motorsports, and others offer full ranges of panhard rods too; if you also get a torque arm, be sure to stick with the same tuner for the panhard rod. *Kenny Brown Performance*

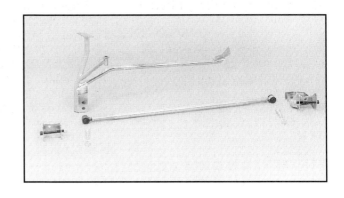

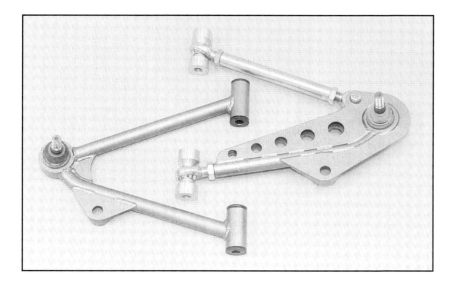

These two Griggs Racing lower front A-arms illustrate the range between street and racing parts. Both work with the Griggs Racing K-member, with the street arm at left offering quiet, smooth operation from its urethane bushings. The racing part is adjustable for caster, camber, and track, is reinforced for higher loads, and employs metal bushings for increased precision. As you'd guess, there is a healthy cost differential, too. Either arm weighs less than a stock arm and is stronger for reduced deflection, and thus provides more precise tire placement.

5.0's springs would have it blobbing up and down like a cube of Jell-O. This explanation also makes it easy to see that shocks and springs are matched parts. Stiffer springs call for stiffer shocks and vice versa. A 5.0 with stiffer springs and stock shocks can have a distinct pogo stick feel to it.

It's also not commonly known that the shock or strut has much more influence on ride quality than the spring. That harsh, jarring ride hammered out by many modified cars comes mainly from the shocks, unless the car is lowered so far it is crashing on the bump stops on every other joint in the pavement (more common than you'd think). It typically doesn't come from the springs.

All this is leading up to the idea that there's no inexpensive way to a good shock that offers premium control with a relatively plush ride. The industry-leading Bilstein, Koni, and Tokico shocks handle the control/ride compromise well, as does the newer Edelbrock offering, but you won't find them at clearance prices. The less expensive dampers, like KYBs, neither handle nor ride as well, but are noticeably less expensive and an improvement over stock.

In drag racing, weight transfer from the front to the back axle is desirable, while movement in the other direction is of no help. Thus, the Lakewood 90/10 front strut is used to allow rapid raising of the front end, coupled with a stiff rebound curve to keep the front end up until about half track. Then the gently lowering front allows better aerodynamics at the high-speed end of the track. Such shocks are typically fixed rate, but HAL offers knob-adjustable drag shocks that range from a 90/10 drag shock to a street-oriented 50/50 configuration. The HALs are rebuildable, too.

Like variable rate springs, 90/10 shocks are hardly optimum for all-around handling. You can drive them on the street for just getting around, but corner-type handling is lost.

Quad Shocks

Because of its rear suspension geometry, the 5.0 Mustang is prone to hopping the rear axle under hard acceleration. Ford's fix was to fit a pair of small shocks in a nearly horizontal position above the axle to dampen the reactive back-and-forth axle motion that is part of the hopping cycle. For a stock or bolt-on Mustang the quad shocks should stay, but as soon as the additional axle control found in traction bars, torque arms, or other fore-and-aft links is fitted, the quad shocks should be removed. At that point they are just slowing suspension reaction time, and their axle dampening function has been taken over by the new control links. Plus, quad shocks limit tire width increases necessary for drag and road race 5.0s.

Caster/Camber Plates

Both caster and camber are set where the top of the front strut attaches to the inner fender structure known as the shock tower. A plate and slotted holes allow the top of the strut to be moved in and out to set the camber. Ford allows limited adjustment of camber and none for caster, and when the car is lowered the stock range of camber adjustment is inadequate. Too much negative camber is achieved and the tires wear rapidly on their inner edges. Also, more caster is desirable, as it gives more camber when the front tires are turned and the suspension is compressed. In other words, extra caster helps keep the outside front tire flatter to the pavement when cornering. It also provides high-speed stability. The downside is that excessive caster raises the steering effort to the point where if you really get carried away, the power steering pump soon wears out.

To allow more caster and camber adjustment, aftermarket adjusting plates are used. These are

Looking straight up at SVD's rear suspension system, it's clear that a total redesign has taken place. Note how the upper control arms, just visible above and to the side of the differential, are straight. This keeps them from binding with the lower control arms, and in any case, this racing suspension is fully outfitted with rod-end bearings for freedom of movement. Lateral location is handled by the horizontal diagonal link; think of it as a panhard rod lying on its side. This design passes Ford crash test criteria, unlike a torque-arm car that can spear the torque arm up through the floorboard in a serious accident.

commonly referred to as camber plates. Installation is a straightforward replacement of the stock fitting atop the strut, complicated only by having to enlarge the holes in the bodywork some to allow the extra movement.

Modern camber plates are actually two plates joined together by clamping cap screws. This arrangement allows caster and camber to be set individually, a huge improvement in convenience over older plates that required getting both adjustments spot on while the retaining bolts were loose.

Camber plates often incorporate an extra inch in height for the strut mounting. This keeps the strut in the midpoint of its travel

on lowered cars, ensuring the strut does not bottom out before the suspension hits the stops.

You'll also have a choice of urethane or metal rod end bearings to locate the top of the strut in the camber plate. Street cars should stick with urethane bushings here to avoid bringing road noise into the body structure. Hardcore cornering types may still want to opt for the rod end bearings, but unless you're racing, there's no real benefit on the street. The metal ends wear faster than urethane, too.

Bump Steer Correction
When a 5.0 is lowered with shorter springs, the relationship between the steering rack and the spindle out at the tires is upset. The steer-

ing rack ends up lower than the tie-rod ends at their spindle ends, which causes the tie-rod ends to run upward at an angle. This is no good, because then the tie-rod ends are swinging through an arc during the critical ranges of suspension travel. Those arcs mean the tie-rod ends are effectively getting shorter and longer as the suspension extends and compresses, which leads to uncommanded steering inputs. This is called bumpsteer; when the tire rolls over a bump, the wheel is steered even though the steering wheel is not moved. This makes for nervous handling and midcorner corrections.

Two cures are generally used, either singly or together. For the usual lowering job, offset rack bushings will get the steering straightened out. The rack bushings fit into holes in the steering rack where it mounts to the K-member. The stock bushings have the mounting stud hole centered, while offset bushings have offset holes. That allows raising or lowering the steering rack, relative to the tires. Raising the rack is what's needed.

The second cure is to lower the outer end of the tie rods, using spacers. A bumpsteer correction kit is a set of such spacers and, typically, bearing-style tie-rod ends. Such kits are useful on heavily lowered cars, or for fine-tuning the tie-rod alignment, as the spacers give some adjustment to the process that offset rack bushings don't. Combinations of lowering and tire diameter can call for both offset rack bushings and a bumpsteer correction kit.

Baer Racing is the primary purveyor of bumpsteer correction kits, while a number of outfits like Maximum Motorsports offer offset rack bushings.

Sway Bars

Normally there is little need to change the sway bars on a 5.0. For bolt-on street cars, the massive sway bars Ford fits are more than enough, so spend your money elsewhere. Aftermarket bars are of benefit on more heavily modified cars, especially when large changes in lowering, spring rate, shock valving, and suspension design (torque arms, three links, and so on) are fitted.

If you are saving every possible pound, then tubular sway bars, like those marketed by Steeda Autosports, are worth the effort. The solid factory bars weigh a ton. Likewise, with drag cars you can disconnect or remove the front sway bar to speed up the reaction time of the chassis and improve weight transfer to the rear suspension. When you take your street car to test-and-tune night to find out what she'll do, simply disconnect one end link from the sway bar to

make it inoperative. Reconnect it before heading home to restore handling. More dedicated drag cars can have the bar removed to save the weight, but don't drive around the streets without the bar. Huge body roll will result, and while you can learn to live with it after a while, your emergency maneuvering is right up there with an ocean liner when the sway bar is disconnected.

SN-95 Spindles

Ford greatly improved the spindles on the 1994 and later Mustangs. An easy bolt-in interchange with earlier Fox-chassied cars, the later spindle offers better geometry for more precise steering and higher cornering power. It is also the spindle most chassis tuners build their kits around, and the one many of the brake kits are built for. I don't point this out so you'll run out and add SN-95 spindles for your earlier car, but rather so you'll understand why so many suspension kits require the change.

Panhard Bars

A panhard bar is a simple tube that runs from one side of the car to the other in the rear suspension. One end of the bar is attached to the rear axle, the other to a bracket hanging from the chassis. The purpose of the bar is to locate the body above the axle, or, in other words, keep the body from flopping back and forth on the rear suspension.

Ford does not use a panhard bar on the Mustang, leaving its job up to the upper control arms. But as we know, these arms bind the rear suspension because they are angled to the lower control arms, so the suspension moves more freely without them. To remove the upper control arms, some sort of lateral locating device, like a panhard bar, is necessary. This is mainly where panhard bars have entered the Mustang world; they're from torque arm manufacturers such as Griggs Racing, Maximum Motorsports, and others.

Because the panhard bar also

Bart's Works front suspension uses a custom A-arm and coil-over shocks to provide excellent front suspension geometry. This relatively affordable front end uses rod ends on the coil-over and tie-rod ends for maximum precision, along with urethane bushing in the A-arm and lower arm for a quiet, smooth ride. SVD also offers a complete coil-over/A-arm front suspension for 5.0 Mustangs.

locates the rear roll center, the point where the chassis rolls about when leaning in a corner, fitting a panhard bar to the stock suspension is also beneficial. This is what Kenny Brown does, for example. It's an easy and effective way of lowering the Mustang's too-high rear roll center for less body roll and reduced understeer.

Two basic panhard bars are offered, adjustable and nonadjustable. For street cars the nonadjustable panhard bar is best, but you want to make sure the bar you buy is compatible with the other suspension components on the car. The best way of doing this is to pick a suspension supplier and stick with his line of parts. They're designed to work together, and mixing a Maximum Motorsports panhard bar with a Griggs Racing torque arm will not give the balanced handling you're looking for.

Keep in mind that any panhard bar working without the upper control arms is the sole locating link for the axle in a lateral direction. You don't want a flimsy bar, or worse yet, a lightly built bracket hanging down from the chassis. This is a load-carrying suspension member, and you don't want the bracket or bar failing in a high-speed corner! Luckily, most of the fly-by-night operators have left this market, but stick with the major manufacturers to ensure quality.

Traction Bars
For decades, a cheap and effective way of increasing traction during acceleration with a live axle car has been to add a set of traction bars. Sometimes they're called slapper bars, or even Lakewood bars among 5.0 people, due to the popularity of that brand. Traction bars are easily affordable and do make a big difference in hooking up the rear tires.

Traction bars work by directing the torque reaction in the rear suspension against the chassis. Thus the bars are trying to either lift the body and chassis or leveraging the rear axle against the ground, depending on how you want to look at it.

The advantages of traction bars are that they are quite effective in planting the rear tires, and allow removing the quad, or kicker, shocks because traction bars also squelch axle hop. This lets the rear suspension react faster, shortening the 60-foot time at the strip.

Traction bar disadvantages are several, but not deal-breaking if all that's desired is simple acceleration traction. For one, traction bars hang low under the lower control arms and can hang up on steep driveways and such. Traction bars

work only when accelerating and don't redirect braking forces like a torque arm or multilink suspension design, nor do they work as well as more sophisticated designs when cornering. However, for a dead-simple street car designed to beat a hot Volkswagen across an intersection, they're hard to beat price wise.

Control Arms
There are several reasons to change the control arms in either the front or rear suspension. Primary of these is to change the geometry of the suspension by using a shorter or longer arm. Plus, the stock arms are fine for street use, but do bend and distort some under high loads, especially when it comes to the rear suspension, drag slicks, and hard launches. A new arm with factory-fitted bushings may be a convenient way to change bushings, too. This is the case with Ford Racing Performance Parts' upper control arms in the rear suspension.

Of all the control arm replacement going on, most of the attention is focused on the rear suspension's lower control arms. This is because these arms have so much to do with carrying acceleration loads, not binding the suspension, holding the coil springs, and connecting all that tire rumble to the bodywork. Thus, we have the beefy but stock dimensioned, urethane-bushing lower arms at one end, and the length-adjustable, rod-end, spring perch-adjustable, reinforced but lightweight arms at the other, with all sorts of variations of bushing and adjustability in between. Bolt-on 5.0s will do fine with just bushings or replacement arms. Handling fans will want to move to a nonadjustable arm in conjunction with probably a torque arm, while those going all out for handling or building open track cars can use the adjustable, lightweight arms.

The rear upper control arms are mainly removed these days, as more 5.0s move into the more

sophisticated torque arm suspensions. However, Ford Racing Performance Parts still offers its heavy-duty upper arms. These use stock bushings at the axle end for the necessary compliance in the stock Ford suspension, but the front bushings are approximately twice as firm for faster, more positive response. These are a good addition to a daily driver bolt-on car, on which road noise should be minimized.

Griggs Racing, Racecraft Performance, HP Motorsports, and South Side Machine offer some of the more popular replacement lower control arms, with the latter two biased toward straight-line traction. Steeda Autosports and Unlimited Performance offer similar designs in weight-saving aluminum. Steeda's design goes so far as to have a three-piece urethane bushing offering a hard center section for straight-line traction and compliant outside bushings for improved cornering.

Pinion Angle
When a car is lowered, the angle between the drive shaft and the differential changes. On high-powered 5.0s with big power adders, this can upset the handling and wear out the U-joints. To restore the proper pinion angle, the axle must be rotated in its control arms. This is done with adjustable-length upper control arms, and pinion angle is the only need for adjustability in those arms. A bolt-on car with standard lowering springs, moderate torque, and standard-height tires should not need its pinion angle reset. Adjustable ride height cars with coil-over shocks that are being adjusted up and down at the strip can use adjustable upper arms. Torque arm suspensions automatically set pinion angle with the torque arm and do not need adjustment.

Bennett Racing, Racecraft Performance, HP Motorsport, and Kenny Brown Performance are among those offering adjustable upper control arms.

Redesigned Suspensions

When handling becomes paramount, either because of huge power levels at the drag strip or the desire to corner faster and with less drama, the difficulties in dealing with the basic 5.0 suspension become overwhelming. Then it is time to move on to fundamentally redesign suspension systems. Because most of the Mustang's handling problems are in the rear suspension, it is best to concentrate there.

Torque Arms

Just as traction bars try to lift the chassis during acceleration, a torque arm is designed to plant the axle during acceleration, but it also transfers the reactive force from braking into the body. The result is a traction device that both plants the axle while accelerating and works to lift the nose under braking. Furthermore, because the traction bar is located by a single bolt at its front end, the traction bar does not locate the axle relative to the chassis to any marked degree. That job is left to the control arms, or control arms and panhard rod. By separating the locating duties from the traction duties, the suspension works freely, with little bind.

Torque arms can be used either with or without the upper control arms. Removing the rear upper control arms and fitting a panhard bar is the best method because it reduces suspension binding. However, the length of a torque arm is specific to the way its designer wants it to work. Thus a Maximum Motorsports torque arm is different from a Griggs Racing torque arm, and the suspension parts from these manufacturers should not be mixed.

Due to its fundamental redesign of the rear suspension, a torque arm has a profound effect on handling. Torque-arm cars absolutely plant the rear tires coming off the turns or at the drag strip. Even in casual braking, the amount of nose dive is greatly reduced and the car feels more stable and predictable at all times. If you haven't driven a torque-arm car, it's worth the trouble to seek one out and sample it before deciding on your suspension plans. The cost of a total torque-arm suspension is quite high, but worth it.

One factor contributing to the torque arm's cost is that the torque arm works so well, the front of the car picks up plenty of understeer. Now, on the street with light to moderate cornering and hard acceleration, this understeer is barely noticeable and can easily be lived with. But corner-carving enthusiasts, especially slalom or open-track fans, will want to work with the front suspension to make it stick better. The usual camber plate, urethane bushing, strut, and spring tricks will work great on most street cars. As more handling prowess is desired, then a tubular K-member is called for.

About the only downside to a torque-arm suspension, aside from the cost, is the introduction of some road noise into the passenger compartment. This isn't bad, but those with really quiet street cars will notice an increase in the tire's presence. There is also the odd clunk and bonk that makes it through, but these are minor.

Independent Rear Suspension

New on the scene as this book was written was the IRS from the 1999 Mustang Cobra. This assembly of subframe, differential, axles, control arms, sway bar, uprights, and brakes is designed as an interchangeable insert with the live axle suspension in the Mustang GT. Thus, the IRS assembly should bolt into nearly any Fox-chassis Mustang, all the way back to 1979 models. Naturally, expect some fabrication issues with the older chassis.

Furthermore, the IRS will require exhaust work (fitting Cobra exhaust seems the easy expedient), and improving the front suspension is a given. The IRS uses an aluminum differential, too, so extremely high-powered engines are likely not a good match. This IRS option seems good for a fast, sophisticated street car where the excellent IRS ride is worth the cost and trouble of installation.

A-Arm Front Suspension

MacPherson strut suspensions are not supposed to be optimum handlers, due mainly to difficulties in obtaining the proper camber while cornering. A-arm front suspensions are better in this regard, and several tuners have either toyed with, or offer, A-arm front ends for 5.0s. Given the tight confines of the Mustang's shock towers, these aftermarket A-arm suspensions all use a tall spindle and a quite short upper A-arm. This gives a rapid camber rise while cornering.

Most popular is the relatively affordable, relatively easy-to-install Bart's Works design. Its key part is a fabricated spindle, and the rest is mainly the upper A-arm and the off-the-shelf ball-joints and such to make it all fit. A well thought out design, the Bart's Works suspension has a great ride, keeps understeer at bay, and offers full suspension travel in a lowered package.

Special Vehicle Developments offers two A-arm front ends, one for street use, another designed purely for racetrack competition. Contex is another A-arm builder, which offers a bewildering array of both front and rear suspensions, but spotty production runs and hit-or-miss factory support make its product line something of a minefield. Saleen Performance Products has also built A-arm front ends for its race cars and a mere handful of ultra-high-end street cars, but has not made a point of offering this system to the public.

Brakes

15

Right off the showroom floor, stock 5.0-liter Mustangs were powerful and underbraked. For a completely stock car, the small front discs and rear drums could best be described as adequate. Early 5.0 Mustangs came with pitifully small 10.06-inch disc brakes in the front and 9-inch drums in back. In 1986, Ford stepped up the rotors minimally to 10.84 inches, but the 9-inch drums remained. Not until 1994 did the standard issue 5.0 Mustang gain 10.5-inch rear disc brakes and better 10.9-inch front brakes—of course, the car picked up a few hundred pounds as well.

Only the 1993–95 SVT Mustang Cobras received braking systems in line with their as-delivered performance. Where all previous 5.0-liter Mustangs got by with single 60-millimeter pistons clamping on rotors around 10 inches in diameter, 1993–95 Mustang Cobras were blessed with dual-piston front calipers clamping 13-inch rotors. The rear discs are also larger than run-of-the-mill Mustangs, measuring 11.65 inches.

Rotors

Since a vehicle does most of its stopping with the front brakes, the rear drums can perhaps be forgiven. Drums, after all, will really stop a vehicle—once. The 10-plus-inch front brakes found on standard issue 5.0s are simply too small. If you have to make more than one hard stop from high speed the brakes will fade fast. Increasing the size of the rotors gives the brakes more leverage to stop a vehicle. This is because the brakes have to convert the vehicle's inertial energy into frictional energy via the brakes. Larger rotors allow this conversion to happen more quickly.

Fortunately there are a number of aftermarket brake kits from Baer Racing, Ford Racing Performance Parts, Stillen, and Wilwood. Making these upgrades to 1979–93 5.0s means replacing or modifying the stock front spindles. It's possible to upgrade to 12-inch rotors and retain 15-inch wheels. Moving up to the more desirable 13-inch front rotors necessitates buying larger wheels and tires, making a brake upgrade quite expensive. Of course, larger wheels and tires are almost always required with the common brake upgrades, as they also mandate a switch to five-lug spindles, thus requiring five-lug wheels. Only Baer Racing offers larger brakes available with the Fox-body 5.0's four-lug pattern. SN95 Mustangs already have five-lug spindles and larger wheels from the factory and offer an easier upgrade path to larger rotors.

In the rear, 1994–95 5.0s feature adequately sized rear rotors, but 1993 and earlier 5.0s really need more than the dinky drum brakes they came with. Ford Racing

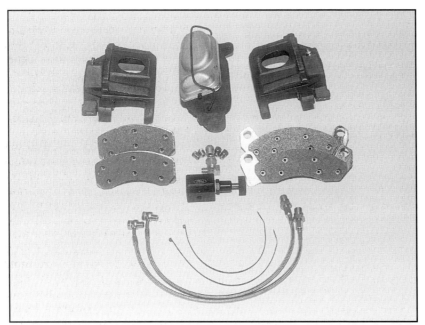

Owners of 1993-and-earlier 5.0 Mustangs looking for an inexpensive braking improvement can get one from Kenny Brown Performance in the form of its Club-Sport brake package. The kit includes calipers with 73-millimeter pistons, a larger master cylinder, an adjustable proportioning valve, streetable performance brake pads, and all necessary fittings and installation hardware. This simple upgrade is available for under $400 and offers a bit more performance potential than junk-yard calipers. While both are sourced from Mark VII, the Kenny Brown calipers feature steel pistons designed to handle high temperatures found in performance applications; the stock phenolic pistons have actually been known to burn when subjected to high heat. The braided steel hoses in the picture are optional.

Performance Parts and Stainless Steel Brakes both offer 10-inch rear disc brake conversions for early 5.0s. Baer, Ford Racing Performance Parts, and Wilwood also offer larger rear disc conversions, which may necessitate larger wheels and tires. Moving to larger rear brakes of any brand may also require an adjustable proportioning valve to balance the braking bias front to rear.

Pads

A sensible upgrade for any braking system in need of more stopping power is a more aggressive set of brake pads. Pads work on the rotors to convert the vehicle's movement into frictional energy. More aggressive brake pads will shorten a vehicle's stopping distance, while hastening rotor wear.

Unlike many parts where racing pieces can pull double duty, brake pads are considerably more application-specific. While high-performance street pads will work in a performance capacity like an open-track event, pad wear will increase dramatically. Conversely, when running a racing brake pad on the street, it rarely reaches ideal

Maximum Motorsports led the way with inexpensive brake upgrades for Fox 5.0 Mustangs. Its package, installed on this stock front brake, includes streetable Hawk Carbotic front brake pads, heavy-duty rear brake shoes, braided stainless-steel brake hoses, and stainless-steel caliper guide sleeves. The pads improve braking, the lines improve pedal feel, and the guide sleeves help even-out pad wear. This package provides a noticeable improvement for a bit more than $200 and could easily be coupled with Mark VII pistons and a rear-disc conversion for a formidable, affordable brake improvement.

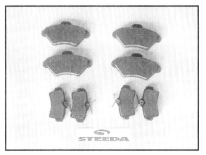

Picking the proper brake pad is tricky. Aggressive street pads can work on the racetrack, but racing pads don't work well on the street. It's best to work with a tuner to select the proper pads for your 5.0 Mustang. Steeda Autosports offers a variety of brake pads and shoes for all years of 5.0 Mustangs, including pads with street, autocross, and competition designations. Steeda and many other vendors also offer stainless-steel caliper guide sleeves, which help even-out pad wear with the stock single-piston calipers. *Steeda Autosports*

operating temperature, so braking performance suffers. One other item worth noting is dusting. Performance pads are often more likely to soil your wheels with brake dust.

In general, an organic/metallic combination designed for street performance offers a good mixture of improved stopping power and acceptable streetability. However, there are a number of brake pad materials, including those containing exotic materials like carbon fiber and Kevlar. Working with a Mustang tuner knowledgeable about brake upgrades is likely the best way to select improved pads. Many shops like Maximum Motorsports and Steeda Autosports even offer streetable pad upgrades for the stock 1979–93 disc/drum brakes.

Calipers

The pistons inside brake calipers hold the brake pads and squeeze them on the rotors to stop a vehicle. Stock 5.0s feature calipers equipped with single 60-millime-

ter pistons. These are small pistons, which naturally have less leverage on the pad than larger pistons. Also, single pistons tend to provide uneven pad wear. They are, however, light and cheap, which is why they are standard issue on 5.0 Mustangs.

There two ways to go to get higher performance pistons onto a 5.0 Mustang. Heavier Lincoln Mark VII's were fitted with calipers that use a single 73-millimeter piston. Naturally, these offer an increase in braking force with a budget price tag. Some 5.0 vendors, like Kenny Brown Performance, even offer budget braking packages built around these packages. The other option is an aftermarket brake package. All aftermarket brakes have at least dual-piston calipers, with racing-oriented packages featuring four- and six-piston calipers. Naturally, these packages command higher prices.

Lines

Some aftermarket braking systems include braided stainless-steel

Wheel Options

Ford Racing Performance Parts

It is possible to upgrade braking power while maintaining four-lug wheels in early 5.0s, but it's worth it to go with five-lug spindles and axles to gain the additional

choices in wheel design. Moving up to 17-inch and larger wheels on 1993 and earlier 5.0s often means bending the fender lips back and banging on the frame rails, but it can be done. Those 5.0s built between 1990 and 1993 came with 16-inch wheels from the factory and have larger fender openings, so they are a bit more adaptable; 18-inch wheels are about the maximum diameter that will fit under a Fox 5.0. Later 1994–95 5.0s have much larger fender openings and can accept up to 20-inch wheels.

Tires in the neighborhood of 10 inches wide can easily be fit inside a Fox 5.0's fenders, using a wheel with a 20- to 25-millimeter offset. Removing the horizontally mounted quad shocks can really help tire clearance in the rear. Among the most popular wheels accompanying a brake upgrade are those from the 1995 Mustang Cobra R. These 17x9-inch wheels are available from Ford Racing Performance Parts in offsets and bolt patterns for 1979–93 and 1994–95 wheels. They will clear most popular brake packages and they look great.

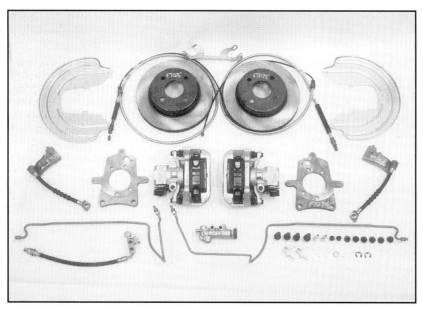

Those choosing a budget route to upgrading the brakes on a 1979–93 5.0 Mustang will likely find the Ford Racing Performance Parts' rear disc brake conversion kit attractive. It uses factory brake parts to convert a 5.0 Mustang to the same rear brakes as the 1987–88 Thunderbird Turbo Coupe. The kit includes 10-inch rotors, a larger master cylinder, and all the lines, fittings, and fasteners necessary for installation. While all cars do most of their braking with the front brakes, these brakes can still help a 5.0 Mustang, as the factory drums aren't really worth too much. *Ford Racing Performance Parts*

brake lines. While these lines are certainly more durable and race ready than standard rubber lines, they also improve braking performance, because as rubber lines age they can weaken. When faced with brake fluid pressure, the older lines swell and don't deliver maximum pressure to the brake calipers' pistons. Swapping to braided stainless-steel lines ensures there is no pressure loss in the flexible brake lines. Baer Racing's comprehensive brake packages include braided stainless lines, and some companies, like Maximum Motorsports, even offer braided lines to upgrade the stock braking system.

Unlike other subsystems on a 5.0 Mustang, brake upgrades are not complicated. Larger is definitely better. It's not really possible to have too much braking power in a heavy, powerful car like a 5.0 Mustang. The only considerations are completeness of the kit and its streetability. Baer Racing, Ford Racing Performance Parts, and Stillen all offer brake systems that are streetable and some that will serve street driving and road racing. Wilwood's 5.0 brake kits, however, are better suited to racing.

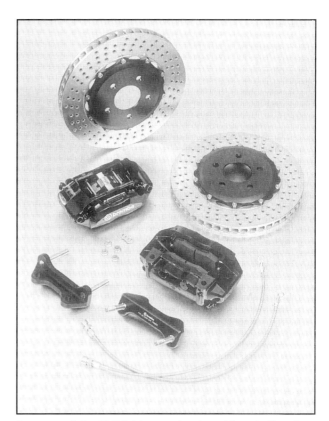

Baer Racing's Serious Street kit is the most attractive kit for 1993-and-earlier 5.0s because it employs 12-inch rotors front and rear and is available with a four-lug bolt pattern. As a result, this kit can be installed with inexpensive 16-inch wheels. The SS kit is also 30 pounds lighter than stock, making it a good fit for street/strip cars as well. In addition to the larger rotors, this kit includes PBR dual-piston front calipers, PBR single-piston rear calipers, braided steel hoses, an adjustable proportioning valve, Performance Friction brake pads, and every last piece of hardware necessary to install it. It should be noted the Baer brakes come preassembled on modified stock spindles, which really eases installation. Baer Racing offers eight different front brake upgrade packages and five different rear disc packages for everything from pure street 5.0s to Trans-Am racers. Stepping up from their fabulous PBR-based systems are their wonderful Alcon-based systems like this Pro package. It features four-piston Alcon calipers. *Baer Racing*

Because of the SN95 Mustang's adaptable spindle, aftermarket brake companies are pursuing easy brake upgrades. Brembo is a well-respected brake in many forms of racing. Brembo offers three stages of brake upgrades for SN95 Mustangs. Pictured here is the mid-level upgrade featuring four-piston calipers; 13-inch, two-piece rotors; braided steel hoses; caliper adapter bridges; and performance street brake pads. The premium Brembo package offers larger calipers and thicker rotors, while the entry-level package features OEM-style one-piece rotors. While Brembo's brake kits are front-only and relatively expensive, they offer premium quality stopping, and the calipers are specifically designed to yield streetable pad wear.

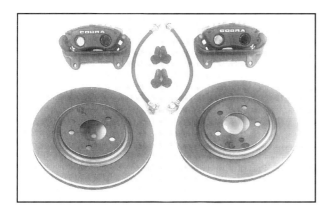

Naturally, many owners of 1993-and-earlier 5.0s were jealous of the quality of brakes found on 1994–95 Mustang Cobras. The only Fox-bodied 5.0s to receive those brakes from the factory were the 109 1993 Mustang Cobra Rs. Fortunately, Ford Racing Performance Parts developed the M-2300-C Cobra Disc Brake Conversion, which allows owners of pre-1994 Mustangs to upgrade to 13-inch front brakes (with dual-piston calipers), 11.65-inch rear brakes, and five-lug wheels. The kit is designed to cover all early models, so it's a bit more difficult to install than an application-specific kit, but it is comprehensive and relatively cost effective. Also, it is based on factory parts, so you can likely get service parts more easily in a pinch. *Ford Racing Performance Parts*

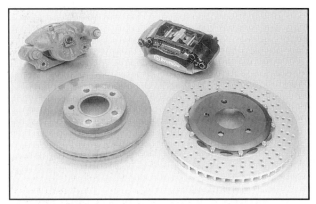

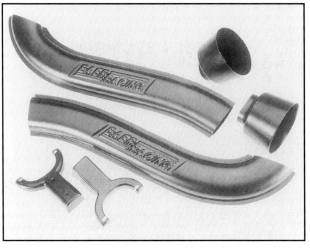

Comparing the stock SN95 single-piston front caliper and 10.9-inch rotor to Brembo's 13-inch rotor and four-piston caliper shows the obvious disparity in braking capability. The four-piston Brembo caliper provides more clamping force and yields more even pad wear than the heavier Ford caliper. It also allows easier pad changes. The larger Brembo rotor obviously offers more frictional area for increased braking. The cross-drilling in the Brembo rotor allows gases expelled from hot brake pads to escape so they don't linger in between the pad and rotor, causing the pad to float above the rotor surface.

In racing or open-track environments, the brakes can really face extreme temperatures, which can lead to premature failure. As such, it is wise to route oncoming air over the brakes for increased cooling. Baer Racing offers Claw Coolers designed to adapt to all 5.0 Mustangs and route air from a Fox or SN95 Mustang's front end over the front brakes.

Installing new brakes means bleeding the system and offers an excellent opportunity to freshen the brake fluid. This rarely changed fluid loses effectiveness over time as it absorbs water from the atmosphere. Brake specialists at Baer Racing recommend Ford's Extra Heavy Duty Brake Fluid for street applications and Castrol's SRF for racing applications. The Castrol has a high wet boiling point to withstand the heated rigors of racing. Both fluids come in metal containers, which protect the fluid from its enemies, water and light, unlike the plastic-bottled Lucas fluid also pictured.

Appearance

16

It's been written that the 5.0 Mustang is the best nearly complete performance car ever built. Ford equipped these cars with excellent horsepower, attractive looks, adequate brakes, and lots of potential. Through the years, 5.0 Mustangs transformed from cars with angular body panels and Spartan interiors to rounded vehicles with stylized interiors. The primary changes were the headlights, taillights, quarter windows, hoods, and rear wings. Over that same time, there were three major interior redesigns, but each year received minor tweaks inside and out. And there was the major SN95 redesign.

The details changed, but the basic premise of affordable, attractive performance remained. These cars aren't perfect, but they are affordable, attractive, and fast. That combination eventually made them the darling of the automotive aftermarket and opened the door to customizing a 5.0 Mustang to any owner's tastes.

Backward Compatibility

Some of the most popular appearance modifications for 5.0 Mustangs

No other aftermarket outfit made more of a mark on the appearance of 5.0 Mustangs than Saleen Performance. Of course, Saleen is best known to the general public as a small-volume producer of high-performance Saleen Mustangs, but each new Saleen Mustang created a look for many owners of pedestrian Mustangs to mimic. This 1989 Saleen SSC shows off the classic rendition of the Fox-bodied Saleen. It wears Saleen's attractive center bumper filler molding, ground effects, and the often-imitated wing. Most of the Saleen parts from any Saleen model are available individually via Saleen Performance.

As attractive as Saleen's Fox body parts are, the SN95 body kit creates one of the most attractive Mustangs ever. This 1995 Mustang shows what a dramatic effect aftermarket body parts can have on a 5.0. It isn't a true Saleen; it's loosely modeled on the top-of-the-line, 351-powered SR, but it features Saleen's ground effects and SR double wing. It was also augmented by a fiberglass cowl-induction hood.

Saleen Mustangs were the most influential cars with regard to exterior modifications—until Ford released its 1995 Mustang Cobra R. This was not a 5.0 Mustang, rather a 5.8 Mustang. The only Fox-platform Mustang to receive a 351W from the factory combined all the good looks of the 1994–95 Mustang Cobras: a unique front fascia with round foglights and a special rear wing. To these items, Ford's Special Vehicle Engineering added a double-rise cowl-induction hood to clear the large engine and beautiful 17x9-inch, five-spoke wheels to clear the large brakes. Cobra R wheels and hoods are de rigueur on many SN95 5.0 Mustangs. HO Fibertrends was the OEM supplier for the 250 Cobra Rs. They offer them for sale, and many other fiberglass outfits sell clones.

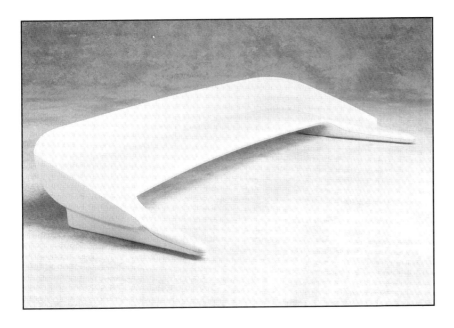

It's difficult to find a modified 5.0 Mustang without an aftermarket wing of some sort bolted to its hatch or trunk lid. The market leader in wings for 5.0s is Saleen Performance. Though its wings were intended for use with their complete body kits, most people combine them with stock and aftermarket body kits. Saleen offers a few other wing designs as well, including those for coupes and hatchbacks, but these are among the most popular.

are those that retrofit later parts on earlier cars. This is so popular because in most cases cars within the same genre (1979–93 and 1994–95) readily accept parts from one another. Some parts will only fit on certain model years and others require minor modifications.

This means you can take an 1982 Mustang and convert it into a 1993 Cobra. You can take a 1994 GT and turn it into a 1995 Cobra R. Or, best of all, you can mix and match parts from your favorite model years and come up with your ultimate Mustang. This isn't just true of body parts, however.

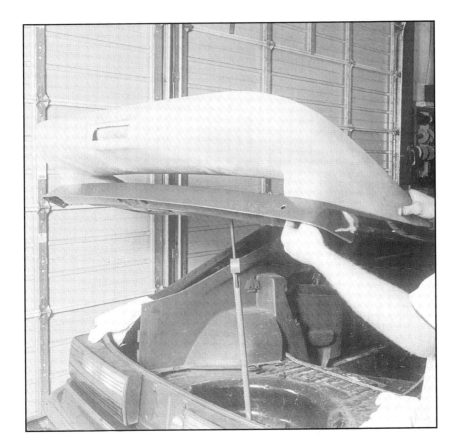

Similar to and nearly as popular as the Saleen wing is Dugan Racing's Whale Tail for 1979–93 5.0s. Dugan's wing appears as more of a one-piece unit. Where the Saleen wing's scooped main body obviously differentiates from the car's body, Dugan's Whale Tail smoothly blends to a point with it mounting feet. This wing is an attractive way to differentiate a 5.0 from the masses of Fox 5.0s with Saleen wings. Both Saleen and Dugan wings utilize Mustang GT third brake lights, so owners of LXs must purchase a GT light to complete their installation on hatchback cars. Coupe owners will have to come up with convertible third brake lights. Dugan also offers, among other things, trick fiberglass fender apron covers that mask the unsightly holes in the factory inner fender aprons.

Next to the Saleen-style wing, a cowl-induction hood is the next most popular modification. Cowl-induction hoods are popular because they offer aggressive styling, which often balances out a wing on the rear end. Fiberglass hoods also offer additional clearance for taller intakes or engines, reduced front-end weight, and improved airflow out of the engine compartment. Cervini's Auto Designs, Design Concepts, Harwood, HO Fibertrends, Motion Performance, Saleen Performance, Sanja Performance, and Steeda Autosports are among those offering fiberglass hoods for 5.0s. This unique Sanja Performance Heat Extractor hood offers a mild cowl rise coupled with vents to route heat out of the engine compartment. Many cowl-induction hoods allow hot air to easily escape the engine compartment, but this hood actually ducts it away after it passes through the radiator. *Sanja Performance*

Interior and drivetrain parts are also open for retrofitting. Vendors that specialize in used parts, like Dugan Racing and Mustang Parts Specialities, can help you make these changes without searching through every junkyard in town.

Keep in mind if you are considering retrofitting your 5.0 with newer parts or going retro with your newer 5.0, that it's cheaper and easier to use parts from model years closer to your vehicle's year. The further apart the two are, the more difficult the fitment can be. Plus, if you are trying to go from a 1979 to a 1993, the conversion can get expensive. Still, this ability to blend parts from various model years is yet another beauty of the 5.0 Mustang.

Paint Scheming

An important aspect of any vehicle's burger-stand appeal is its paint job. Those going for a restoration look simply must focus on getting a high-quality repaint. Those wanting to make a splash will need something a bit out of the ordinary. The key is looking for a scheme you like, say flames or

Cervini's Auto Designs offers perhaps the widest variety of fiberglass body parts for 5.0 Mustangs. Pictured are its Ram Air hood, Stalker bumper cover, Cobra-style wing, and Cobra rear valance for Fox-bodied Mustangs. Cervini also offers Cobra, Cobra R, and Saleen-style hoods and body kits for Fox-body Mustangs, as well as hoods and a Stalker body kit for SN95 cars. Cervini's parts aren't the lightest or cheapest fiberglass parts on the market, but they are some of the highest quality body parts out there.

A specialist in complementary body tweaks for Fords, particularly 5.0 Mustangs, is Classic Design Concepts, best known for the Classic Light Bar and Classic Side Exhaust on this 1994 Mustang Cobra. These two pieces provide a dramatic aesthetic improvement for SN95 Mustangs, and CDC also offers these parts for Fox-body 5.0s as well. CDC also markets hoods, Cobra grille inserts, gas tank AeroShields, and Side Scoops for SN95 Mustangs. *Classic Design Concepts*

a monochromatic look, picking your colors and shopping for a price. If you are looking to get your 5.0 featured in a magazine, don't paint it black or white unless you plan to spice it up with some colorful graphics.

Also, it's easy to save money by removing moldings and trim pieces before taking it to the body shop, but be sure to set this up ahead of time. You may also want to purchase any aftermarket body parts (hoods, wings, body kits) you

want to add and have them painted along with the rest of the car to ensure a good match. Above all, the key is finding a paint shop that performs quality paint jobs within your budget.

Just Looking

There is little theory to discuss with regard to aesthetic modifications. It's an understatement to say there are enough 5.0 appearance modifications to fill another book. Clearly it's impossible to show every possible appearance modification, but there is enough to cover the most popular modifications. However, it won't do much good to write about all of them if you can't see them, so in this chapter the pictures will do the talking. If you don't see what you like, it's likely someone somewhere makes what you want for your 5.0 Mustang.

Whereas exterior modifications are a way to stand out, interior modifications are a way to make your driving experience more enjoyable. Here's an example of a tricked-out interior from a 1987–93 5.0 Mustang, Dugan Racing's Super Viper project car. The interior treatment includes vinyl-covered aftermarket bucket seats, a Hurst Chrome-Stick shifter handle, Auto Custom Carpets and floor mats, Auto Meter gauges, Florida 5.0's gauge pods, Dugan's white-face gauges, and a Grant Challenger steering wheel. It was also converted to the tan interior hue found in SN95 Mustangs.

I took a similar path remaking my 1989 5.0's interior. I chose to swap in a complete black interior from a 1993 Coupe and augment it with a passel of aftermarket goodies. The black interior is the rarest and most attractive interior found in Fox-body cars. Mustang Parts Specialties supplied the interior parts. I spiced up the stock black interior by choosing a carbon-fiber dash trim kit from Tora Sport, a gauge cluster (which allows installing aftermarket gauges in place of the stock gauge cluster) and gauge pod from Florida 5.0, Auto Meter Phantom gauges, Kustom Fit bucket seats, a Cobra leather parking brake handle, Dugan Racing pedal covers, B&M carbon-fiber-look shift knob, and a Grant Corsa GT wheel, replete with Mustang-specific cruise control adapter. Not only do these items improve the car's looks, they make it a blast to drive.

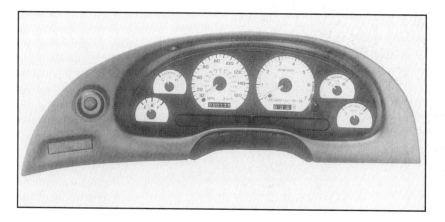

White-face gauges are exceedingly popular additions to 5.0 Mustangs and were introduced into the common lexicon in Saleen Mustangs. Naturally, Saleen sells them as piecemeal add-ons for Fox and SN95 Mustangs. It also offers a trick gauge pod that replaces the clock on SN95 Mustang dashes with a twin-gauge pod. The problem with white-face gauges is that they can be difficult to read at night. BBK Performance, Dugan Racing, NR Automotive Accessories, and others also offer white-face gauge kits. All give that sports-car look to 5.0s.

Because they serve aesthetic and performance needs, gauges are among the most popular interior modifications. This Phantom tachometer offers a 10,000-rpm sweep, an easy-to-see red pointer, and a large Shift-Lite. Shift lights are critical for racers, as there is rarely time to actually look at the needle, so the flash of light can save your engine. Auto Meter offers gauges for just about any need. Boost, fuel pressure, and nitrous pressure gauges are also popular 5.0 additions. While Auto Meter seems the most popular supplier, Ford Racing Performance Parts, Saleen Performance, and VDO also offer quality gauges. *Auto Meter Gauge Works*

Another popular way to add aftermarket gauges to a Fox 5.0 Mustang is Auto Meter Gauge Works' Gauge Cage, which allows placing gauges in the car's center air conditioning vents. Gauge Works first offered these innovative mounting plates independently, but was purchased by Auto Meter. It offers two varieties of Gauge Cage: one with three gauge holes and one with two gauge holes and two A/C vents. These Cages are also available in black, silver, and carbon-fiber-look to accommodate most interior themes. Gauge Works also markets pillar-mount gauge pods, which place one, two, or three gauges in ready view on the car's A-pillar.

Especially when spiffing up an older 5.0, the factory carpet has long since been worn, faded, and stained. An easy way to renew an interior's luster is to replace the carpet and floor mats. Auto Custom Carpets has molded carpets like this one being installed by Mark Houlahan of Mustang Monthly magazine. ACC offers carpet and mats to match any factory color, plus a full range of custom colors and pile configurations. ACC also sells floor mats embroidered with text and logos of your choosing.

Designed to mimic the two-seater look of Saleen's SSC, Dugan Racing's Two-Seater conversion eliminates the cramped, rarely used rear seats of any Fox-bodied 5.0. In place of the seats, the conversion uses attractively formed fiberglass panels to continue the trunk or hatch floor to where the front of the rear seats once was. The two-piece lower section is then capped by an armrest piece that replaces the stock armrest and carries its lines to the rear of the car. Dugan's fiberglass two-seater panels are sold unupholstered, so you'll have to match it to your interior, which is easy enough to do but could be farmed out to an upholstery shop. These panels offer myriad opportunities for customization, providing hidden storage space or displayed mounting for car audio or computerized EFI hardware.

They are most often installed for racing or aesthetic reasons and are good for both, but aftermarket seat belts can make everyday driving more pleasant as well. These Harnessbelts from Schroth Restraint Systems are the only street-legal harnesses on the market. They are available in a variety of colors, so they can be used to match or contrast a car's color scheme. Their hidden advantage is improved safety, thanks to Schroth's (pronounced "shrote") Anti-Submarining technology, which prevents the driver from sliding out of his lap belt during a crash. Another Harnessbelt bonus is that they make the driver feel more comfortable and connected-in to the vehicle, thanks to the security and support provided by the belts. These belts can be installed in a 5.0 Mustang using factory seat belt mounting bolts.

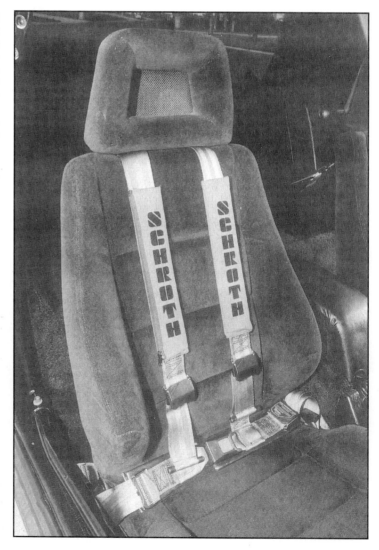

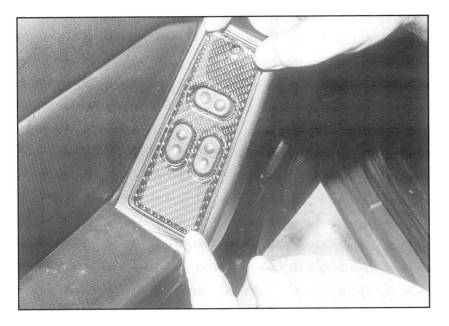

A carryover from their immense popularity in the import car scene, carbon-fiber and carbon-fiber-look trim overlays became fashionable for 5.0 Mustangs. This is one piece of Tora Sport's real carbon fiber kit for 1987–93 Mustangs. It is the most complete kit for the Fox Mustangs and is easily attached via high-quality 3M adhesive. No bolting, trimming, or custom work is required to install the kit. Simply clean the area with alcohol, let it dry, and apply the overlay. Tora Sport also offers carbon-fiber kits for SN95 Mustangs. Several other manufacturers offer carbon-fiber-look kits for Mustangs as well. These trim pieces add an exotic look to a Mustang's interior.

Like seat belts, seats are usually bought for racing or showing off. While they provide the necessary lateral support for racing and the burger-stand appeal to set a 5.0 apart from a stocker, seats can also make driving more enjoyable. The same lateral support necessary from racing is comforting in daily driving. Recaro is the most popular and respected seat maker around. It offers a wide variety of seat styles and designs, from streetable units like the Trend (pictured) to carbon-fiber racing seats. While Recaros are high-quality units, they are also quite expensive. For those wanting similar seats for less, Flofit, Jamex, Kustom Fit, and Sube Sports (Cobra) offer several seat styles in affordable price ranges. *Recaro North America*

Another easy, affordable interior upgrade is a set of pedal covers, like these from Saleen Performance. These brushed aluminum pedal covers offer an aesthetic counter point in the usually dark and drab footwell, but they also provide more pedal grip, thanks to raised edges on the stylized round holes. These covers require drilling into the stock pedals to secure them. Some other covers on the market offer more stylized looks and actually clamp over the stock pedals.

Car audio upgrades are as much a part of modifying a street car as any other modification. There are too many options to even scratch the surface in this book, but one company worth talking about is JL Audio. Not only is it a respected maker of subwoofers, it also offers Mustang-specific subwoofer-and-housing packages. Pictured here is its Fox-body Mustang enclosure, which takes the place of the spare tire in the spare tire well. It includes a 12-inch sub and a display case for an amplifier. It is expensive, but working with Mustang specific parts can reduce headaches when installing car audio equipment. By the way, it sounds great too.

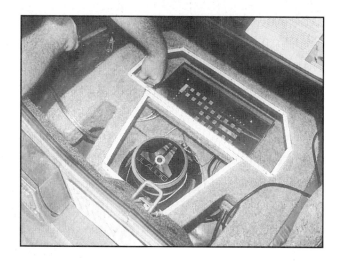

Moving parts from under the hood to a 5.0's interior is not common, but when it comes to transferring battery weight from the front of the car to the rear, the positives outweigh the negatives. Relocating the battery from the driver-side front (1987–95) or the passenger-side front (1979–85) to the passenger-side rear improves the vehicle's front-to-rear weight ratio. This provides better handling, straight-line traction, and improved drag strip weight transfer. This battery relocation kit from MAD Enterprises includes all the necessary, high-quality hardware to get the job done safely and cleanly. Using an Optima battery is a good idea with any battery relocation, as its sealed Spiral Cell design reduces the risks of battery acid leakage inside the vehicle.

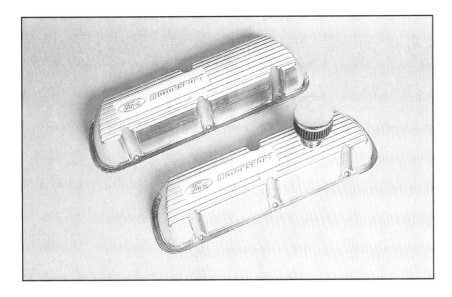

Aftermarket valve covers have always been a staple of engine compartment modifications. Ford Racing Performance Parts has the widest variety of 5.0 valve covers in various styles. These polished pieces were further livened up by ELD Performance. They sprayed the top of the finned covers with yellow high-temp paint, then removed it from the top of the fins, with paint thinner, before it dried. Comp Composites valve covers are also a popular choice. They are light, tall enough to clear aftermarket rocker arms, and available in black, blue, red, and yellow.

This GT-40 intake has likewise been spruced up by an ELD paint job. Moreover, it wears one of Boss, Inc.'s intake cover plates. Boss offers these plates for stock and GT-40 intakes. It also sells similarly styled, adhesive-backed fender badges meant to replace the stock 5.0 badges with aggressive 302 or 351 script.

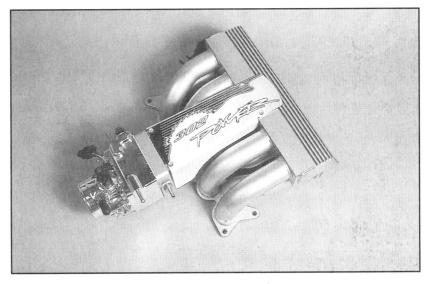

ELD Performance does everything from engine to suspension modifications on most any car or truck. It is best known for adding its polished-and-painted look to an engine compartment. ELD offers chrome and polished covers, brackets, hood prop rods, valve covers, bolts, and just about anything you want to shine in a 5.0 engine compartment. This kind of treatment makes the difference between a grocery-getter and an attention-getter at a car show or on cruise night.

153

Appendix

10,000 RPM
42541 6th St. East
Lancaster, CA 93535
(805) 942-1312/(805) 942-1312 fax

ABC Exclusive
1825 Summit Ave., #209
Plano, TX 25076
(972) 578-2267/(972) 578-2490 fax

Accessible Technologies, Inc.
14014 W. 107th St.
Lenexa, KS 66215
(913) 338-2886/(913) 338-2879 fax

Accufab
1514-B East Francis
Ontario, CA 91761
(909) 930-1751/(909) 930-1753 fax

Advanced Autosport
132 98th Ave.
Oakland, CA 94603
(510) 568-4466/(510) 635-9066 fax

Aeroform
6300 St. John Ave.
Kansas City, MO 64123
(816) 241-9711

Aerohead Industries
8621 Southeastern Ave.
Indianapolis, IN 46239
(317) 862-0223/(317) 862-6300 fax

Aerospace Components
P.O. Box 3015
Seminole, FL 34645
(813) 545-4943/(813) 545-4943 fax

Alternative Auto Performance
145 Malow
Mt. Clemens, MI 48043
(810) 463-0010/(810) 463-3194 fax

American Sports Car Design
324 Home Ave.
Maryville, TN 37801
(423) 982-3091/(423) 983-4418 fax

Anderson Ford Motorsport
P.O. Box 638
Clinton, IL 61727
(217) 935-2384/(217) 935-4611 fax

Apex Motorsports
2555 Lafayette St., #105
Santa Clara, CA 95050
(408) 562-1000

ARB Air Locker-USA
1425 Elliott Ave. W.
Seattle, WA 98119-3104
(206) 284-5906

ARP
531 Spectrum Circle
Oxnard, CA 93030-8988
(805) 278-7223/(805) 981-1329

Art Carr Performance Transmissions
10575 Bechler River Ave.
Fountain Valley, CA 92708
(714) 962-6655/(714) 968-7743 fax

Auburn Gear
400 E. Auburn Dr.
Auburn, IN 46706
(219) 925-3200

Auto Custom Carpet
P.O. Box 1350
Anniston, AL 36202-1350
(205) 236-1118/(205) 236-7375 fax

Auto Meter Products
413 West Elm St.
Sycamore, IL 60178
(815) 895-8141

Auto Specialties
13313 Redfish, #106
Stafford, TX 77477
(281) 261-5811

AutoTrans Group, Inc.
14849 124 Ave.
Edmonton, Alberta, Canada T5L 3B2
(403) 453-3767/(403) 453-2208 fax

Autumn Fleet Sales
7301 Deering Ave.
Canoga Park, CA 91303
(818) 340-9444/(818) 340-0531 fax

AVO Performance Shocks
P.O. Box 1129
Palm City, FL 34990
(407) 221-0164/(407) 221-0561 fax

B&M Automotive
9152 Independence Ave.
Chatsworth, CA 91311
(818) 882-6422/(818) 882-3616 fax

Baer Racing
3108 W. Thomas Rd, #1201D
Phoenix, AZ 85017
(602) 233-1411/(602) 352-8445 fax

Barts Works
1546 B South Euclid
Tucson, AZ 85713
(520) 884-7599/(520) 884-7618 fax

Bassani Manufacturing
2900 E. La Jolla St.
Anaheim, CA 92806-1305
(714) 630-1821/(714) 630-2980 fax

Baumann Engineering
P.O. Box 63
Clemson, SC 29633
(803) 646-8920/(803) 646-8925 fax

BBK Performance
1611 Railroad St.
Corona, CA 91720
(909) 735-2400/(909) 735-8882 fax

Be Cool
377 S. River Rd.
Bay City, MI 48708
(517) 895-9699/(517) 892-9213 fax

Bennett Racing
P.O. Box 593
Haleyville, AL 35565-0593
(205) 486-5520/(205) 486-8441 fax

Bilstein Shock Absorbers
8845 Rehco Road
San Diego, CA 92121
(619) 453-7723/(619) 453-0770 fax

Borla Performance Industries
5901 Edison Dr.
Oxnard, CA 93033
(805) 986-8600/(805) 986-8940 fax

Boss, Inc.
7672 Montgomery Rd.
Cincinnati, OH 45236
(513) 530-0390/(513) 794-0170 fax

Brembo Brake
1567 Sunland Ln.
Costa Mesa, CA 92626
(714) 641-0104/(714) 641-5827 fax

Briante Racing
48 Gleneida Ridge Rd.
Carmelle, NY 10512
(914) 769-3728/(914) 769-9124 fax

Brodix
P.O. Box 1347
Mena, AZ 71953
(501) 394-1075/(501) 394-1996 fax

Brothers Performance Warehouse
2012 Railroad St.
Corona, CA 91720
(909) 735-8880/(909) 735-8093 fax

BXR Manifolds, Inc.
199 McNamara Rd.
Spring Valley, NY 10977
(914) 354-0585/(914) 354-0859 fax

C&L Performance, Inc.
13015 South Memorial Parkway
Huntsville, AL 35803
(205) 882-6813/(205) 882-2508 fax

Carolina Mustang Performance
302 W. Chatham St.
Cary, NC 27511
(919) 467-2900/(919) 460-5810

Centerforce Clutches
2266 Crosswind Dr.
Prescott, AZ 86301
(520) 771-8422/(520) 771-8322 fax

Central Coast Mustang
708 B W. Betterravia
Santa Maria, CA 93455
(805) 925-8848/(805) 925-3193 fax

Central Florida Motorsports
320 North St.
Longwood, FL 32750
(407) 339-9211/(407) 339-9661 fax

Cervini's Auto Designs
3656 N. Mill Rd.
Vineland, NJ 08360
(609) 691-5306/(609) 691-5331 fax

Charlie's Mustangs
766-A N 9th St.
San Jose, CA 95112
(408) 275-6511/(408) 275-6432 fax

Classic Design Concepts, Inc.
1880 W. Maple
Walled Lake, MI 48390
(248) 624-7997/(248) 624-7987 fax

Coast High Performance
2070 Del Amo Blvd.
Torrance, CA 90503
(310) 781-1441/(310) 781-1444 fax

Competition Cams
3406 Democrat Rd.
Memphis, TN 38118
(901) 795-2400/(901) 366-1807 fax

Compucar Nitrous Oxide Systems
614 Atomic Rd.
N. Augusta, SC 29841
(803) 442-9206

Constant Velocity
1429A Wentker Ct.
Two Rivers, WI 54241
(920) 794-2869/(920) 793-4590 fax

Corbeau USA
9503 South 560 West
Sandy, UT 84070
(801) 255-3737/(801) 255-3222 fax

Crane Cams
530 Fentress Blvd.
Daytona Beach, FL 32014
(904) 252-1151/(904) 258-8846 fax

Currie Enterprises
1480-B N. Tustin Ave.
Anaheim, CA 92807
(714) 528-6957/(714) 528-2338 fax

D&D Performance
49676 Martin Rd.
Wixom, MI 48393
(248) 926-6220/(248) 926-6222 fax

Diversified Products Marketing
6110 Gotfredson Rd.
Plymouth, MI 48170
(313) 459-0130/(313) 455-2173 fax

Dominion Performance
2537-D Pacific Coast Hwy., Box 418
Torrance, CA 90505
(818) 709-4794/(818) 709-4788 fax

Downs Ford
360 Rt. 37
Toms River, NJ 08753
(908) 349-2240

Dr. Gas Inc.
1672 East 10770 South
Sandy, UT 84092
(801) 571-6097/(801) 571-6090 fax

D.S.S., Inc.
960 Ridge Ave.
Lombard, IL 60148
(630) 268-1630/(630) 268-1649 fax

Dugan Racing
1175 Highway 23, Suite 101
Suwanee, GA 30174
(770) 932-5480/(770) 932-9842 fax

DynoMax
111 Pfingsten Rd.
Deerfield, IL 60015
(847) 267-8366/(847) 267-8363 fax

Edelbrock Corporation
2700 California St.
Torrance, CA 90509
(310) 781-9303/(310) 533-0844 fax

Eibach Springs
17817 Gillette Ave.
Irvine, CA 92714
(714) 752-6700/(714) 752-6788 fax

Energy Suspension
1131 Via Callejon
San Clemente, CA 92673
(714) 361-3935/(714) 361-3940 fax

Every Last Detail Performance
2421 Crofton Lane, Suite 9
Crofton, MD 21114-1324
(410) 768-9368/(410) 730-5140 fax

Excessive Motorsports
2909A West 40 Hwy.
Blue Springs, MO 64015
(816) 737-7610/(816) 322-1090 fax

Extrude Hone
8075 Pennsylvania Ave.
Irwin, PA 15642
(412) 863-5900/(412) 863-8759 fax

Fel-Pro Inc.
7450 N. McCormick Blvd.
Skokie, IL 60076
(847) 674-7700/(847) 568-1916 fax

Flaming River Industries
17851 Englewood Dr.
Cleveland, OH 44130
(216) 826-4488/(216) 826-0780 fax

Flex-a-lite
4540 S. Adams St.
Tacoma, WA 98409-2907
(253) 922-2700/(253) 922-0226 fax

Florida 5.0
5480 SW 25th St.
Hollywood, FL 33023
(954) 966-5523

Flow Tech
2605 W. First St.
Tempe, AZ 85281
(602) 966-1511/(602) 966-1197 fax

FlowKooler
289 Prado Rd.
San Luis Obispo, CA 93401
(805) 544-8841/(805) 544-5615 fax

Flowmaster
2975 Dutton Ave., #3
Santa Rosa, CA 95407
(707) 544-4761/(707) 544-4784 fax

Fluidampr
11980 Walden Ave.
Alden, NY 14004-9790
(716) 937-7903/(716) 937-4692 fax

Ford Performance Solutions
1004 Orange Fair Lane
Anaheim, CA 92801
(714) 773-9027/(714) 773-4178

Ford Racing Performance Parts
44050 N. Groesbeck Hwy.
Clinton Township, MI 48036-1108
(810) 468-1356

Forte's Parts Connection
474 Moody St.
Waltham, MA 02154
(617) 647-1530/(617) 647-3278 fax

Fox Lake Power Products
6512 Dalton Fox Lake Rd.
North Lawrence, OH 44666
(216) 682-8800

FP Performance Products
P.O. Box 1966
Detroit, MI 48235
(810) 225-2700/(810) 354-8950 fax

Global West
1423 E. Philadelphia
Ontario, CA 91761-5708
(909) 923-6176/(909) 923-6180 fax

Grant Products
700 Allen Ave.
Glendale, CA 91201
(323) 849-3171/(818) 241-4683 fax

Griffin Radiator
100 Hurricane Creek Rd.
Piedmont, SC 29673
(803) 287-4898

Griggs Racing
29175 Arnold Dr.
Sonoma, CA 95476
(707) 939-2244/(707) 939-2249 fax

Hanlon Motorsports
3621 St. Peters Rd.
Elverson, PA 19520
(610) 469-2695/(610) 469-2694 fax

Hedman Hedders
16410 Manning Way
Cerritos, CA 90703
(562) 921-0404/(562) 921-7515 fax

HO Fibertrends
235 Route 674 S.
Asheville, OH 43103
(614) 983-3864

Holcomb Motorsports, Inc.
P.O. Box 1473
Lumberton, NC 28358
(910) 739-0747/(910) 739-0731 fax

Holley Performance Products
1801 Russellville Rd.
Bowling Green, KY 42102
(502) 782-2900/(502) 745-9590 fax

Hooker Headers
1024 W. Brooks St.
Ontario, CA 91761
(909) 983-5871/(909) 986-9860 fax

Hotchkis Performance
12035 Burke St., #13
Santa Fe Springs, CA 90670-2685
(562) 907-7757/(562) 907-7765 fax

HPC
550 W. 3615 S.
Salt Lake City, UT 84115
(801) 262-6807/(801) 262-6307 fax

HP Motorsport
5055 S. 36th St.
Omaha, NE 68107
(402) 731-7301

Hypertech
1910 Thomas Rd.
Memphis, TN 38134
(901) 382-8888/(901) 373-5290 fax

Incon Systems
1090 W. Bagley Rd.
Berea, OH 44017
(440) 234-2450/(440) 234-5355 fax

Interactive Systems & Technologies
1105 Hasty Trail
Canton, GA 30115
(770) 720-1259/(770) 720-1249 fax

J&P Performance
325 Nantucket Blvd., Unit 14
[AUTHOR: NEED A CITY/PROVINCE]
Canada M1P 4V5
(416) 751-9766/(416) 751-2983 fax

Jamex
4975 C Energy Way
Reno, NV 89509
(702) 857-4888/(702) 857-1635 fax

JBA Headers
7149 Mission Gorge Rd.
San Diego, CA 92120
(619) 229-7797/(619) 229-7761 fax

Jet-Hot Coatings
55 E. Front St.
Bridgeport, PA 19405
(610) 277-2444/(610) 277-0135 fax

K&N Engineering, Inc.
P.O. Box 1329
Riverside, CA 92502-1329
(909) 684-9762/(909) 684-0716 fax

Kar Kraft Engineering
P.O. Box 51831
Livonia, MI 48151
(313) 422-8510/(313) 421-7605 fax

Keith Craft Racing
Rt. 3, Box 329
Arkadelphia, AR 71923
(501) 246-7460

Kenne Bell
10743 Bell Ct.
Rancho Cucamonga, CA 91730
(909) 941-1375/(909) 944-4883 fax

Kenny Brown Performance
57 Gasoline Alley
Indianapolis, IN 46222
(317) 247-5320/(317) 247-5347

Koni Shock Absorbers
1961 International Way
Hebron, KY 41042
(606) 586-4100/(606) 334-3340 fax

KS Reproduction Corp.
P.O. Box 763
S. Plainfield, NJ 07080-3806
(908) 754-7155/(908) 754-4224 fax

La Rocca's Performance
1600 Englishtown Rd.
Old Bridge, NJ 08897
(908) 723-1111/(908) 723-9640

Lentech Automatics
3487 Joys Rd.
Richmond, Ont., Canada K0A-2Z0
(613) 838-5390

Level 10 Transmissions
1888 Route 94
Hamburg, NJ 07419
(973) 827-1000

LPW Racing Products
632 E. Marion St.
Lancaster, PA 17602
(717) 394-7432/(717) 394-1198 fax

Lugo Performance Automotive
2401 N. Orange Blossom Trail
Orlando, FL 32804
(407) 294-6003

MAC Products
43214 Black Deer Loop
Temecula, CA 92590
(909) 699-9440/(909) 308-0081 fax

March Performance
5820 Hix Rd.
Westland, MI 48185
(313) 729-9070/(313) 729-9075

Mark Ray Motorsports
5155 Pit Rd. S.
Harrisburg, NC 28075
(704) 455-5058/(704) 455-5159 fax

Match Port Engineering
P.O. Box 1917
Benson, AZ 85602
(520) 327-8917

Maximum Motorsports
736B Foothill Blvd.
San Luis Obispo, CA 93405
(805) 544-8748/(805) 544-8645 fax

McLeod Industries, Inc.
600 Sierra Madre Circle
Placentia, CA 92870
(714) 630-2764/(714) 630-5129 fax

Mor-Flow Performance
P.O. Box 25547
Tempe, AZ 85285-5547
(602) 839-7057/(602) 839-7057

Moser Engineering
1616 N. Franklin St.
Portland, IN 47371
(219) 726-6689/(219) 726-4159

Mr. Gasket
8700 Brookpark Rd.
Cleveland, OH 44129-6899
(216) 398-8300/(216) 749-0442

MSD Ignition
1490 Henry Brennan Dr.
El Paso, TX 79936
(915) 857-5200/(915) 857-3344

Mustang Parts Specialties
P.O. Box 1533
Winder, GA 30680-6533
(770) 867-2644/(770) 307-0403 fax

Mustang Specialties, Inc.
1401 S. Dixie Hwy.
Pompano Beach, FL 33060
(954) 942-5202

Mustangs Unlimited
185 Adams St.
Manchester, CT 06040
(860) 647-1965/(860) 649-1260 fax

Mustangs Unlimited
5182 Brook Hollow Parkway
Norcross, GA 30071
(770) 446-1965/(770) 446-3055 fax

Neuspeed
3300 Corte Malpaso
Camarillo, CA 93012
(805) 388-8111/(805) 388-0030 fax

Nitrous Express
4923 Lake Park Dr.
Wichita Falls, TX 76302
(940) 767-7694/(940) 767-7697 fax

Nitrous Oxide Systems, Inc.
2970 Airway Ave.
Costa Mesa, CA 92626
(714) 545-0580/(714) 545-8319 fax

The Nitrous Works
1450 McDonald Rd.
Dahlonega, GA 30533
(706) 864-7009/(706) 864-2206 fax

Nology Engineering
7360 Trade Street
San Diego, CA 92121-2422
(619) 578-4688/(619) 578-4388 fax

North American Motorsports
2973 Harbor Blvd.
Costa Mesa, CA 92626
(714) 718-0824/(714) 718-0825 fax

North East Mustang
796 Lake Ave.
Bristol, CT 06010
(860) 585-6929

Nowak & Company
249 E. Emerson Ave.
Orange, CA 92665-3303
(714) 282-7996/(714) 637-0425 fax

N.R. Automotive
2760 Woodwardia Dr.
Los Angeles, CA 90077
(213) 470-8092

Optima Batteries
17500 E. 22nd Ave.
Aurora, CO 80011
(303) 340-7440/(303) 340-7474 fax

Panhandle Performance
106 W. Peachtree Dr.
Lynn Haven, FL 32444
(904) 265-9818/(904) 265-9840 fax

Paul's High Performance
3715 Commerce St.
Jackson, MI 49203
(517) 764-7661/(517) 764-7674 fax

Paxton Automotive
1260 Calle Suerte
Camarillo, CA 93012
(805) 987-5555/(805) 389-1154 fax

Performance Automatic, Inc.
8174 Beechcraft Ave.
Gaithersburg, MD 20879
(301) 963-8078/(301) 963-5076 fax

Performance Distributors
2699 Barris Dr.
Memphis, TN 38132
(901) 396-5782/(901) 396-5783 fax

Performance Parts, Inc.
13120 Lazy Glen Ct.
Herndon, VA 22071
(703) 742-6207/(703) 742-6208 fax

Perma-Cool
671 E. Edna Pl.
Covina, CA 91723-1314
(818) 967-2777/(818) 915-2665 fax

Powerdyne Automotive Products
104-C East Ave., K-4
Lancaster, CA 93535
(805) 723-2803/(805) 723-2802 fax

Powered By Ford
1516 S. Division Ave.
Orlando, FL 32805
(407) 843-3673/(407) 841-7223 fax

Powertrax
245 Fischer Avenue
Costa Mesa, CA 92626
(714) 545-5425

Precision Gear, Inc.
12351 Universal Dr.
Taylor, MI 48180-4077
(313) 946-0524/(313) 946-2981 fax

Precision Industries
5804 Ferguson Rd.
Bartlett, TN 38134
(901) 383-1555/(901) 382-7009 fax

Pro-5.0
P.O. Box 454
Kenilworth, NJ 07033
(908) 241-0107/(908) 755-8497 fax

Probe Industries
42257 6th St. West 307
Lancaster, CA 93534-7163
(805) 945-3363/(805) 945-4703 fax

Pro-Flow Technologies
25760 John R. Rd.
Madison Heights, MI 48071
(248) 399-9223/(248) 399-4054 fax

R&E Racing
44533 Sierra Hwy.
Lancaster, CA 93534
(800) 776-6792/(805) 945-5801 fax

Racecraft Performance
5301 N.W. 15th St.
Margate, FL 33063
(305) 978-5388

Racers Chassis
565 Brennen Rd.
Lakeland, FL 33813
(941) 646-4755/(941) 646-3204 fax

Racers Edge
4100 Powerline Rd., Suite F-4
Pompano Beach, FL 33073
(954) 968-6844/(954) 968-6697 fax

Ram Automotive Co.
201 Business Park Blvd.
Columbia, SC 29203
(803) 788-6034/(803) 736-8649 fax

Ramsey's Performance
5403-D Southern Comfort Blvd.
Tampa, FL 33634
(813) 886-5597/(813) 960-0166 fax

Recaro North America
905 W. Maple Rd.
Clawson, MI 48017
(248) 288-6800/(248) 288-0811 fax

Reider Racing Enterprises, Inc.
12351 Universal Dr.
Taylor, MI 48180
(313) 946-1330/(313) 946-8672 fax

Richmond Gear
1208 Old Norris Road
Liberty, SC 29657
(864) 843-9231/(864) 843-1276 fax

ROL Manufacturing of America
154 F St.
Perrysburg, OH 43551
(800) 253-6272/(419) 666-7419 fax

Roush Performance, Inc.
32675 Schoolcraft Rd.
Livonia, MI 48150
(313) 513-4410/(313) 513-4422 fax

Saleen Performance Parts
9 Whatney
Irvine, CA 92618
(714) 597-3860/(714) 597-4917 fax
Sanja Performance
183 Hugh Paxton Rd.
Greensburg, KY 42743
(502) 932-3216/(502) 789-3907 fax

Schroth Restraint Systems Corp.
1942 Broadway St., #400
Boulder, CO 80302-5239
(303) 447-1700/(303) 447-1847 fax

Southside Machine
6400 N. Honeytown Rd.
Smithville, OH 44677
(330) 669-3556/(330) 669-2020 fax

Special Vehicle Development
337 Blacks Rd.
Cheshire, CT 06410
(203) 272-7928/(203) 272-7561 fax

Stage 8 Fasteners
15 Chesnut Ave.
San Rafael, CA 94901-1057
(415) 485-5340

Stainless Steel Brakes Corp.
11470 Main Rd.
Clarence, NY 14031
(716) 759-8666/(716) 759-8688 fax

Steeda Autosports, Inc.
1351 NW Steeda Way
Pompano Beach, FL 33069
(954) 960-0774/(954) 960-1449 fax

Strange Engineering
1611 Church St.
Evanston, IL 60201
(847) 745-9168/(847) 745-5449 fax

Superchips, Inc.
134 Baywood Ave., #B
Longwood, FL 32750-3447
(407) 260-0838

Supertrapp Industries
4540 W. 160th St.
Cleveland, OH 44135
(216) 265-8400

TA Performance Products
16167 N. 81 St.
Scottsdale, AZ 85260
(602) 922-6808/(602) 922-6811 fax

TCI
One TCI Dr.
Ashland, MS 38603
(601) 224-8972/(601) 224-8255 fax

Taylor Cable Products
301 Highgrove Rd.
Grandview, MO 64030
(816) 765-5011

Tokico Gas Shocks
1330 Storm Parkway
Torrance, CA 90501
(310) 534-4934

Tommie Vaughn Motors
1145 North Shepherd
Houston, TX 77008
(713) 869-4661/(713) 869-5168 fax

Tractech, Inc.
11445 Stephens Drive
Warren, MI 48090

TransGo
2621 Merced Ave.
El Monte, CA 91733
(626) 443-7456/(626) 401-2715 fax

Trick Flow
P.O. Box 909
Akron, OH 44309
(330) 630-5343/(330) 630-5343 fax

Turbo Technology
6229 S. Adams St.
Tacoma, WA 98409
(206) 475-8319/(206) 475-8319 fax

Unlimited Performance
145 S. Congress Ave.
Del Rey Beach, FL 33445
(561) 279-0179/(561) 272-1680 fax

VDO Performance Instruments
188 Brooke Road
Winchester, VA 22603
(540) 665-0100/(540) 722-4198

Vortech Engineering Inc.
5351 Bonsai Ave.
Moorpark, CA 93021
(805) 529-9330/(805) 529-7831 fax

Weiand Automotive Industries
2316 San Fernando Rd.
Los Angeles, CA 90065
(213) 225-4138

Weldon Pump
640 Golden Oak Parkway
Oakwood Village, OH 44146
(216) 232-2282/(216) 232-0606 fax

Wild Rides
30 Roosevelt Ave.
Carteret, NJ 67008
(908) 541-1516/(908) 541-1144 fax

Wilwood Disc Brakes
4700 Calle Bolero
Camarillo, CA 93012
(805) 388-1188/(805) 388-4938 fax

Windsor-Fox
P.O. Box 2683
Apple Valley, CA 92307
(619) 946-3835/(619) 242-8548 fax

World Products, Inc.
80 Trade Zone Ct.
Ronkonkoma, NY 11779
(516) 737-0372/(516) 737-0467 fax

Index